INTERPLAY
The Process
of
Interpersonal Communiction

HOLT, RINEHART AND WINSTON
New York   Chicago   San Francisco
Atlanta   Dallas   Montreal   Toronto   London   Sydney

INTERPLAY

The Process
of
Interpersonal Communication

RONALD B. ADLER
Santa Barbara City College

LAWRENCE B. ROSENFELD
University of New Mexico

NEIL TOWNE
Grossmont College

Cover: A detail from *Children's Games* by Pieter Bruegel. Reproduced by permission of Saskia and Kunsthistorisches Museum, Vienna.

Library of Congress Cataloging in Publication Data

Adler, Ronald B.
  Interplay.

  Includes index.
  1. Interpersonal communication—psychological aspects. I. Rosenfeld, Lawrence B., joint author. II. Towne, Neil, date, joint author. III. Title.
BF637.C45A33   302.2   80–11169

ISBN 0–03–049586–5

1 2 3 4 5 0 3 2 9 8 7 6 5 4 3 2

Acknowledgments

page 2 "Let It Be a Dance" from *Speaking Poems* 2ed. by Ric Masten. Reprinted by permission of the author, Sunflower Ink, Monterey, California.

page 3 From *Zorba The Greek* by Nikos Kazantzakis. Copyright © 1952 by Simon & Shuster, Inc.

page 4 "Frank & Ernest" cartoon by Schnieder. Reprinted by permission. © 1976 NEA, Inc.

page 7 Cartoon by Hamilton from *William Hamilton's Anti-Social Register* by Wm. Hamilton. Copyright © William Hamilton 1974. By permission of Cronicle Books.

page 8 Excerpt abridged from pp. 64, 66–67 in *Dancer from the Dance* by Andrew Holleran. Copyright © 1978 by William Morrow and Company, Inc. By permission of the publishers.

page 31 Cartoon by Chon Day. Used by permission of Chon Day and Copyright © by *Saturday Review*.

page 33 Reprinted from *Shyness: What It Is, What to Do About It* by Philip Zimbardo. Copyright © 1977, by permission of Addison-Wesley Publishing Co., Reading, Mass.

page 40 Excerpt from *Come Be With Me* by Leonard Nemoy. Reprinted by permission of International Creative Management. Copyright © Leonard Nemoy, 1978.

page 50 "Peanuts" cartoon by Charles Schultz. © 1967 United Feature Syndicate Inc.

page 60 From *The Best of Sydney J. Harris*, By Sydney J. Harris. Copyright © 1975 by Sydney J. Harris. Reprinted by permission of Houghton Mifflin Company.

page 62 from *The Poetry of Robert Frost* edited by Edward Connery Lathem. Copyright 1930, 1938, © 1969 by Holt, Rinehart and Winston. Copyright © 1958 by Robert Frost. Copyright © 1967 by Lesley Frost Ballantine. Reprinted by permission of Holt, Rinehart and Winston, Publishers and Jonathan Cape Ltd.

page 67 "Hands" from *Voice of the Hive* 1st ed. by Ric Masten. Reprinted by permission of the author, Sunflower Ink, Monterey, California.

page 71 Used by permission of Charles Scribner's Sons and William Heinemann Ltd. From *Look Homeward, Angel* by Thomas Wolfe. Copyright 1929 Charles Scribner's Sons; renewal copyright © 1957 Edward C. Aswell, Administrator, C.T.A. and/or Fred Wolfe.

page 72 *Miss Peach* by Mell Lazarus. Courtesy of Mell Lazarus and Field Newspaper Syndicate.

page 74 "Peanuts" cartoon by Charles Schultz. © United Feature Syndicate Inc.

page 87 Reproduced by permission from *Introduction to Psychology* by Dennis Coon, Copyright © 1977 West Publishing Company. All rights reserved.

page 88 © 1979 By permission of Redbook Magazine and Jerry Marcus.

page 94 "Coming & Going" from *His & Hers: A Passage Through the Middle-Age Crazies* by Ric Masten. Reprinted by permission of the author, Sunflower Ink, Monterey, California.

page 112 Cartoon by Richard Stine. Reprinted by permission of Carolyn Bean Associates, Publishing. © 1974 Richard Stine. Drawing from *Smile in a Mad Dog's i* by Richard Stine.

page 119 "Ziggy" cartoon by Tom Wilson reprinted by permission of Universal Press Syndicate.

page 120 From *Benchley Beside Himself* by Robert Benchly. Copyright 1930 by Robert C. Benchley. Reprinted by permission of Harper & Row, Publishers, Inc.

page 121 "Peanuts" cartoon by Charles Schultz. © 1963 United Feature Syndicate Inc.

page 173 "Peanuts" cartoon by Charles Schultz. © 1965 United Feature Syndicate Inc.

page 196 Reprinted courtesy of the San Francisco *Examiner*, September 1, 1968.

page 204 Poem by Lenni Shender Goldstein. Used by permission of the author.

page 205 "Peanuts" cartoon by Charles Schultz. © 1977 United Feature Syndicate Inc.

page 208 From *The Best of Sydney J. Harris*, by Sydney J. Harris. Copyright © 1975 by Sydney J. Harris. Reprinted by permission of Houghton Mifflin Company.

page 219 From *Merce Cunningham*, edited by James Klosty. Copyright © 1975 by James Klosty. Reprinted by permission of E. P. Dutton/Saturday Review Books.

page 223 "Nothing" in *Love Poems for the Very Married* by Lois Wyse (World Publishing Company). Copyright © 1967 by Lois Wyse. Reprinted by permission of Harper & Row, Publishers, Inc.

As we write these words, the text of *Interplay* is already being typeset. Thus, writing a preface is something of an anticlimax. But while the book lies behind us, it is ahead of you; and so it seems appropriate here to briefly state our purposes and methods.

We had four goals in mind as we wrote *Interplay*. First: to provide a thorough introduction to the field of interpersonal communication, and to do so in a way that would attract readers taking their first concerted look at the subject. Second: to present information in a clear, understandable manner. As students and professors, all three of us have suffered through the dry, often convoluted writing that seems to characterize most academic work. Having paid these dues, we vowed to share our message in the most straightforward, unpretentious way we knew. Third: to demonstrate the many fascinating ways in which the principles of interpersonal communication occur outside of textbooks and classrooms. Toward this end we included a variety of quotations, excerpts, photographs, cartoons, and poetry which effectively and dramatically illustrate the points we make.

Our final, and perhaps most important, goal has been to provide a means for our readers to skillfully apply the principles of interpersonal communication to their everyday interactions. This has been made possible through Susan R. Glaser's skills book, *Toward Communication Competency: Developing Interpersonal Skills*. This book draws upon the most recent and productive findings of learning theory to present readers with a step-by-step plan for improving communication in their important relationships. If you do not have a copy of the skills book handy, and if you are interested in turning theory into practice, we suggest you obtain one. It is the component that makes *Interplay* complete.

Anyone who has written a book knows that the authors' acknowledgements are more than just good manners. Whatever success *Interplay* enjoys will be due in great measure to the help of many people. Susan Glaser must be mentioned first, for her book completes the goals we set for our book. We also owe a big debt to Jean Civikly for her contribution in the chapter on relationships.

We are also lucky to have been blessed with the best editorial and design help imaginable. Our editor, Roth Wilkofsky, proved as usual to be a good friend and helpful guide through the perils of scheduling, budgets, promotion, reviews, and other mysteries. The copy editor, Stuart Kenter, did a fine job of strengthening language and setting style. The market analysis and other help of Kathleen

Preface

Domenig helped us keep our writing on target. Our designer, Janet Bollow, has shown her ability to turn several hundred pages of typed manuscript into an inviting piece of work that enhances the messages within. Nancy Myers at Holt, Rinehart and Winston has done an admirable job of making a five-way transcontinental project run smoothly, proving that nothing is impossible. We also are grateful to Marge Mahoney for her professional work in typing the manuscript, and to Iris Koch and Susan Gorton for their help in gathering materials.

We also owe a thank you to those friends and colleagues whose feedback helped us keep our writing focused: Al Anderson, University of Texas, Austin; Keith Erickson, Texas Tech University; Tim Hopf, Washington State University; Dick Johnston, Diablo Valley College; Daniel J. O'Keefe, University of Michigan; Lynn A. Phelps, Miami University; Barbara Walker, Florida State University; Barbara Warnick, Tulane University; John Wiemann, University of Calfironia, Santa Barbara; William A. Yaremchuk, Monmouth College.

And, finally, we want to say thanks to our wives. Whatever glamour might have initially come with being married to an author has long ago evaporated, and our wives deserve great credit for putting up with our stresses and strains while pursuing interests of their own.

Ronald B. Adler
Lawrence B. Rosenfeld
Neil Towne

Contents

10 Language   251

11 Conflict   275

INTERPLAY
The Process
of
Interpersonal Communication

Interpersonal Process

1

1 let a dancing song be heard
    play the music say the words
        and fill the sky with sailing birds
        and let it be a dance
    learn to follow learn to lead
    feel the rhythm fill the need
 to reap the harvest plant the seed
 and let it be a dance
    everybody turn and spin
        let your body learn to bend
            and like a willow in the wind
        let it be a dance
    a child is born the old must die
 a time for joy a time to cry
 take it as it passes by
    and let it be a dance
        the morning star comes out at night
            without the dark there can be no light
        and if nothing's wrong then nothing's right
    so let it be a dance
 let the sun shine let it rain
 share the laughter bear the pain
    and round and round we go again
        so let it be a dance

Ric Masten

Communicating is like dancing. Dancing is like communicating. Both are expressive. Both can take many forms—they can be done with a partner, in a group, in an empty café, or before an audience of hundreds. Both require cooperation to be successful. And both demand skill, though skill by itself isn't enough. A dance performed with no feeling and words not spoken from the heart will be only clever motions, without spirit.

Why We Communicate

Dancing may be beautiful, but it's not necessary. You can live a long and happy life without being able to dance beautifully, or even at all. But communicating is another matter. As you'll now see, it's absolutely essential that we are able to communicate effectively. There are several reasons for this.

In the first place, the sheer amount of time we spend communicating is staggering. This alone provides a major reason for studying the subject. In research done at the University of Cincinnati, Rudolph Verderber, Ann Elder, and Ernest Weiler measured the amount of time a sample of college students spent on various activities. These researchers found that the group they observed spent an average of over 61 percent of their waking time engaged in some form of communication. Whatever one's occupation, the results of such a study would not be too different. Of course, some people spend relatively little time interacting with others, but most of us spend the bulk of our time relating to family, friends, coworkers, teachers, and strangers.

There's a good reason why we speak, listen, read, and write so much: Communication satisfies most of our needs.

Physical Needs   In his landmark book *Motivation and Personality*, Abraham Maslow identifies five basic types of needs which each of us must satisfy if we are to live a safe and fulfilled life. Maslow argues that these needs are hierarchical; that is, we strive to satisfy the more basic ones before we move on to meeting others. Maslow states that the most fundamental category of needs is *physiological*. We

"Come on, Zorba," I cried, "teach me to dance!"

Zorba leaped to his feet, his face sparkling. . .

"Watch my feet, boss," he enjoined me. "Watch!"

He put out his foot, touched the ground lightly with his toes, then pointed the other foot; the steps were mingled violently, joyously, the ground reverberated like a drum.

He shook me by the shoulder.

"Now then, my boy," he said. "Both together!"

We threw ourselves into the dance. Zorba instructed me, corrected me gravely, patiently, and with great gentleness. I grew bold and felt my heart on the wing like a bird.

"Bravo! You're a wonder!" cried Zorba, clapping his hands to mark the beat. "Bravo, youngster! To hell with paper and ink! To hell with goods and profits! To hell with mines and workmen and monasteries! And now that you, my boy, can dance as well and have learnt my language, what shan't we be able to tell each other!"

He pounded on the pebbles with his bare feet and clapped his hands.

"Boss," he said, "I've dozens of things to say to you. I've never loved anyone as much before. I've hundreds of things to say, but my tongue just can't manage them. So I'll dance them for you!

Nikos Kazantzakis *Zorba the Greek*

must have sufficient food, air, water, and rest in order to live. Also, as a species, we must reproduce in order to survive. Unless we satisfy these basic physiological needs, we have no future.

The next category of needs involves *safety*. Once assured of nutrition and atmosphere, we have to find shelter and clothing to protect ourselves from the sometimes hostile elements. We must also ensure that we are safe from any forces that threaten our lives or health, including dangerous animals or people as well as life-threatening diseases.

It's obvious that the ability to communicate well plays a critical role in satisfying these basic needs. For most of us, earning the money that puts food on the table and clothes on our backs comes from holding a job, and both getting and carrying out that job requires an ability to express yourself and to understand others. Even if you chose to spend the rest of your life on welfare, you would have to convince an eligibility worker that you deserved public support, which would require communicative skills.

Communication also plays an important role in such basic needs as maintaining your health. Selecting a good physician and describing "where it hurts" requires you to speak clearly, and following the doctor's instructions calls for the ability to listen and to understand.

Of course, you're aware of the importance of skillful communication in satisfying the basic need of sexual fulfillment.

Social Needs Once our basic physiological and safety needs are satisfied, the next most fundamental human concern, according to Maslow, is to establish and maintain social contact. Virtually all people have the desire to be accepted, appreciated, or loved by others. We become lonesome in the absence of human company, and thus tend to seek out others even when our physiological and safety needs do not require that we do so.

Psychologist William Schutz describes three basic interpersonal needs which we strive to satisfy by social interaction: We want to be included in what other people do and also include them in our activities (inclusion); we need to exercise some control over others (control); and we need to have others care about us and in turn to care about them (affection). Like Maslow, Schutz argues that the desire to achieve inclusion, control, and affection aren't just desirable, but are *essential*. We interact with others because this is the only way to satisfy these basic needs. In other words, "people who need people" aren't the "luckiest people in the world," they're the *only* people in the world!

Ego Needs As you'll read in Chapter 2, defining and confirming our personal identity provides the foundation for much of our behavior. Maslow recognizes this fact when he discusses the human need for *self-esteem*. We strive to respect ourselves and be respected by others, and much of our communication is devoted to these goals. We put in extra effort at school or on the job not so much for the pay increase or the high grade, but to be able to think "I've done well; I'm competent," and to hear others say this about us.

Another category of ego needs involves what Maslow describes as *self-actualization*—the need to maximize our potential, to become everything we are capable of being. Just as a mountaineer climbs a challenging peak "because it's there," we sometimes express ourselves because we feel some kind of drive to say what needs to be said for the simple purpose of creating a message. This need for self-actualization explains why many people write, paint, dance, and otherwise express themselves. After we're physically and socially secure, a need to reach out and create messages still exists—because the ideas and feelings are there.

The Need for Better Communication

The needs we've just discussed are obviously important. If most people were able to satisfy them on their own, there would be no reason to have written this book. The truth, however, is that few people communicate well enough to satisfy their physiological, social, and ego needs completely. Many fall desperately short of these goals. In the next few pages we'll look at three areas in which there is a need for better communication.

Life and Health   We've already seen that failure to satisfy our physiological needs may prove fatal. It would be an overstatement to say that there are many incidents where people communicate so poorly that they starve, or meet some similar fate. But consider the other types of needs we've discussed. What happens if we don't satisfy our desire for inclusion, control, or affection? Do we die in such cases? At first, the answer would seem to be "no"; but, in fact, there does seem to be a connection

Man lives by affirmation even more than he lives by bread.

Victor Hugo

between social interaction and physical health—and even longevity.

In a nine-year study of 7,000 subjects, Lisa Berkman, an epidemiologist for the California Department of Health, found that people with few or no strong social relationships died at a rate of from two to four and one-half times greater than more socially oriented people. The context in which social interaction occurred did not seem to matter: Some of the longer-lived subjects gained support from marriages, others had friendships, and still others were members of some organization. But people with no such affiliations apparently failed to meet a life-sustaining need.

Suicide figures are also indicative of people's inability to meet interpersonal needs. In the United States in 1975 there were 12.6 deaths by suicide for every 100,000 population. In 1965 there were 11.6 suicides per 100,000. This increase amounts to a bit more than 8 percent in ten years. In the last fifteen years there has been a 90 percent increase in suicides among young people between the ages of fifteen and twenty-one. In this age group suicide now ranks second to automobile accidents as the cause of death.

This depressing picture is based on officially reported figures. The number of suicides disguised as auto accidents, poisonings, and so on will never be known. Moreover, sociologists working in this area estimate that seven to eight times as many people attempt suicide as those who actually succeed in killing themselves. This statistic means that every year in the United States about 175,000 to 200,000 individuals evidently want to give up the struggle to live a satisfying life. Many suicides take their lives to escape from loneliness or unhappy relationships. Hence, an inability to communicate is again a problem.

Of course, not everyone who has trouble communicating dies prematurely. But even for the survivors, life can be unhappy. Figures on mental illness indicate that 10 percent of all Americans are considered maladjusted or mentally ill. A look at any medical text concerned with the problems of mental illness makes it clear that they are due in great part to unsatisfying relationships in which little effective communication has occurred. It's additionally said that many people who experience such difficulties are either unwilling or unable to take the step of asking for help.

Better Relationships "What about me?" you might ask. "I'm alive, I'm not suicidal, and although I have my ups and downs, I'm not mentally ill. Why should I worry about communicating better?" We answer this question by suggesting that while your life might not be terrible, it's probably not as good as it could be. One reason why you may be less than totally satisfied is that your important relationships are sometimes unrewarding. And one source of relationship problems is a difficulty in communicating.

Family relationships certainly suffer when members have trouble communicating effectively. This situation is probably most apparent in households with adolescents. As writers such as Jay Haley, Harold Mosak, and Rudolph Driekers (see the *Readings* section at the end of this chapter) describe, the teen years are a difficult time. Between the ages of twelve and nineteen or twenty the body goes through changes which leave the teenager acting in ways older adults find exasperating. For instance, the slouch that parents constantly reprimand teenagers for is partially a response to rapid physical growth and, as such, a natural part of the maturing process. To an older observer, however, such slouching is often a condition for criticism. Similarly, the rapid pace and impatience of teens comes partially from another physiological change taking place during adolescence. G. G. Luce points out that as an individual grows from childhood to maturity, the rate at which he or she consumes oxygen declines, resulting in a slowing of the metabolism. Luce goes on to suggest that this higher metabolic rate may account for teenagers' seemingly slow passage of time, and for their frustration with the admonitions of older adults to "slow down and wait."

Along with these physiological changes, stages in the emotional development of family members lead to communication breakdowns. For instance, while family

"If you want to talk, why don't you call up a radio talk-show?"

relationships may be of prime importance to parents, to teenagers the associations with peers become the most critical. Teenagers need to break away from the family (usually to reestablish emotional ties later), while parents often want to hang on to their children. As this struggle develops, the family union loses its previous stability, or homeostasis. Typical patterns of interaction are disrupted and the predictability which is often a prime benefit of family life is shattered. During this stressful period the friction between family members grows, often becoming intolerable.

While learning to communicate effectively certainly won't evaporate these generational differences, it can help family members cope with them in a way that doesn't threaten their relationships with each other. If families can use communication skills such as this book describes, their ability to share and adapt to each others' needs will provide a foundation which can survive the turbulence of stressful periods.

Husbands and wives often have as much trouble communicating with each other as with their children. In 1975 there were 2.1 million marriages and 1 million divorces recorded officially. That works out to about one marriage dissolved for every two started. Ten years earlier, in 1965, there was one divorce for every four marriages. In California in 1975 there were 130,000 divorces and 160,000 marriages, or thirteen divorces for every sixteen marriages. Of course, marriage in itself doesn't guarantee

While his life was impeccable on the surface, he felt he was behind glass: moving through the world in a separate compartment, touching no one else. This was painful. . . . One night going home on the train to Connecticut he found himself in the air-conditioned car staring at a page of *The New Yorker* on his lap. His mind stopped. The page gleamed with a high, cold gloss in the fluorescent light: He stared at its shining surface, the pale gray pinstripe of his dark pants leg. Eventually his stop appeared. He got off in a somnambulistic daze. No one met him at the station. He felt he should call someone for help—but who?

Andrew Holleran
Dancer from the Dance

social compatibility, increased self-esteem, or self-actualization. And divorce isn't always a sign of failure. It does seem fair to assume, however, that many marriages end because the partners are unable to communicate with each other successfully. Furthermore, partners incapable of meeting each others' needs in one relationship may have the same problem in subsequent ones.

Outside of the family, the inability to communicate keeps many people from having the amount and quality of friendships they desire. In a survey of students at Pennsylvania State University, Gerald Phillips and Nancy Metzger explored the relationship between communication and friendship. The responses of their subjects indicated a strong need for better communication skills. A majority of the people Phillips and Metzger questioned reported that their friendships needed improving. Of these, many expressed frustration over their efforts to explain their behavior to others, while another group had trouble explaining to others how they wanted them to behave. The three main sources of pain in friendships were all communication-related: failure of friends to live up to promises; betrayal of confidences; and the friends' use of confessed weaknesses to intimidate the subjects.

These results demonstrate a wider problem, and one that also stems at least partially from an inability to communicate well. In his book, *We, The Lonely People,* Ralph Keyes takes a careful look at contemporary society and concludes that the loss of community contributes greatly to the difficulty we have in meeting our needs:

The problem of community, which sociologist Robert Nisbet calls "the single most impressive fact in the twentieth century in Western Society," is relatively modern. For most of man's history, group life was a given, and grew naturally out of the ways we were forced to be with each other—to live, work, wash clothes, and die.

This is no longer true. We have less and less necessity to be together, and fewer ways of knowing each other, while our need for community remains constant. So we're forced back

on the only immutable reason for joining hands: the human need for company. Without place, without cause, common work or religion most of us must make that humiliating admission: I can't live alone.

. . . But to join that community, each one of us must take the hard, terrifying first step—saying—even to one other person— "I need you."

Keyes' message comes through loud and clear—we are doomed to disappointment if we can't reestablish community in some way to provide the kind of social intercourse necessary to meet our interpersonal needs.

Self-Understanding So far, we've seen that communication problems can estrange parents and their children, contribute to failing marriages, threaten friendships, weaken communities, and even shorten our lives. There is one final reason for learning to communicate more skillfully. By relating clearly with others we can come to understand ourselves better.

The fact that many people seek self-understanding becomes apparent as soon as you survey the amount of written material currently available on that subject. Almost any bookstore (not to mention airport, supermarket, and drugstore) has a large number of books devoted to teaching you more about yourself, often through bettering your communication. Besides the obvious social benefits, these books promise— though they don't always deliver—other benefits of improved communication.

Communication can lead to better self-understanding in two ways. First, by be-coming open to the way others view us we can learn more about ourselves. As you'll read in Chapter 2, the reflected appraisals of others serve as a kind of mirror in which we may view ourselves. The more we open ourselves up to such appraisals, the better idea we'll have of how we appear.

Secondly, besides learning about ourselves by listening to others, we can gain self-understanding from speaking. Virtually everyone has had the experience of understanding their own position better after having explained it to another. There are benefits in expressing our thoughts and feelings about almost any subject, from the process for factoring a quadratic equation to how to bake a cheesecake to why you are or aren't in love.

Probably the most dramatic validation of self-expression as a road to understanding is evidenced by the handsome living that many psychotherapists earn by primarily allowing their clients to talk themselves into better mental health. Of course, it would be an oversimplification to suggest that the only skill a therapist must possess is to keep quiet and let the patient rattle on, but few therapists would dispute the value of being a supportive, empathetic listener.

We don't want to overstate our case and suggest that communicating better will solve every problem. Loneliness, illness, confusion about oneself, conflict, and other unsatisfying conditions often have causes that go far beyond communicative behaviors. It would be a mistake to think that simply reading this book will leave you with a completely trouble-free life. But as you'll see from reading on, research does suggest that personal functioning and social relationships improve as we become more effective communicators.

What Is Communication?

So far we've been talking about communication as if the actions described by this word were perfectly clear. We've found, however, that most people aren't aware of all that goes on whenever two or more people share ideas. Before going further we want to show you what does happen when one person expresses a thought or feeling to another. By doing so, we can introduce you to a common working vocabulary that will be useful as you read on, and at the same time preview some of the activities we'll cover in later chapters.

A Communication Model A model is a simplified representation of some process. For instance, consider what a model of "digestion" might look like. At one end of a page we could draw a mouth with food going into it, followed by tubes running into and out of a baglike object representing the stomach. To represent the intestines we could draw a coiled hose that connects the two.

While this representation may tell us something about digestion, it also tells us a great deal about the following characteristics of models:

1. *Models can represent the relevant elements of a process.* Even though our diagram is crude, it does provide a good introduction to the basic parts of the digestive tract.

2. *Models organize the parts of a process and indicate how they are related to each other.* For example, an uninformed viewer would learn from our drawing that the stomach is below the esophagus and above the intestines.

3. *Most models make a complex event simple.* This simplification helps promote understanding. It's certainly easier to an uninitiated learner to start exploring the digestion process with a simple model than by delving into the intricacies of an extremely complex event.

4. *A model provides an opportunity to look at a familiar process in a new way.* By doing so, models sometimes make us aware that we've been operating on misconceptions. For instance, by adding an explanation of what goes on in each part of our digestion model, it becomes clear how little digestion actually goes on in the stomach, contrary to the belief of many people.

While models clearly offer several advantages, they also suffer from a number of potential drawbacks. First, in an attempt to make a complex event simple, a model may oversimplify and lead viewers into thinking that the event itself is simple. This mistaken assumption has the highest probability of occurring if a learner has little information on what the event is really like. For instance, someone not versed in physics might actually believe that an atom is quite similar to one or more marbles spinning around a grapefruit.

It's also important to remember that a model is an analogy, and nothing more. The danger of confusing the map with the territory is illustrated by the story of an elementary school child who, having studied geography by using the classroom map, was surprised to discover that Spain was not a pink country, France green, and so on.

Finally, a model can cause us to stop thinking about the process that it represents and can cause us to conclude that we know everything significant about the subject. This mistake is termed *premature closure,* and, of course, should be avoided.

Keeping the advantages and dangers of models in mind, we can begin to build a representation of what goes on in the process of communication. Since we need to begin somewhere, let's start with you wanting to express an idea. If you think about it for a moment, you'll realize that most ideas you have don't come to you already put into words. Rather, they're more like mental images, often consisting of unverbalized feelings, such as anger, and how you want a job to look when it is finished. We can represent your mental image like this:

Figure 1-1

Since people aren't mind readers, you have to translate this mental image into symbols (usually words) that others can understand. No doubt you can recall times when you actually shuffled through a mental list of words to pick exactly the right ones to explain an idea. This process, called *encoding,* goes on every time we speak.

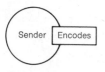

Figure 1-2

Once the idea is encoded, the next step is to send it. We call this step the *message* phase of our model. You have a number of ways by which you can send a message. For instance, you might consider expressing yourself in a letter, over the telephone, or face to face. In this sense, writing, talking on the phone, and speaking in person are three of the *channels* through which we send our messages. In addition to these channels we transfer our thoughts and feelings by touch, posture, gestures, distance, clothing, and many other ways. The important fact to realize now is that there are a number of such channels.

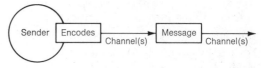

Figure 1-3

When your message reaches another person, much the same process we described earlier occurs in reverse. The receiver must make some sense out of the symbols you've sent by *decoding* them back into feelings, intentions, or thoughts that mean something to her (see Figure 1-4).

Ideally, at this point the mental images of the sender and receiver ought to match. If this happens, we can say that an act of successful communication has occurred. However, as you know from your own experience, things often go wrong somewhere between the sender and the receiver. For instance:

Your constructive suggestion is taken as criticism;

Your carefully phrased question is misunderstood;

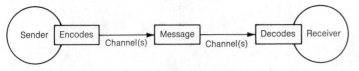

Figure 1-4

Your friendly joke is taken as an insult;
or
Your hinted request is missed entirely.

And so it often goes. Why do such misunderstandings occur? To answer this question we need to add more detail to our model. We recognize that without several more crucial elements our model would not represent the world.

First, it's important to recognize that communication always takes place in an *environment*. By this term we do not mean simply a physical location, but also the personal history that each person brings to a conversation. The problem here is that each of us has a different environment because of our differing backgrounds. While we certainly have some experiences in common, we also see each situation in a unique way. For instance, consider how two individuals' environments would differ if:

A was well rested and B was exhausted;

A was rich and B was poor;

A was rushed and B had nowhere special to go;

A had lived a long, eventful life and B was young and inexperienced; or

A was passionately concerned with the subject and

B was indifferent to it.

Obviously this list could go on and on. The problem of differing environments is critical to effective communication. Even now, though, you can see from just these few items that the world is a different place for sender and receiver. We can represent this idea on our model shown in Figure 1-5.

Notice that we've overlapped the environments of A and B. This overlapping represents those things that our communicators have in common. This point is important because it is through our shared knowledge and experiences that we are able to communicate. For example, you are able to at least partially to understand the messages we are writing on these pages because we share the same language, however imprecise it often may be.

Different environments aren't the only cause of ineffective communication. Com-

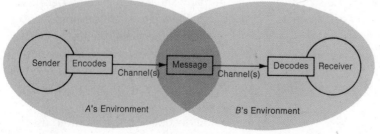

Figure 1-5

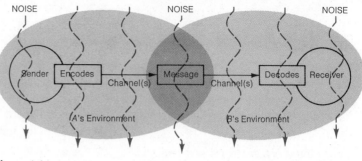

Figure 1-6

municologists use the term *noise* to label other forces that interfere with the process, and point out that it can occur in every stage (see Figure 1-6).

There are primarily two types of noise that can block communication—physical and psychological. Physical noise includes those obvious things that make it difficult to hear, as well as many other kinds of distractions. For instance, too much cigarette smoke in a crowded room might make it hard for you to pay attention to another person, and sitting in the rear of an auditorium might make a speaker's remarks unclear. Physical noise can disrupt communication almost anywhere in our model—in the sender, channel, message, or receiver.

Psychological noise refers to forces within the sender or receiver that make these people less able to express or understand the message clearly. For instance, an outdoorsman might exaggerate the size and number of fish caught in order to convince himself and others of his talents. In the same way, a student might become so upset upon learning that he failed a test that he would be unable (perhaps unwilling

is a better word) to clearly understand where he went wrong. Psychological noise is so important a problem in communication that we have devoted Chapter 7 to investigating its most common form, defensiveness.

So far we've talked only about one-way communication, consisting of a single sender and receiver who never switch roles. There certainly are situations in which this is an accurate picture of what goes on: television, radio, and newspapers represent one-way communication, as do some unfortunate families where parents expect to do all the talking while their children are placed in the position of being merely listeners.

At this point you can probably recognize that there are cases where communication must be *two-way*, with each participant both sending and receiving. Two-way communication is appropriate and important in many situations, not only because it gives us a chance to share our ideas with others, but also because it helps us check and verify our understanding of the messages others have sent. This use of two-way communication for verification is termed *feedback*.

Without feedback it is difficult to assess how effective you are as a communicator

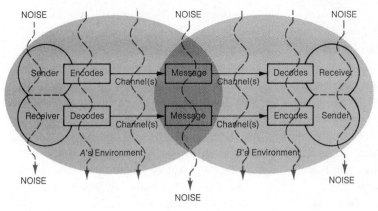

Figure 1-7

(although feedback is no guarantee of accurate understanding). Teachers seem to have an uncanny ability to talk for hours without realizing that once-active listeners have nodded off to sleep, nibbled through their lunches, or slipped quietly out of the room. The feedback is there, but the teacher either ignores it or fails to analyze it.

On the other hand, students have been taught how to shake their heads in agreement, smile, and look contemplative, without any of these behaviors serving as an accurate reflection of their response to what's happening for them. Without questioning a student's feedback, it becomes impossible to determine the actual state of affairs—who is bored and who is not. Ignoring feedback, or not checking it to determine its accuracy, leads to misunderstandings.

This completes our representation. Take a moment and look at the detailed model of the communication process which we've built (see Figure 1-7).

This picture is probably more complicated than a definition you might once have given. But now you can probably see that every step is important and can't be omitted. Given this model, perhaps you can better understand why effective communication is often so difficult and why spending some time learning the skills that make it possible can be worth your while.

Characteristics of Communication   Although our model has almost certainly increased your understanding of communication, we need to explain some additional important characteristics of that phenomenon.

Communication is a process   Although the model on page 13 suggests that there are specific, discrete acts of communication, the truth is that the process is continuing, ongoing. In this sense, a more accurate representation would require a motion picture, rather than a single drawing. We could argue that communication has neither beginning nor end. After all, the environment that shapes your understanding has been developing from birth—or even before, if you consider the genetic characteristics shaping perception. (We'll have a great deal to say about this in Chapter 4.) And the events that make up your history of relating to the other person affect your behavior in a given situation. For example, the way you behave around an attractive person of the opposite sex, a police officer, or a stranger you encounter in a dark alley is certainly influenced by your background. Keeping this in mind, you can see that it's not accurate to suggest that an "act" of communication begins when you first encounter someone else.

Communication is irreversible   Picture yourself sitting in a movie theater, watching a film. You know that the projectionist could stop the film, run it in reverse, or start it over at any point by backing it up. Communication may be thought of as a film which *cannot* be stopped, put in reverse, or started over. It continues on, much like the "river which cannot be stepped into twice," the river which continues to flow and change regardless of how much it seems to look the same.

This book that you're reading is part of the communication process—an element of it. What you read you cannot "unread," and what you read affects you many ways: It affects the other communication events in which you engage, and will continue to do so, whether you are always aware of this or not.

Communicators are simultaneously senders and receivers   Our model implies that at any given point in time a person is either sending or receiving a message. Actually, at any point we are doing both. The two sender-receiver representations in our model should not be one under another, but rather superimposed (hard to represent in a two-dimensional drawing!). The process does not involve A sending a message to B, who in turn sends a message back to A. Rather, A and B are both sending and receiving messages *at the same time.* Although at a given moment A may appear to be the predominant sender and the predominant receiver, A and B are performing both roles simultaneously.

For example, consider this book. It may appear that we are the senders and you are the receiver, that you are affected by what is written here, and we are not. In fact, this view isn't completely accurate. For us, the process of writing was a process of listening—to our students, teachers, colleagues, and ourselves. We wrote, listened to feedback, rewrote, received more feedback, and rewrote! Also, as we dealt with and wrote down the ideas in this book, we found ourselves dealing with other people differently and, we believe more effectively. We lived what we wrote, and this changed our own behavior, just as we hope that "living" what's here may change the way you act.

Interpersonal Communication Defined
Now that you have a clearer understanding of the overall process of communication, it's time to see what distinguishes interpersonal communication from other varieties. The most obvious distinction involves the context in which the communication occurs. We can look at how many people are involved, whether they're close or far from each other, and how much access they have to each other (for

example, how much of each other they can see, hear, and touch, and how easy it is to offer each other feedback). Interpersonal communication using this approach is defined as involving a "small number" of communicators who are "close" together and who have a "great deal" of access to each other.

Using a situational approach we can see that mass communication is easily distinguished from interpersonal communication because it involves more people with greater distances between them, and with very limited access to each other. In some cases, mass communication may involve feedback which takes months to process, as in the case of letters to TV stations about the most and least popular shows.

Public communication—usually consisting of a speech given before an audience—is also easily distinguished from interpersonal communication. Greater numbers of communicators at greater distances from each other are involved in public communication and access—especially in the form of feedback—is relatively limited, although not so much as in the case of mass communication.

Matters become a little more confusing when we compare interpersonal and small group communication. However, clear differences between these modes do exist. For example, issues such as conformity, leadership, division of labor, and decision making are much more prominent in groups due to the greater number and complexity of interrelationships.

On the other hand, there are strong similarities in one-to-one and small group interaction. Both involve a small number of communicators who are physically close and who have great access to each other.

And certainly there is a strong degree of "interpersonalness" in many group settings. Consider, for instance, a small work, study, or social group to which you've belonged. The relationships in such a group almost certainly involved elements you'll be studying in this interpersonal text: resolution of conflicts, issues of self-disclosure, the expression of feelings, changes in the emotional climate, and so on.

This fact suggests another definition of interpersonal communication—one which doesn't involve context so much as the way in which the participants deal with each other. If we use this second definition, one characteristic of interpersonal communication is, then, the disposition to *respond to others as individuals*. In less personal relationships we tend to classify the other person using sociological or cultural labels such as "Anglo," "Black," "teacher," "student," "doctor," and so on. As long as we rely primarily on such general—and possibly irrelevant—data, the relationship is not likely to become a personal one.

A second element of "interpersonalness" in relationships is the degree to which communicators rely on standardized rules to guide their interactions. When we meet someone for the first time we know how to behave because of the established social rules we have been taught. We shake hands, speak politely, and rely on socially accepted subjects: "How are you?" "What do you do?" "Lousy weather we've been having." The rules governing our interaction have little to do with us or the people with whom we interact; we are not responding to each other as individuals.

As we continue to interact, however, we sometimes gain more information about each other, and use that information as the basis for our communicating. As we share experiences, the rules that govern our behavior will be less determined by cultural rules, and more determined by the unique features of our own relationship. This doesn't mean that we abandon rules altogether, but rather that we often create our *own* conventions, ones which are appropriate for us. For example, one pair of friends might develop a procedure for dealing with conflicts by expressing their disagreements as soon as they arise, while another could tacitly agree to withhold a series of gripes, then clear the air periodically. While we could digress here and speculate about which procedure is more productive, the important point to recognize is that in both cases the individuals created their own rules.

A third characteristic of interpersonal qualities in a relationship involves the amount of information the communicators have about each other. When we meet people for the first time we have little information about them, usually no more than what we are told by others and the assumptions we make from observing what they wear and how they handle their bodies. As we talk, we gain more information in a variety of areas. The first topics we talk about are usually nonthreatening, nonintimate ones. If we continue talking, however, we may decide to discuss relatively few impersonal things. We may decide to increase the number of topics we talk about and choose to be more revealing of ourselves in doing so.

As we learn more about each other, and as our information becomes more intimate,

the degree to which we share an interpersonal relationship increases. This new degree of intimacy and sharing can come almost immediately, or else may grow slowly over a long period of time. In either case, we can say that the relationship becomes more interpersonal as the amount of self-disclosure increases. We'll have a great deal to say about this subject in Chapter 3.

If you accept the characteristics of individual regard, creation of unique rules, and sharing of personal information as criteria for an interpersonal relationship, you can see that many one-to-one relationships never reach this stage. And conversely, it's possible for groups, both small and large, to achieve an interpersonal relationship. As you read on, keep these facts in mind and realize that while interpersonal communication is most likely to occur in two-person settings, it's not restricted to them.

Characteristics of Effective Communicators

Now that you have an idea of exactly what constitutes communication—both interpersonal and otherwise—it's time to see what distinguishes effective communicators from their less successful counterparts. In an attempt to discover the difference, Paul Feingold conducted an exhaustive review of research in the various disciplines concerned with communication: speech, psychology, guidance counseling, sociology, and human relations. After gathering and evaluating a large body of information,

Feingold concluded that there are five general characteristics a person must exhibit in order to be perceived as an effective communicator. He suggests that these are important for all types of communicators: Walter Cronkite, a favorite teacher, the President of the United States, your best friend, or yourself. Let's take a brief look at these five characteristics.

The man who lives by himself and for himself is apt to be corrupted by the company he keeps.

Charles H. Parkhurst

Adeptness at Creating Messages   There are several characteristics that constitute adeptness. The first is an ability to speak about the world in a way that *coincides with a receiver's perceptions*. In order to make a message intelligible and acceptable, the sender has to have some awareness of how the receiver perceives the world. This includes a knowledge of the receiver's sociological and cultural background as well as his or her present psychological state. To understand the importance of this ability, think about both effective and ineffective instructors you've known. Often the difference between helpful and obscure instructors involves their ability to put a concept in terms with which you're familiar—to imagine how the field of chemistry, philosophy, or electronics appears to you.

The second aspect of adeptness is the ability to express ideas *clearly*. Consider the following quotes taken from letters written by individuals to their welfare departments in application for support:

This is my eighth child. What are you going to do about it?

I cannot get sick pay. I have six children. Can you tell me why?

In accordance with your instructions, I have given birth to twins in the enclosed envelope.

Unless I get my husband's money pretty soon, I will be forced to lead an immortal life.

You have changed my little boy to a girl. Will this make a difference?

My husband had his project cut off two weeks ago and I haven't had any relief since.

Letters to school from parents explaining the absence of their child are no clearer:

My daughter was absent from school. She is totally exhausted. She spent the weekend maneuvering with the Marines.

John was late for class because he was home in bed with the doctor.

Mary was late for school because she had to run to the doctor with a swollen foot.

Although we can decipher the meaning of each of these, the conclusion we must draw is that the writer is not a clear communicator!

Feingold identifies *credibility* as a third component of adeptness, and it's certainly true that we only allow others to influence us when we view them as competent and trustworthy. Robert Young has established himself with millions of television viewers over the years as a warm, loving father (*Father Knows Best*) and a compassionate, dedicated physician (*Marcus Welby*), and so people now follow his commercial advice and buy the brand of decaffeinated coffee which he recommends. While this consumer behavior may not be logical, it certainly demonstrates the persuasive power of credibility.

The last aspect of the adeptness principle is one that is most obviously connected with our notion of "interpersonalness": A communicator we perceive as effective *reveals something personal about himself* in his messages. We've already seen that self-disclosure is one characteristic of close relationships, and it should be no surprise to find that most people judge communicators as most understandable and believable when they offer personal information to support their messages.

Similarity with the Receiver   Similarity can be demographic—including such factors as age, sex, and social class—or attitudinal, involving beliefs, likes, and dislikes. All we have to do is examine the current crop of television commercials to gain ample evidence of the principle. Advertisers know that one way to influence the public is to present people who are "average," people the viewers can identify as being like themselves. One commercial for a product aimed at relieving heartburn and acid indigestion presents, in one short spot on television, a fat person, a thin person, an Anglo, an Hispanic-American, a Black, a teacher, a carpenter, an executive, and a

secretary—all of varying ages, of course—to spell out their favorite product.

The more we perceive someone as similar to ourselves, the more we think we know about the person. This knowing extends beyond sociological and cultural data, and we get the feeling that we also share psychological characteristics. This assumption is often incorrect, but the feeling that we share an interpersonal relationship with the speaker persists.

Adaptability   The third characteristic that causes us to identify communicators as effective involves their ability to adapt to the situation at hand. We perceive effective communicators as those able to meet the demands placed on them by varying circumstances. We probably appreciate this adaptability most when it allows others to meet our needs. For instance, think about how much you appreciate those people (probably few in number) who can recognize when you're having some personal problem and find a way to help you cope with it. Truly flexible helpers have a wide repertoire of behaviors available—offering advice, lending support, clarifying our feelings, and even simply listening quietly. Furthermore, effective communicators know when to use each style.

Adaptability extends into other areas as well. Some communicators seem able to get along well with a wide range of people from various ages, ethnic backgrounds, or educational levels. Others seem comfortable in diverse settings. In any case, we admire flexible, adaptable communicators.

> **Instead of loving your enemies, treat your friends a little better.**
>
> Edgar Watson Howe

Commitment to the Receiver   Not surprisingly, we view people who are responsive and interested in us as effective communicators. Commitment can be demonstrated in many ways. In a business setting it might be an obvious desire for the relationship to be mutually profitable. On a personal level commitment might appear as a genuine concern for our emotional welfare. Sometimes commitment can show up in small but significant ways: arriving on time for appointments, spending time with us when other demands beckon, remembering special occasions, or defending us from the attacks of others.

Adeptness at Receiving Messages   The fifth characteristic of effective communicators changes our emphasis somewhat. So far we have focused on communicators primarily as senders, identifying the kind of messages they send to us. We also value those people who are skillful receivers. This ability actually ties in closely with the previous ones, for skillful listening requires adaptability, a certain amount of similarity with the speaker, and most certainly a commitment to us. As you'll see in Chapter 8, listening involves much more than simply sitting quietly and occasionally nodding your head.

So now we've taken a first look at the subject of communication. We've outlined a number of reasons why people communicate, demonstrated that we often need to do a better job, explained in some detail exactly what goes on in the communication process, distinguished interpersonal communication from other types, and talked about the qualities of effective communicators. In the remainder of this book we'll build on this foundation. By the time you're finished, you should not only understand the concepts of communication better, but should also be able to express yourself better and understand others better as well.

Readings

Berelson, Bernard and Gary A. Steiner. *Human Behavior: An Inventory of Scientific Findings.* New York: Harcourt, Brace and World, 1964.

Berkman, Lisa. "Social Relationships and Longevity." In *Organizational Communication, (2nd, Ed.),* Gerald M. Goldhaber, ed., Dubuque, Iowa: Wm. C. Brown, 1979: 65–66.

Dance, Frank E. X. "The 'Concept' of Communication." *Journal of Communication,* 20, (1970): 201–210.

Feingold, Paul. *Toward a Paradigm of Effective Communication: An Empirical Study of Perceived Communicative Effectiveness.* Doctoral dissertation, Purdue University, 1976.

Haley, Jay. *Uncommon Therapy: The Psychiatric Techniques of Milton H. Erickson.* New York: W. W. Norton, 1973.

Herzberg, Frederick. "One More Time: How Do You Motivate Employees?" *Harvard Business Review,* 46, (1968): 53–62.

Holtzman, Paul D. and Donald Ecroyd. *Communication Concepts and Models.* Skokie, Ill.: National Textbook Co., 1976.

Keyes, Ralph. *We, The Lonely People: Searching for Community*. New York: Harper and Row, 1973.

Luce, Gay G. *Biological Rhythms in Psychiatry and Medicine*. Washington, D.C. National Institute of Mental Health, 1970.

Maslow, Abraham H. *Motivation and Personality* (Revised Ed.). New York: Harper, 1970.

Maslow, Abraham H. *Toward a Psychology of Being*. New York: Van Nostrand Reinhold, 1968.

Miller, Gerald. "On Defining Communication: Another Stab." *Journal of Communication,* 16, (1966): 88–98.

Miller, Gerald and Mark Steinberg. *Between People: A New Analysis of Interpersonal Communication*. Chicago: Science Research Associates, 1975.

Mosak, Harold H. and Rudolph Driekers. "Adlerian Psychotherapy." In *Current Psychotherapy,* Raymond Corsini, ed., Itasca, Ill.: F. E. Peacock, 1973.

Phillips, Gerald and Nancy Metzger. *Intimate Communication*. Boston: Allyn and Bacon, 1976.

Schutz, William. *The Interpersonal Underworld*. Palo Alto, Calif.: Science and Behavior Books, 1966.

Stevens, S. S. "Introduction: A Definition of Communication." *Journal of the Acoustical Society of America,* 22, (1950): 689.

Verderber, Rudolph, Ann Elder and Ernest Weiler. "A Study of Communication Time Usage Among College Students." Unpublished study, University of Cincinnati, 1976.

Wenburg, John and William Wilmot. *The Personal Communication Process*. New York: Wiley, 1973.

2

Who are you?

Before reading on, take a few minutes to answer this question by trying the following simple exercise. First, make a list of the ten words or phrases that describe the most important features of who you are. Some of the items on your list might involve social roles: student, son or daughter, employee, and so on. Or you could define yourself through physical characteristics: fat, skinny, tall, short, beautiful, ugly. You might focus on your intellectual characteristics: smart, stupid, curious, inquisitive. Perhaps you can best define yourself in terms of moods, feelings, or attitudes: optimistic, critical, energetic. Or you could consider your social characteristics: outgoing, shy, defensive. You may see yourself in terms of belief systems: pacifist, Christian, vegetarian, libertarian. Finally, you could focus on particular skills (or lack of): swimmer, artist, carpenter. In any case, choose ten words or phrases which best describe you and write them down.

Now choose the one item from your list that is the most fundamental to who you are and copy it on another sheet of paper. Then pick the second most fundamental item and record it as number two on your new list. Continue ranking the ten items until you have reorganized them all.

Now comes the most interesting part of the experience. Find a place where you won't be disturbed and close your eyes. Take a few moments to relax and then create a mental image of yourself. Try to paint a picture that not only captures your physical characteristics, but that also reflects the attitudes, aptitudes, feelings,

and/or beliefs included on your list. Take plenty of time to create this image.

Now recall (or peek at) your second list noting the item you ranked as number ten—the one least essential to your identity. Keeping your mental image in focus, imagine that this item suddenly disappeared from your personality or physical makeup. Try to visualize how you would be different without that tenth item. How would it affect the way you act? The way you feel? The way others behave toward you? Was it easy to give up that item? Do you like yourself more or less without it? Take a few minutes with your eyes closed to answer these questions.

Now, without regaining the item you've just given up, continue your fantasy by removing item number nine. What difference does its absence make for you?

Now slowly, at your own pace, continue the process by jettisoning one item at a time until you have given them all up. Notice what happens at each step of the process. After you've gone through your entire list, reclaim the items one by one until you are back to where you started.

How do you feel after trying this exercise? Most people find the experience a strong one. They say that it clarifies how each of the items selected are fundamental to their identity. Many people say that they gain a clear picture of the parts of themselves they value and the parts with which they are unhappy.

What you've accomplished in developing this list is to partially describe your *self-concept*. There are many different ways of defining self-concept, but probably the clearest way to think of the term is as the image you hold of yourself. If you had a special mirror that not only reflected physical features, but also allowed you to view other aspects of yourself—emotional states, talents, likes, dislikes, values, roles, and so on—then the reflection in that mirror would be your self-concept.

You probably recognize that the self-concept list you recorded is only a partial one. To make the description of yourself complete, you'd have to keep adding items until your list ran into hundreds of words. Take a moment now to uncover the many parts of your self-concept by simply responding to the question "Who am I?" over and over again. Add these responses to the list you have already started.

Of course, not every item on your self-concept list is equally important. For example, the most significant part of one person's self-concept might consist of social roles, whereas for another it might be physical appearance, health, friendships, accomplishments, or skills.

"All right," you say, "now I have a clearer picture of my self-concept, but what does this have to do with the way I communicate?" We can begin to answer this question by looking at how your present self-concept developed.

How the Self-Concept Develops

Researchers generally agree that the self-concept does not exist at birth. An infant lying in a crib has no notion of self, no notion—even if verbal language were miraculously made available—of how to answer the question at the beginning of this chapter. Consider what it would be like to have no idea of your characteristic moods,

physical appearance, social traits, talents, intellectual capacity, beliefs, or important roles. If you can imagine this experience— *blankness*—you can start to understand how the world appears to someone with no sense of self. Of course, you have to take one step further and *not know* you do not have any notion of self.

Soon after birth the infant begins to differentiate among the things in the environment: familiar and unfamiliar faces, the sounds that mean food, the noises that frighten, the cat who jumps in the crib, the sister who tickles—each becomes a separate part of the world. Recognition of distinctions in the environment probably precedes recognition of the self.

At about six or seven months the child begins to recognize "self" as distinct from surroundings. If you've ever watched children this age you've probably marveled at how they can stare with great fascination at a foot, hand, and other body parts which float into view, almost as if they were strange objects belonging to someone else. Then the connection is made, almost as if the child were realizing "The hand is *me*"; "The foot is *me*." These first revelations form the child's earliest concept of self. At this early stage, the self-concept is almost exclusively physical, involving the child's basic realization of existence and of possessing certain body parts over which some control is exerted. This self-concept is a rather limited one, and barely resembles more fully developed self-concepts held by older children.

What happens next? What are the next influences that help expand this rudimentary self-concept? There are two theories defining how a person's self-concept develops: *reflected appraisal* and *social comparison*. These theories are complementary, each explaining a distinct way in which people come to an image of who they are.

Reflected Appraisal Before examining this view of self-concept development, try the following exercise. Either by yourself or aloud with a partner, recall someone you know or once knew who was an "upper"—who helped enhance your self-concept by acting in a way that made you feel accepted, worthwhile, important, appreciated, or loved. Your upper needn't have played a crucial role in your life, as long as the role was positive. Often one's self-concept is shaped by many tiny nudges as well as a few giant events. For instance, Ron's upper was Sam, who when Ron was six or seven years old treated him to "special days"—a morning spent together exploring the treasures in Sam's jewelry store, followed by a lunch in a restaurant. Another was Abe, Lawrence's grandfather, who always told Lawrence that he could become a playwright if that's what he wanted.

After thinking about your upper, recall a "downer" from your life—some person who acted in either a big or small way to diminish your self-esteem. Among the downers teachers recall are students who yawn in the middle of their classes. (The students may be tired, but it's difficult for

teachers not to think that they are doing a poor, boring job.) Another downer is Joyce, a former girlfriend of Neil's, who shrugged off his romantic overtures by refusing to take them seriously.

After thinking about your uppers and downers, you should begin to see that everyone's self-concept is shaped by those around them. To the extent that you have received upper messages, you have learned to appreciate and value yourself. To the degree that you have received downer signals, you are likely to feel less valuable, lovable, and capable. In this sense it's possible to see that the self-concept you described in your list is a product of the upper and downer messages you've received throughout your life.

The family is the first place we receive upper and downer messages. It provides us with our first feelings of adequacy (and inadequacy), acceptance (and rejection), and what constitutes an acceptable goal in life. Even before children can speak, people are making evaluations of them. The earliest months of life are full of messages—the first uppers and downers shaping the self-concept. The amount of time parents allow their children to cry before attending to their needs communicates nonverbally to the children over a period of time just how important they are to the parents. The parental method of handling infants speaks volumes: Do they affectionately play with the child, joggling her gently and holding her close, or do they treat her like so much baggage, changing diapers or carrying out feeding and bathing in a brusque, businesslike manner? Does the tone of voice with which they speak to the child express love and enjoyment or disappointment and irritation?

Of course, most of these messages are not intentional ones. It is rare when a parent deliberately tries to tell a child he or she is not lovable; but whether the messages are intentional or not doesn't matter—nonverbal statements play a big role in shaping a youngster's feelings of being "OK" or "not OK."

As children learn to speak and understand language, verbal messages also contribute to their developing self-concept. Close your eyes for a moment and think about messages you heard when you were being raised.

"What a beautiful child!"

"Can't you do anything right?"

"Come give me a hug."

"I don't know what to do with you!"

As you can clearly see, each of these messages implies some sort of appraisal. And because a child has no way of defining "self" other than through the eyes of surrounding adults, these evaluations have a profound influence on the developing self-concept.

In a review of self-concept literature, William Fitts summarizes parental influence on self-concept formation. Parents with healthy self-concepts tend to have children with healthy self-concepts, and parents with poor, negative, or deviant self-concepts tend to have children who view themselves in primarily negative ways. Interestingly, if one parent has a good self-concept and the other a poor self-concept the child is most likely to choose the more positive parent as a model. If neither parent has a strong

CHILDREN LEARN WHAT THEY LIVE

If a child lives with criticism
 he learns to condemn.
If a child lives with hostility
 he learns to fight.
If a child lives with ridicule
 he learns to be shy.
If a child lives with shame
 he learns to feel guilty.
If a child lives with tolerance
 he learns to be patient.
If a child lives with encouragement
 he learns confidence.
If a child lives with praise
 he learns to appreciate.
If a child lives with fairness
 he learns justice.
If a child lives with security
 he learns to have faith.
If a child lives with approval
 he learns to like himself.
If a child lives with acceptance and
 friendship
 he learns to find love in the world.

Dorothy Law Nolte

self-concept, it is likely that the child will seek an adult outside the family with whom to identify.

In families where one parent has a strong, positive self-concept, the child is usually provided with a secure environment in the form of love and attention. A child brought up in such an environment is able to face the world as a secure, confident person. If both parents have strong, positive self-concepts, then the effect is even more pronounced.

In late life the self-concept continues to be shaped by how others respond to us, especially when messages come from what sociologists term "significant others"— those people whose opinions we especially value. A look at the uppers and downers you described earlier (as well as others you can remember) will show that the evaluations of a few especially important people can have long-range effects. A teacher from long ago, a special friend or relative, or perhaps a barely known acquaintance whom you respected can all leave an influential imprint on how you view yourself. To see the importance of significant others, ask yourself how you arrived at your opinion of yourself as a student, as a person attractive to the opposite sex, as a competent worker, and you'll see that these self-evaluations were probably influenced by the way others regarded you.

What determines whether an appraisal is accepted or rejected? At least four requirements must be met for an appraisal to be regarded as important:

1. First of all, the person who offers a particular appraisal must be someone we see as competent to offer it. Parents satisfy this requirement extremely well because as young children we perceive that our parents know so much about us—more than we know about ourselves some-times—and thus are able to make any number of accurate evaluations of us.

2. The person who offers the evaluation must be perceived as being highly personal. The more the other person indicates that he or she knows a great deal about us and the more he or she adapts what is being said to accurately describe us, the more likely we are to accept judgments from this person.

3. The appraisal must be reasonable in light of what we believe about ourselves. If an appraisal is *similar* to one we give ourselves we will believe it; if it is *somewhat dissimilar* we will probably still accept it; but if it is *completely dissimilar* we will probably reject it.

4. Appraisals that are consistent and numerous are more persuasive than those that contradict usual appraisals or those that only occur once. As long as only a *few* students yawn in class, a teacher can safely disregard them as a reflection of teaching ability. In like manner, you could safely disregard the appraisal of the angry date who may have told you in no uncertain terms what kind of person behaves as you did. Of course, when you get a second or third similar appraisal in a short time, the evaluation becomes harder to ignore.

In addition to specific influential individuals, each of us also formulates a self-concept based on the influence of various reference groups to which we are exposed. A youngster who is interested in ballet and who lives in a setting where such preferences are regarded as weird will start to accept this label if there is no support from significant others. Adults who want to share their feelings but find themselves in a society that discourages such sharing might, after a while, think of themselves as oddballs, unless they can get some reassurance that such a desire is normal. Again, we encounter the idea of knowing ourselves through the "mirrors" of others. To a great degree, we judge ourselves by the way others see us.

You might argue that not every part of your self-concept is shaped by others, that there are certain objective facts recognizable by self-observation alone. After all, nobody needs to tell you whether you are taller than others, speak with an accent, have curly hair, and so on. These facts are obvious.

While it's true that some features of the self are immediately apparent, the *significance* we attach to them—that is, the rank we assign them in the hierarchy of our list and the interpretation we give them—depends greatly on the opinions of others. After all, there are many of your features that are readily observable, yet you don't find them important at all because nobody has regarded them as significant.

Recently we heard a woman in her eighties describing her youth. "When I was a girl," she declared, "we didn't worry about weight. Some people were skinny and others were plump, and we pretty much accepted the bodies God gave us."

"Guess who Miss Price picked to play poison ivy in the class play."

In those days it's unlikely that weight would have found its way onto the self-concept list you constructed, since it wasn't considered significant. Compare this attitude with what you find today: It's seldom that you pick up a popular magazine or visit a bookstore without reading about the latest diet fads, and TV ads are filled with scenes of slender, happy people. As a result you'll rarely find a person who doesn't complain about the need to "lose a few pounds."

Obviously the reason for such concern has a lot to do with the attention paid to slimness these days. Furthermore, the interpretation of characteristics such as weight depends on the way people important to us regard them. We generally see fat as undesirable because others tell us it is. In a society where obesity is the ideal (and there are such societies) a person regarded as extremely heavy would be admired. In the same way, the fact that one is single or married, solitary or sociable, aggressive or passive takes on meaning depending on the interpretation society attaches to those traits. Thus, the importance of a given characteristic in your self-concept has as much to do with the significance you and others attach to it as with the existence of the characteristic.

Man wishes to be confirmed in his being by man, and wishes to have a presence in the being of the other . . . secretly and bashfully he watches for a Yes which allows him to be and which can come to him only from one human person to another.

Martin Buber

Social Comparison   Whereas it's true that each one of us is to a large extent a product of our environment, we are not totally passive recipients of environmental influence. Both consciously and unconsciously we each create our environment as well as respond to it.

In *The Concept of Self,* Kenneth Gergen describes the theory of social comparison and how it shapes our self-concept. Gergen explains that people have a continuing need to establish the value and correctness of their beliefs, something that is often difficult to do since exact standards are

hard to come by. Therefore, people often look at others as a way of judging themselves. They compare their beliefs, attitudes, and behaviors with those around them in order to establish the value of their own position. Just as we determine height or size by comparison (a five-foot, seven-inch warrior would be a giant in pygmy territory), we also determine other characteristics by comparison. For instance, if you see people all around you as being generally miserable, then you might view yourself as a happy, content person; whereas, in a different environment you could wind up looking unfulfilled by comparison with others.

At first glance, social comparison theory seems pretty deterministic. Besides being the product of how others see us, we are also shaped by how we measure up to others. At second glance, however, the concept of social comparison offers a way of reshaping an unsatisfying self-concept.

Since, to some degree, we're in control of who is available for comparison, it's possible to seek out people with whom we compare favorably. This technique may bring to mind a search for a community of idiots in which you could appear as a genius, but there are healthier ways of changing your standards for comparison. For instance, you might decide that it's foolish to constantly compare your athletic prowess with professionals or campus stars, your looks with movie idols, and your intelligence with only Phi Beta Kappas. Once you place yourself alongside a truly representative sample, your self-concept may change.

Besides offering a chance for boosting an unnecessarily low self-concept, the social comparison theory allows for delusions

Friday in Mrs. Gainey's sixth-grade class at P.S. 25 in New York City was the weekly day of reckoning for us. The mornings were spent taking tests which she graded during lunch period (who ate?). When we reassembled after recess, all thirty of us cleared out our belongings from the "old" desks and stood at attention around the perimeter of the classroom. We waited to discover for whom the bells would toll and for whom the chimes would ring out. On the basis of a combined average of the test scores, each child was ranked from one to thirty and seated accordingly. The best and the brightest would be placed up front from left to right in the first row closest to the teacher's desk. There would always be a lot of tension between these ambitious little hotshots to determine if they would keep their exalted places or move even further toward Row 1, Seat 1. There was also the sex thing: would a boy beat out Joanie this week or would the girls continue their stranglehold on the top spot?

After the first ten names were sung out by the teacher and the pupils took their seats, the tension eased somewhat as the insignificant middle-level kids were put into their places. As Mrs. Gainey got down to the final ten kids already standing nervously at the back of the room, all forty eyes were riveted on them. Accompanying each name called was the math grade, spelling grade, history grade, and science grade. Smiles broke into snickers as these grades got lower and lower. Sometimes you'd have to bite the inside of your mouth not to laugh out loud as these unfortunates squirmed in agony. It didn't help to have the teacher remind us not to laugh at them because one day we might be in the same boat and then we'd be sorry. Unimaginable! As usual, "Baby" Gonzales brought up the rear. I was sure he did so on purpose as a status thing to hear the teacher say, "And last again this week, Mr. Gonzales." No one laughed or looked his way; "Baby" was the biggest kid in the class and did not "work and play well with others."

Philip Zimbardo

of grandeur. For instance, suppose you wanted to think of yourself as a tremendously effective communicator (many people do), even though others disagreed with this image. You could achieve your goal by choosing those with whom to compare yourself. If you chose to be a big fish in a small pond you could hang around with extremely shy or aggressive or ignorant people, and thereby assure yourself of looking topnotch in comparison with them.

Another way of using comparison to (unrealistically) boost self-esteem would be to argue that those who don't approve of you have worthless opinions, whereas others who think as you do have excellent judgment. Also, you could set up standards which only you and a few other people meet and thereby argue that you are a rare individual indeed. Somewhat illogical, but when a self-concept is at stake, who worries about logic?

Evidence that we exercise a great deal of control over our self-concepts comes from investigations of changes in self-concepts over time. Fitts summarizes an investigation that found that the degree to which a self-concept is positive *increases with age*. Measurement of the self-concepts of people twenty, thirty, forty, fifty, sixty, and sixty-nine years old indicate that there is a steady increase in positive self-concept; generally, people feel better about themselves as they get older. Although the correlation is between self-concept and age, the real relationship is between self-concept and what happens as we get older. And one of the things that happens is we gain more and more control over our lives, we gain the opportunity to structure things to ensure that we'll have good feelings about ourselves.

With age we seek interpersonal relationships and work at tasks that reinforce our view of ourselves. For example, if you think of yourself as a "bad person" you might surround yourself with people who do not like you so that you can say, "Gee, I must really be a bad person because look at all the people who don't like me." And if you think of yourself as a "failure" you might continuously take on jobs that are too difficult so that you can fail and prove to yourself you really are a failure. Of course, given that the self-concept seems to improve with age, the opposite is probably happening: You tell yourself that you're a "good person" and surround yourself with people who like you, and that you're competent and take on jobs that are both important and within your capability of accomplishing. This principle makes sense when we realize that children have less control over their lives than adults, and so have less opportunity to structure positive events for themselves, all of which makes them more prone to believe evaluations presented by adults.

Dimensions of the Self-Concept

Now that you have a better idea of how your self-concept has developed, we can take a closer look at some of its characteristics.

The Self-Concept Is Multidimensional   Just as the universe is composed of countless galaxies, each person's self-concept is a conglomeration of many beliefs. Various dimensions of the self-concept can be measured in an instrument called the Tennessee Self-Concept Scale, developed by William Fitts. According to Fitts, our core, the internal self-concept, is made up of three different perceptions we have of ourselves: what we *do,* what we *are,* and how we *feel* about what we are.

The first perception Fitts labels the *Behavioral Self*. We see ourselves behave, and these perceptions form the basis for this aspect of our self-concept. For

example, in the fantasy at the beginning of this chapter, you may have listed your talents. You might have indicated you like to work on your car, to do the minor repair work. The behaviors involved in that activity would form the behavioral part of your self-concept.

The second perception, what we *are,* Fitts labels the *Identity Self.* For example, although you may like to do the minor repairs on your car, you may not think of yourself as a mechanic. What you *do* is differentiated from what you *are.* On the other hand, you may indeed see yourself as a mechanic—that may be a part of your identity—and so what you *do* is intimately connected with what you *are.* The labels and symbols you use to identify yourself, whether it's "mechanic," "student," "son," or "daughter," make up your Identity Self.

Fitts labels the third perception, how we *feel* about what we are, as the *Judging Self.* First we observe ourselves to see what we do, then we generalize these observations and label what we are, and finally we judge the product. You may like to do minor repairs on your car, may see yourself as a mechanic, and may also judge yourself as a good mechanic.

This third self-perception—the judgments we make—forms the basis for the most crucial aspect of our self-concept: *self-esteem.* (When the term self-concept is used without clarification, it's likely that what is being referred to is self-esteem, the generalization from the Judging Self.) If the bulk of evaluations made by the Judging Self are positive, the result is positive self-perception and high self-esteem; if most are negative, the result is low self-esteem.

If the core, or *internal* part of the self-concept is made up of these three self-perceptions, then the outside, or *external* part is made up of all the numerous "selves" we present to the world in the countless situations we encounter.

The Tennessee Self-Concept Scale measures five dimensions of the external self, each of which is composed of a Behavioral Self, an Identity Self, and a Judging Self. The first subself is the *physical self,* which includes our view of our bodies, state of health, skills, and sexuality. This subself, like the other four, can be analyzed in terms of the three internal selves. For example, the Behavioral Self: "I *play* racquetball"; the Identity Self: "I *am* a racquetball player"; the Judging Self: "I am a *mediocre* racquetball player."

The second subself, the *moral-ethical self,* describes our relationship to the supernatural and our feelings of being a "good" and "bad" person. The third subself, the *personal self,* reflects our sense of personal worth apart from the feelings we have about our bodies and the kinds of relationships we have with others. The fourth subself, the *family self,* reflects our feelings about ourselves as family members. The fifth and last subself, the *social self,* reflects our feelings of self-worth in interactions with other people in general.

Keep these categories in mind and take another look at the terms you used to describe yourself at the beginning of this chapter. Now, which dimensions of self seem to predominate in your self-concept: physical, moral-ethical, personal, family, or social? And how do you perceive yourself internally: in terms of your behaviors, your identity, or the value of your attributes?

The Self-Concept Is Subjective   The way you view yourself isn't always the same as the way others view you. Sometimes the image you hold of yourself might be more favorable than the way others regard you. You might, for instance, see yourself as a witty joketeller when others can barely tolerate your attempts at humor. You might view yourself as highly intelligent while one or more instructors would see your scholarship as substandard. Perhaps you consider yourself an excellent worker, in contrast to the employer who wants to fire you.

There are several reasons why some people have a self-concept that others would regard as being unrealistically favorable. First, a self-estimation might be based on obsolete information. Perhaps your jokes used to be well received, or your grades were high, or your work was superior, and now the facts have changed. As you'll soon read, people are reluctant to give up a familiar self-image. This principle makes especially good sense when it's possible to avoid the unpleasant truth of the present by staying in the more desirable past.

A self-concept might also be excessively favorable due to distorted feedback from others. A boss may think of himself as an excellent manager because his assistants lavish him with false praise in order to keep their jobs. A child's inflated ego may be based on the praise of doting parents.

A third reason for holding what appears to be an unrealistically high self-concept has to do with the expectations of a society that demands too much of its members. Much of the conditioning we receive in our early years implies that anything less than perfection is unsatisfactory, so that admitting one's mistakes is often seen as a sign of weakness. Instructors who fail to admit they don't know everything about a subject are afraid they will lose face with their colleagues and students. Couples whose relationships are beset by occasional problems don't want to admit that they have failed to achieve the "ideal" relationship they've seen portrayed in fiction. Parents who don't want to say, "I'm sorry, I made a mistake," to their children are afraid they'll lose the youngsters' respect.

Once you accept such an irrational idea—that to be less than perfect is a character defect—admitting your frailties becomes difficult. Such a confession becomes the equivalent of admitting one is a failure—and failure is not an element of most peoples' self-concept. Rather than label themselves failures, many people engage in self-deception, insisting to themselves and to others that their behavior is more admirable than the circumstances indicate. We'll have more to say about the reasons behind such behavior and its consequences when we discuss defense mechanisms in Chapter 7.

In contrast to the cases we've just described are times when we view ourselves *more* harshly than the objective facts suggest. You may have known people, for instance, who insist that they are unattractive or incompetent in spite of your

honest insistence to the contrary. In fact, you have probably experienced feelings of excessively negative self-evaluation yourself. Recall a time when you woke up with a case of the "uglies," convinced that you looked terrible. Remember how on such days you were unwilling to accept even the most sincere compliments from others, having already decided how wretched you appeared. Whereas many of us only fall into the trap of being overly critical occasionally, others constantly have an unrealistically low self-concept.

Sidney Simon, in a delightful book called *Vulture: A Modern Allegory on the Art of Putting Oneself Down*, describes how we are experts at putting ourselves down. A vulture—the psychological type—is an imaginary bird we create who sits within view and swoops down whenever we feel the need to pick on ourselves. What do you say when you trip over something? "Boy, am I a klutz!" And the vulture drops down from its perch on the nearby fence to claw and bite (remember, vultures only come after the weak and helpless—preferably the dead). What do you say when you fail to get the high grade on the exam you thought you would get? "If I only had half the brains of a snail, I . . ." And you can feel the vulture picking at you from its new perch on your shoulder. Think of the negative messages you give yourself. Do you tend to call yourself stupid, crazy, inadequate, immature, horrible, dumb, lazy, ugly, rotten, vicious, filthy, dirty, low-life, bum, tramp, fool? The list can go on and on. If you do, you probably have so many vultures they have to fight for room on the fence!

What are the reasons for such excessively negative self-evaluations? As with an unrealistically high self-esteem, one source for an overabundance of self-put-downs is obsolete information. A string of past failures in school or with social relations can linger to haunt a communicator long after they have occurred, even though such events don't predict failure in the future. Similarly, we've known slender students who still think of themselves as fat and clear-complexioned people who still behave as if they were acne-ridden.

Distorted feedback can also create a self-image that is worse than a more objective observer would see. Having grown up around overly critical parents is one of the most common causes of a negative self-image. In other cases the remarks of cruel friends, uncaring teachers, excessively demanding employers, or even memorable strangers can have a lasting effect. As you read earlier, the impact of significant others and reference groups in forming a self-concept can be great.

A third cause for a strongly negative self-concept is again the myth of perfection, which is common in our society. From the time most of us learn to understand language we are exposed to models who appear to be perfect at whatever they do. This myth is most clear when we examine the stories commonly told to children. In these stories the hero is wise, brave, talented, and victorious, whereas the villain is totally evil and doomed to failure. This kind of model is easy for a child to understand, but it hardly paints a realistic picture of the world. Unfortunately, many parents perpetuate the myth of perfection by refusing to admit that they are ever mistaken or unfair. Kids, of course, accept this perfectionist facade for a long time, not

---

You've no idea what a poor opinion I have of myself, and how little I deserve it.

W. S. Gilbert

---

being in any position to dispute the wisdom of such powerful beings. And from the behavior of the adults around them comes the clear message: "A well-adjusted, successful person has no faults."

Thus children learn that in order to gain acceptance, it's necessary to pretend to "have it all together," even though they know this isn't the case. Given this naive belief that everyone else is perfect and the knowledge that you aren't, it's easy to see how one's self-concept would suffer. We'll have a great deal to say about perfection and other irrational ideas, both in this chapter and in Chapter 5. In the meantime, don't get the mistaken impression that we're suggesting it's wrong to aim at perfection as an *ideal*. We're only suggesting that achieving this state is usually not possible, and to expect that you should do so is a sure ticket to an inaccurate and unnecessarily low self-concept.

A final reason people often sell themselves short is also connected to social expectations. Curiously, the perfectionistic society to which we belong rewards those people who downplay the strengths we demand they possess (or pretend to possess). We term these people "modest" and find their behavior agreeable. On the other hand, we consider those who honestly appreciate their own strengths to be "braggarts" or "egotists," confusing them with the people who boast about accomplishments they do not possess. This convention leads most of us to talk freely about our shortcomings while downplaying our accomplishments. It's all right to proclaim that you're miserable if you have failed to do well on a project, whereas it's considered boastful to express your pride at a job well done. It's fine to remark that you feel unattractive, but egocentric to say that you think you look good.

After a while we begin to believe the types of statements we repeatedly make. The self-put-downs are viewed as modesty and become part of our self-concept, whereas the strengths and accomplishments go unmentioned and are thus forgotten. And in the end we see ourselves as much worse than we are.

Like a snapshot
    You develop
Unlike a snapshot . . .
    You never stop

Leonard Nimoy

A Healthy Self-Concept Is Flexible   People change. From moment to moment we aren't the same. We wake up in the morning in a jovial mood and turn grumpy before lunch. We find ourselves fascinated by a conversational topic one moment, then suddenly lose interest. One moment's anger often gives way to forgiveness the next. Health turns to illness and back to health. Alertness becomes fatigue, hunger becomes satiation, and confusion becomes clarity.

We also change from situation to situation. You might be a relaxed conversationalist with people you know but at a loss for words with strangers. You might be patient when explaining things on the job but have no tolerance for such explanations at home. You might be a wizard at solving mathematical problems but have a terribly difficult time putting your thoughts into words. We change over long stretches of time. We grow older, learn new facts, adopt new attitudes and philosophies, set and reach new goals, and find that others change their way of thinking and acting toward us.

Since we change in these and many other ways, our self-concept must also change in order to keep a realistic picture of ourselves. Thus an accurate self-portrait of the type described would probably not be exactly the same as it would have been a year ago or a few months ago or even the way it would have been yesterday. This doesn't mean that you will change radically from day to day. There are fundamental characteristics of your personality that will stay the same for years, perhaps for a lifetime. It is likely, however, that in other important ways you are changing— physically, intellectually, emotionally, and spiritually.

The Self-Concept Resists Change   In spite of the fact that we change and that a realistic self-concept should reflect this change, the tendency to resist revision of our self-perception is strong. When confronted with facts that contradict the mental picture we hold of ourselves, we tend to dispute the facts and cling to the outmoded self-perception.

It's understandable why we're reluctant to revise a previously favorable self-concept. As we write these words, we recall how some professional athletes doggedly insist that they can be of value to the team when they are clearly past their prime. It must be tremendously difficult to give up the life of excitement, recognition, and financial rewards that comes with such a talent. Faced with such a tremendous loss, it's easy to see why the athlete would try to play one more season, insisting that the old skills are still there.

In the same way a student who did well in earlier years but now has failed to study might be unwilling to admit that the label "good scholar" no longer applies. Or a previously industrious worker, citing past commendations in a personnel file, might insist on being considered a topnotch employee despite a supervisor's report of increased absences and low productivity. (Remember that the people in these and other examples aren't *lying* when they insist that they're doing well in spite of the facts to the contrary; they honestly believe that the old truths still hold precisely because their self-concepts have been so resistant to change.)

Curiously, the tendency to cling to an outmoded self-perception also holds when the new image would be more favorable than the old one. We recall a former student who almost anyone would have regarded as being beautiful, with physical features attractive enough to appear in any glamour magazine. In spite of her appearance, this woman characterized herself as "ordinary" and "unattractive" in

Most people cling to pretensions of self as a drowning man grasps at a straw.

Karen Horney

a class exercise. When questioned by her classmates, she described how as a child her teeth were extremely crooked, and how she had worn braces for several years in her teens to correct this problem. During this time she was often kidded by her friends, who never let her forget her "metal mouth," as she put it. Even though the braces had been off for two years, our student reported that she still saw herself as ugly, and brushed aside our compliments by insisting that we were just saying these things to be nice—she knew how she *really* looked.

Examples such as this show one problem that occurs when we resist changing an inaccurate self-concept. Our student denied herself a much happier life by clinging to an obsolete picture of herself. In the same way some communicators insist that they are less talented or worthy of friendship than others would suggest, thus creating their own miserable world when it needn't exist. These unfortunate souls probably resist changing because they aren't willing to go through the disorientation that comes from redefining themselves, correctly anticipating that it *is* an effort to think of one's self in a new way. Whatever their reasons, it's sad to see people in such an unnecessary state of mind.

A second problem that comes from trying to perpetrate an inaccurate self-concept involves self-delusion and lack of growth. If you hold an unrealistically favorable picture of yourself, you won't see the real need for change that may exist. Instead of learning new talents, working to change a relationship, or improving your physical condition, you'll stay with the familiar and comfortable delusion that everything is all right. As times goes by this delusion becomes more and more difficult to maintain, leading to a third problem.

To understand this third problem you need to remember that communicators who are presented with information that contradicts their self-perception have two choices: They can either accept the new data and change their perception accordingly, or they can keep their original viewpoint and in some way refute the new information. Since most communicators are reluctant to downgrade a favorable image of themselves, their tendency is to opt for refutation, either by discounting the information and rationalizing it away or by counterattacking the person who holds it.

Personality Correlates of Self-Concept

People with high or low self-concepts behave in significantly different ways. Research in this area recently reviewed by Mary Ann Sheirer and Robert Draut shows that there is a strong correlation between the type of self-concept a person has and the patterns of thought and actions that person displays. It is unclear whether the self-concept causes these behaviors, whether the behaviors shape the self-concept, or whether the relationship is reciprocal. In any case, the link between a positive self-concept and personal adjustment is a strong one.

One element of a positive self-concept is *security*, a firm belief in the correctness of one's actions and values—a belief that is relatively immune to the judgments of others. For example, a person with a strong positive self-concept would not be terribly bothered by criticisms that career plans or personal relationships were flawed, whereas a less secure person would find such evaluations upsetting.

Along with security, the characteristic of *self-acceptance* goes hand in hand with a positive self-concept. People who accept themselves possess a number of valuable assets: the ability to change their opinions, to utilize new ideas, to more easily accept the opinions and feelings of others, to be sensitive to others, and to comfortably engage in appropriate self-disclosure.

A third aspect of a positive self-concept is *high self-esteem*. People with high self-esteem have all the benefits that accompany self-acceptance, plus the following: popularity, little nervousness or defensiveness, few if any feelings of inferiority, and strong feelings of security. People having high self-esteem usually do well in school, are generally happy with their lives, tend to reach out more to others, make others feel welcome and less alienated. They are more involved with high self-concept people than those with low self-concepts, and more able to "hook into" people with whom they share an interpersonal relationship.

In addition to all of the characteristics just mentioned, high self-concept people enjoy a proportionately greater share of the benefits that come with their richer vocabularies, their ability to give and take criticism comfortably, their more confident tone of voice, and their optimistic attitude toward competition.

A dramatic illustration of the effect of self-concept on communication comes from a comparison between kindergarten children with high and low self-concepts. Children with high self-concepts generally exhibit the following characteristics:

1. They are unafraid of new situations;
2. They make friends easily;
3. They experiment with new materials without much hesitation;
4. They trust their teacher, even though the teacher is a stranger;
5. They are cooperative and can follow rules;
6. They are largely responsible for controlling their own behavior;
7. They are creative, imaginative, and have ideas of their own;
8. They talk freely and are eager to share their own experiences;
9. They are independent and need only a minimal amount of direction;
10. They are happy.

Typical kindergarten children with low self-concepts demonstrate the following characteristics:

1. They rarely show initiative;
2. They rely on others for direction;
3. They ask permission to do most everything;
4. They seldom show spontaneity;
5. They seldom enter new activities;
6. They isolate themselves;
7. They talk very little;
8. They are possessive of objects;
9. They make excessive demands;
10. They either withdraw or aggress;
11. They act frustrated.

Although these behaviors refer to children about six years old, research with older children and adults indicates that this is a good list of the general characteristics of both high and low self-concept people regardless of age.

Though it would be simplistic to divide the world into people having high self-concepts and those having low ones, the picture here is rather clear. The more positively we feel about ourselves, the more easily we will form and maintain interpersonal relationships, and the more rewarding those relationships will be.

The Self-Fulfilling Prophecy and Communication

The self-concept is such a powerful force on the personality that it not only determines how you see yourself in the present, but can actually influence your future behavior and that of others. Such occurrences come about through a phenomenon called the self-fulfilling prophecy.

A self-fulfilling prophecy occurs when a person's expectation of an event makes the outcome more likely to happen than would otherwise have been true. Self-fulfilling prophecies occur all the time, although you might never have given them that label. For example:

1. You expected to become nervous and botch a job interview and later did so;
2. You anticipated having a good (or terrible) time at a social affair and found your expectations being met;
3. A teacher or boss explained a new task to you, saying that you probably wouldn't do well at first; you did not do well;
4. A friend described someone you were about to meet, saying that you wouldn't like the person, which turned out to be correct—you didn't like the new acquaintance.

In each of these cases there is a good chance that the event happened because it was predicted. You needn't have botched the interview, the party might have been boring only because you helped make it so, you might have done better on the job if your boss hadn't spoken up, and you might have liked the new acquaintance if your friend hadn't given you preconceptions. In other words, what helped make each event take place as it did was the expectation that it would happen exactly that way.

There are two types of self-fulfilling prophecies. The first occurs when your own expectations influence your behavior. Like the job interview and the party just described, there are many times when an event that needn't have occurred does happen because you expected it to. In sports you've probably psyched yourself into playing either better or worse than usual, so that the only explanation for your unusual performance was your attitude that you'd behave differently. Similarly, you've

. . . problems which are caused by communication are due not to *inadequate* communication but to *too adequate* communication, since what is transmitted most accurately between people is how they feel rather than what they say. Thus, if the boss really feels his research scientist is not very important, that feeling will be communicated to the scientist much more readily than any words that pass between them.

William Schutz

probably faced an audience at one time or another with a fearful attitude and forgotten your remarks, not because you were unprepared, but because you said to youself, "I know I'll blow it."

Certainly you've had the experience of waking up in a cross mood and saying to yourself, "This will be a bad day." Once you have decided this, you may have acted in ways that made it come true. If you approached a class expecting to be bored, you most probably did lose interest, due partly to a lack of attention on your part. If you avoided the company of others because you expected that they had nothing to offer, your suspicions would have been confirmed—nothing exciting or new did happen to you. On the other hand, if you approached the same day with the idea that it had the potential of being a good one, this expectation probably would also have been met. Smile at people, and they'll probably smile back. Enter a class

> There is an old joke about a man who was asked if he could play a violin and answered, "I don't know. I've never tried." This is psychologically a very wise reply. Those who have never tried to play a violin really do not know whether they can or not. Those who say too early in life and too firmly, "No, I'm not at all musical," shut themselves off prematurely from whole areas of life that might have proved rewarding. In each of us there are unknown possibilities, undiscovered potentialities—and one big advantage of having an open self-concept rather than a rigid one is that we shall continue to expose ourselves to new experiences and therefore we shall continue to discover more and more about ourselves as we grow older.
>
> S. I. Hayakawa

determined to learn something, and you probably will—even if it's how not to instruct students! Approach many people with the idea that some of them will be good to know, and you'll most likely make some new friends. In these cases and similar ones your attitude has a great deal to do with how you see yourself and how others will see you.

A second type of self-fulfilling prophecy occurs when the expectations of one person govern another's actions. The classic example was demonstrated by Robert Rosenthal and Lenore Jacobson in a study they described in their book, *Pygmalion in the Classroom:*

Twenty percent of the children in a certain elementary school were reported to their teachers as showing unusual potential for intellectual growth. The names of these 20 percent were drawn by means of a table of random numbers, which is to say that the names were drawn out of a hat. Eight months later these unusual or "magic" children showed significantly greater gains in IQ than did the remaining children who had not been singled out for the teachers' attention. The change in the teachers' expectations regarding the intellectual performance of these allegedly "special" children had led to an actual change in the intellectual performance of these randomly selected children.

In other words, some children may do better in school, not because they are any more intelligent than their classmates, but because they learn that their teacher—a significant other—believes they can achieve.

To put this phenomenon in context with the self-concept, we can say that when a teacher communicates to a child the message, "I think you're bright," the child accepts that evaluation and changes self-concept to include that evaluation. Unfortunately, the same principle holds for students whose teachers send the message, "I think you're stupid."

This type of self-fulfilling prophecy has been shown to be a powerful force for shaping the self-concept and thus the behavior of people in a wide range of settings outside the schools. Medical patients who unknowingly use placebos—substances such as injections of sterile water or doses of sugar pills that have no curative value—often respond just as favorably to treatment as people who actually receive an active drug. The patients believe they have taken a substance that will help them feel better, and this belief actually brings about a "cure." In psychotherapy Rosenthal and Jacobson describe several studies suggesting that patients who believe they will benefit from treatment do so, regardless of the type of treatment they receive. In the same vein, when a doctor believes a patient will improve, the patient may do so precisely because of this expectation, whereas another person for whom the physician has little hope often fails to recover. Apparently the patient's self-concept as being sick or well—as shaped by the doctor—plays an important role in determining the actual state of health.

In business the power of the self-fulfilling prophecy was proved as early as 1890. A new tabulating machine had just been installed at the U.S. Census Bureau in Washington, D.C. In order to use the machine the bureau's staff had to learn a new set of skills that the machine's inventor believed to be quite difficult. He told the clerks that after some practice they could expect to punch about 550 cards per day; to process any more would jeopardize their psychological well-being. Sure enough, after two weeks the clerks were processing the anticipated number of cards, and reported feelings of stress if they attempted to move any faster.

Sometime later an additional group of clerks was hired to operate the same machines. These workers knew nothing of the devices, and no one had told them about the upper limit of production. After only three days the new employees were each punching over 2,000 cards per day with no ill effects. Again, the self-fulfilling prophecy seemed to be in operation. The original workers believed themselves capable of punching only 550 cards and so behaved accordingly, whereas the new clerks had no limiting expectations as part of their self-concepts and so behaved more productively.

The self-fulfilling prophecy operates in families as well. If parents tell children long enough that they can't do anything right, each child's self-concept will soon incorporate this idea, and each will fail at many or most of the tasks attempted. On the other hand, if children are told that they are capable or lovable or kind, there is a much greater chance of their behaving accordingly.

Our beliefs are so important to us that we will do anything to keep them intact. One way we do this is by claiming that an exception to our belief is "the exception that proves the rule." For example, in our organizational consulting work, we have heard male executives argue that "women don't make good managers." When presented with evidence that sex is not a determinant of good managerial behavior, the usual response is, "Oh, sure, but those women behaved like men!"

The self-fulfilling prophecy is an important force in interpersonal communication, but we don't want to suggest that it explains *all* behavior. There are certainly times when the expectation of an event's outcome won't bring about that occurrence. Believing you'll do well in a job interview when you're clearly not qualified for the position is unrealistic. In the same way, there will probably be people and situations you won't enjoy no matter what your expectations. Thus, to connect the self-fulfilling prophecy with the "power of positive thinking" is an oversimplification.

In other cases your expectations will be borne out because you're a good predictor, and not because of the self-fulfilling prophecy. For example, children are not equally well equipped to do well in school. In such cases it would be wrong to say that the child's performance was shaped by a parent or teacher, even though the behavior did match that which was expected. In the same way, some workers excel and others fail, some patients recover and others don't, all according to our predictions but not *because* of them.

Keeping these qualifications in mind, it's important to recognize the tremendous influence that self-fulfilling prophecies play in our lives. To a great extent we are what we believe we are. In this sense we and those around us constantly create our self-concepts and thus our "selves."

Changing Your Self-Concept

After reading this far, you've probably begun to realize that it is possible to change an unsatisfying self-concept. In the next sections we'll discuss some methods for accomplishing such a change.

Have Realistic Expectations   It's extremely important to realize that some of your dissatisfaction might come from expecting too much of yourself. If you demand that you handle every act of communication perfectly, you're bound to be disappointed. Nobody is able to handle every conflict productively, to be totally relaxed and skillful in conversations, to always ask perceptive questions, or to be 100 percent helpful when others have problems. Expecting yourself to reach such unrealistic goals is to doom yourself to unhappiness at the start.

Sometimes it's easy to be hard on yourself because everyone around you seems to be handling themselves so much better than you. It's important to realize that much of what seems like confidence and skill in others is a front to hide uncertainty. They may be suffering from the same self-imposed demands of perfection that you place on yourself.

Even in cases where others definitely seem more competent than you, it's important to judge yourself in terms of your own growth, and not against the behavior of others. Rather than feeling miserable because you're not as talented as an expert, realize that you probably are a better, wiser, or more skillful person than you used to be and that this is a legitimate source of satisfaction. Perfection is fine as an ideal, but you're being unfair to yourself if you actually expect to reach that state.

Have a Realistic Perception of Yourself
One source of a poor self-concept is inaccurate self-perception. As you've already read, such unrealistic pictures sometimes come from being overly harsh on yourself, believing that you're worse than the facts indicate. Of course it would be foolish to deny that you could be a better person than you are, but it's also important to recognize your strengths. A periodic session of "bragging"—of acknowledging the parts of yourself with which you're pleased and the ways you've grown—is often a good way to put your strengths and shortcomings into perspective.

To love oneself is the beginning of a lifelong romance.

Oscar Wilde

An unrealistically poor self-concept can also come from the inaccurate feedback of others. Perhaps you are in an environment where you receive an excessive number of downer messages, many of which are undeserved, and a minimum of upper messages. We've known many housewives, for example, who have returned to college after many years spent in homemaking where they received virtually no recognition for their intellectual strengths. It's amazing that these women have the courage to come to college at all, their self-concepts are so low; but come they do, and most are thrilled to find that they are much brighter and more competent intellectually than they suspected. In the same way, workers with overly critical supervisors, children with cruel "friends," and students with unsupportive teachers are all prone to suffering from low self-concepts due to excessively negative feedback.

If you fall into this category, it's important to put the unrealistic evaluations you receive into perspective, and then to seek out more supportive people who will acknowledge your assets as well as point out your shortcomings. Doing so is often a quick and sure boost to the self-concept.

Have the Will to Change Often we say we want to change, but aren't willing to do the necessary work. In such cases it's clear that the responsibility for growing rests squarely on your shoulders. Often, we maintain an unrealistic self-concept by claiming that we "can't" be the person we'd like to be, when in fact we're simply not willing to do what's required. You *can* change in many ways, if only you are willing to put out the effort.

Have the Skill Needed to Change Often trying isn't enough. There are some cases where you would change if you knew of a way to do so.

First, you can seek advice—from books such as this one, the references listed at the end of each chapter, and other printed sources. You can also get advice from instructors, counselors, and other experts, as well as from friends. Of course, not all the advice you receive will be useful, but if

© 1967 United Features Syndicate, Inc.

you read widely and talk to enough people, you have a good chance of learning the things you want to know.

A second method of learning how to change is to observe models—people who handle themselves in the ways you would like to master. It's often been said that people learn more from models than in any other way, and by taking advantage of this principle you will find that the world is full of teachers who can show you how to communicate more successfully. Become a careful observer. Watch what people you admire do and say, not so that you can copy them, but so that you can adapt their behavior to fit your own personal style.

At this point you might be overwhelmed at the difficulty of changing the way you think about yourself and the way you act. Remember, we never said that this process would be an easy one (although it sometimes is). But even when change is difficult, you know that it's possible if you are serious. You don't need to be perfect, but you *can* improve your self-concept—*if you choose to.*

Readings

Briggs, Dorothy C. *Your Child's Self-Esteem.* Garden City, N.Y.: Doubleday, 1975.

Campbell, Colin. "Our Many Versions of the Self: An Interview with M. Brewster Smith." *Psychology Today,* 9, (February 1976): 74–79.

Fitts, William H. *The Self Concept and Self-Actualization.* Nashville, Tennessee: Counselor Recordings and Tests, 1971.

Gergen, Kenneth J. "The Healthy, Happy Human Being Wears Many Masks." *Psychology Today,* 5, (May 1972): 31–35, 64–66.

Gergen, Kenneth J. *The Concept of Self.* New York: Holt, Rinehart and Winston, 1971.

Insel, Paul M. and Lenore Jacobson. *What Do You Expect? An Inquiry Into Self-Fulfilling Prophecies.* Menlo Park, California: Cummings Publishing Co., 1975.

Rosenfeld, Lawrence B. "Self-Concept and Role Behavior." In *Now That We're All Here . . . Relations in Small Groups.* Columbus, Ohio: Charles E. Merrill Publishing Co., 1976.

Rosenthal, Robert, "The Pygmalion Effect Lives." *Psychology Today,* 7, (1973): 56–63.

Rosenthal, Robert and Lenore Jacobson. *Pygmalion in the Classroom.* New York: Holt, Rinehart and Winston, 1968.

Samuels, Shirley C. *Enhancing Self-Concept in Early Childhood: Theory and Practice.* New York: Human Sciences Press, 1977.

Scheirer, Mary Ann and Robert E. Kraut. "Increasing Educational Achievement Via Self-Concept Change." *Review of Educational Research,* 49, (Winter 1979): 131–150.

Simon, Sidney B. *Vulture: A Modern Allegory on the Art of Putting Oneself Down.* Niles, Illinois: Argus Communications, 1977.

Survant, A. "Building Positive Self-Concepts." *Instructor,* 81, (1972): 94–95.

Self-Disclosure

3

3 The dream is a common one. You suddenly find yourself without clothes—on the street, at work, at school, or maybe in a crowd of strangers. Everyone else is fully dressed, while you stand alone, naked and vulnerable. Maybe others see you and respond with curiosity or hostility or laughter. Or possibly you seem to be invisible, searching for shelter before you are recognized. Whatever the details, dreams of this sort are usually disturbing.

You needn't be a psychoanalyst to figure out that the nakedness here is symbolic, representing the fear of disclosing oneself in other ways: dropping the masks and facades that we often show to the world. Laughter hides pain, a relaxed pose covers tension, a veneer of certainty masks confusion. And we fear being found out.

Why are we so often afraid of being real, of letting others know who we really are? In his thoughtful book, *What Are You Afraid Of?: A Guide to Dealing With Your Fears,* John T. Wood suggests an answer:

I am afraid to be who I am with you . . . I am afraid to be judged by you, I am afraid you will reject me. I am afraid you will say bad things about me. I am afraid you will hurt me. I am afraid, if I really am myself, you won't love me—and I need your love so badly that I will play the roles you expect me to play and be the person that pleases you, even though I lose myself in the process.

There probably isn't a person over the age of six who wouldn't understand these words. At one time or another all of us are afraid to be real with others. As Wood suggests, the biggest reason for hiding our true selves is usually fear of rejection. As we'll soon see, there are other reasons as well. Because the issue of self-disclosure is such a crucial one in interpersonal communication, we want to spend this chapter looking at it in detail. We'll talk about what self-disclosure is and how it differs from other types of communication, we'll see how one's sex influences disclosure. We will look at the benefits and apparent drawbacks of disclosing. Finally, we'll offer some suggestions for when self-disclosure is appropriate. Let's begin by defining our terms.

What Is Self-Disclosure?

A Model of Self-Disclosure   To *disclose* means to show, make known, reveal. *Self*-disclosure, then is the act of making yourself known to another person, showing yourself in a way so that others can perceive you. (We'll offer a more detailed definition shortly.)

One way to illustrate how self-disclosure operates in communication is to look at a device called the *Johari Window,* developed by Joseph Luft and Harry Ingham.

Imagine a frame which contains everything there is to know about you: your likes and dislikes, your goals, your secrets, your needs—everything.

Everything
about
you

Figure 3–1

Of course, you aren't aware of everything about yourself. Like most people you're probably discovering new things about yourself all the time. To represent this aspect, we can divide the frame containing everything about you into two parts: The part you know about, and the part of which you're not aware (see Figure 3–2).

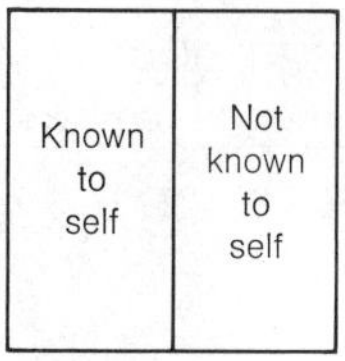

Figure 3–2

We can also divide the frame containing everything about you in another way. In this division one part represents the things about you that others know, and the second part contains the things about you that you keep to yourself. Figure 3–3 represents this view.

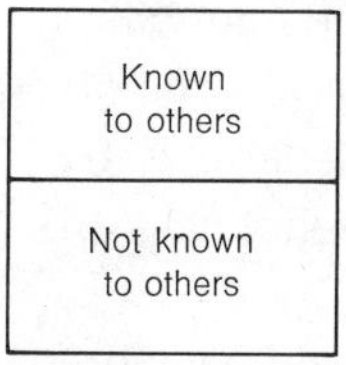

```
┌─────────────────┐
│    Known        │
│   to others     │
├─────────────────┤
│  Not known      │
│   to others     │
└─────────────────┘
```

Figure 3–3

When we impose these two divided frames one atop the other, we have a Johari Window. By looking at Figure 3–4 you can see that Johari divides everything about you into four parts.

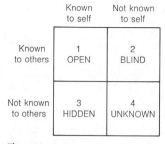

Figure 3–4

Part 1 represents the person of which both you and others are aware. This area is labeled your *open area*. Part 2 represents the part of you that you yourself are not aware of, but others are. This is called your *blind area*. Part 3 represents your *hidden area;* you're aware of this part of yourself, but you don't allow others to know it. Part 4 represents the part of you that is known neither to you nor to others and is therefore referred to as the *unknown area*.

Interpersonal communication of any significance is virtually impossible if the individuals involved have little open area. And taking this a step further, you can see that a relationship is limited by the individual who is less open, that is, who possesses the smaller open area. Figure 3–5 illustrates this situation with Johari Windows.

We've set up *A's* window in reverse so that the Number 1 areas of both *A's* and *B's* Joharis appear next to each other. Note that the amount of successful communication (represented by the arrows connecting the two open areas) is dictated by the size of the smaller open area of *A*. The arrows originating from *B's* open area and being

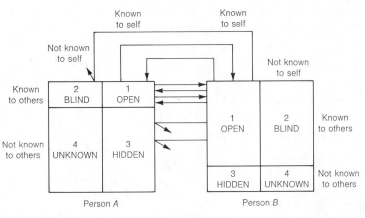

Person A   Person B

Figure 3–5

turned aside by *A's* hidden and blind areas represent unsuccessful attempts to communicate.

Can you put yourself into one of the windows in Figure 3–5? Have you had the experience of not being able to "really get to know" someone because he or she was too reserved or closed? Or perhaps you've frustrated another person's attempts to build a relationship with you in the same way. Whether you picture yourself as more like Person *A* or Person *B* in Figure 3–5, the fact is that self-disclosure is necessary for the success of any interpersonal relationship.

A Definition of Self-Disclosure You might argue that aside from secrets, it's impossible *not* to make yourself known to others. After all, every time you open your mouth to speak you're revealing your tastes, interests, desires, opinions, beliefs, or some other bit of information about yourself. Even when

the subject isn't a personal one, your choice of what to speak about tells the listener something about who you are. And, if you've looked ahead to Chapter 9, you've seen that each of us communicates nonverbally even when we're not speaking at all. For instance, a yawn might mean that you're tired or bored, a shrug of your shoulders might indicate uncertainty or indifference, and how close or how far you choose to stand from your listener may be taken as a measure of your friendliness or comfort with others.

If every verbal and nonverbal behavior in which you engage is self-revealing, how can self-disclosure be distinguished from any other act of communication? According to psychologist Paul Cosby there is a difference. In order for a communication act to be considered self-disclosing it must meet the following criteria: (1) It must contain personal information about the sender; (2) the sender must verbally communicate this information; and (3) another person must be the target. Put differently, the content of self-disclosing communication is the *self,* and information about the self is *purposefully communicated to another person.*

Although this definition is a start, it ignores the fact that some messages intentionally directed toward others are not especially revealing. For example, telling a companion that you dislike eating clams is quite different from announcing that you dislike some aspect of her or him. Let's take a look at several factors that further distinguish self-disclosure from other types of communication.

Honesty It almost goes without saying that true self-disclosure has to be honest. It's not revealing to say, "I've never felt this way about anyone before" to every Saturday night date, or to preface every lie with the statement, "Let me be honest . . ."

What about cases where individuals do not know themselves well enough to present accurate information? Are these unintentionally false statements self-disclosing? For our purposes, the answer is yes. As long as you are honest and accurate to the best of your knowledge, the communication can qualify as an act of self-disclosure. On the other hand, both painting an incomplete picture of yourself (telling only part of what's true), or avoiding saying anything at all about yourself, are not self-disclosive acts.

Depth A self-disclosing statement is generally regarded as being personal—containing relatively "deep" rather than "surface" information. Of course, what is personal and intimate for one person may not be for another. For example, Lawrence, Ron, and Neil might respond differently to a question about their undergraduate grade point averages, depending on how intimate or personal each feels the information is. For Lawrence it might be highly personal (it was a lousy average), whereas for Ron and Neil it may come under the heading of surface information. Even simple statements such as a response to the question "How old are you?" can be extremely revealing for some people.

Availability of information Several researchers in the area of self-disclosure (Lawrence among them) are concerned with the question of what makes a given act of communication qualify as self-disclosure. They argue that such communication must be information the other person is not likely to know at the time or be able to obtain from another source without a great deal of effort, if at all.

Letting people in is largely a matter of not expending energy to keep them out.

Hugh Prather

For example, describing your conviction for a drunk driving accident might feel as if it were an act of serious disclosure, for the information concerns you, is offered intentionally, is honest and accurate, and considered personal. However, if the other person could obtain that information elsewhere without much trouble—from a glance at the morning

newspaper or from various gossips, for example—your communication would not be an act of self-disclosure.

Context of sharing   Sometimes the self-disclosing nature of a statement comes from the setting in which it is uttered. For instance, relatively innocuous information about family life seems more personal when a teacher shares it with her class. This sort of sharing creates a more personal atmosphere because it changes the relationship from a purely "business" level to a more intimate one.

We can summarize our definitional tour by saying that an act of self-disclosure: (1) has the self as content; (2) is intentional; (3) is directed at another person; (4) is honest; (5) is revealing; (6) contains information unavailable from other sources; and (7) gains much of its intimate nature from the context in which it is expressed.

Nondisclosing Communication

Now that we've looked at the preceding characteristics, it's clear how few of our communications are really self-disclosing. Since we spend so little of our time engaging in this kind of sharing, let's take a look at the messages that do make up the bulk of our communicating. We'll start at the "bottom," with the activity that is least productive, and work upward.

Rituals   Much of our communication is designed to keep people at a distance. Rituals are a prime example of this variety. They are uninvolving acts of communication which have highly predictable outcomes. There is little, if any, risk in performing a ritual. There is also very little payoff in terms of developing a relationship with the other person:

"Hi, how are you?"

"Fine, how are you?"

"See ya."

"Sure."

Activities   These are the behaviors that help define most of our social roles and that occupy much of our time. Studying, working on the job, shopping, and the hundreds of other well-defined behaviors we seem to accomplish without conscious effort all fall into this category. As with rituals, it's possible to carry out many activities without becoming personally involved with others. The impersonal lectures of a professor, the mechanical behavior of a grocery checker, and the seemingly uninterested examinations of some busy physicians are all examples of nondisclosing activities.

Of course, it is possible to be more personal when carrying out activities. We've all had the occasional surprising pleasure of having real person-to-person contact in our activity-based interactions. But most of the time it seems as if our activities would be just as successful—and rewarding—if we carried them out with efficient machines.

Pastimes   These consist of the chitchat that passes for conversation. More varied than rituals, pastimes serve many of the same functions: They acknowledge the other person's presence and indicate liking, or at least goodwill. And, as their name implies, pastimes provide a way of relating together when there doesn't seem to be anything else to do.

Although we might not like to admit it, there are common pastimes for men, for women, as well as those shared by both sexes. In the past, male pastimes have often included conversations about such topics as:

1.   The great football/basketball/baseball/hockey/soccer game;
2.   Mechanical information—cars, home repairs and so forth;
3.   Sex.

The personality of man is not an apple that has to be polished, but a banana that has to be peeled. And the reason we remain so far from one another, the reason we neither communicate nor interact in any real way, is that most of us spend our lives in polishing rather than peeling.

Man's lifelong task is simply one, but it is not simple: To remove the discrepancy between his outer self and his inner self, to get rid of the "persona" that divides his authentic self from the world.

This persona is like the peeling on a banana: It is something built up to protect from bruises and injury. It is not the real person, but sometimes (if the fear of injury remains too great) it becomes a lifelong substitute for the person.

The "authentic personality" knows that he is like a banana, and knows that only as he peels himself down to his individuated self can he reach out and make contact with his fellows by what Father Goldbrunner calls "the sheer maturity of his humanity." Only when he himself is detached from his defensive armorings can he then awaken a true response in his dialogue with others.

Most of us, however, think in terms of the apple, not the banana. We spend our lives in shining the surface, in making it rosy and gleaming, in perfecting the "image." But the image is not the apple, which may be wormy and rotten to the taste.

Almost everything in modern life is devoted to the polishing process, and little to the peeling process. It is the surface personality that we work on—the appearance, the clothes, the manners, the geniality. In short, the salesmanship: We are selling the package, not the product.

Sydney J. Harris

Common female pastime subjects have included:

1. Dieting;
2. Exercise;
3. How great/rotten men are.

And there are some pastimes about which both sexes seem to converse equally:

1. Vacation;
2. The party last night;
3. How things were "way back when."

Of course either sex may engage in chitchat about any of these topics, as well as hundreds of others. Traditionally, male and female topics are simply a matter of social convention, and change over time. The point is that while chitchatting, people are not dealing with *each other;* they're passing time.

Pastimes can be risky if you don't want to play by the rules. We know a woman who learned this when she was invited to join a morning coffee group in her neighborhood. She just moved in and had a month before her job started, so she viewed the invitation as an opportunity to meet the neighbors. The pastime for the morning was, "What my husband did most recently that was horrible." When her turn to talk came she told the others that their complaining was a waste of time, and that they should be doing something more productive with the morning. She broke the rules by not playing along. And some potential friends became immediate enemies.

Games   These are the riskiest kinds of nondisclosing communication. Whereas rituals, activities, and pastimes are often honest, if superficial, ways of relating, games are highly structured interactions based on ulterior motives. And most significantly, most of these motives involve ill feelings.

As the well-known psychiatrist and author Eric Berne pointed out, typical games are designed to prove that the other person is wrong and should be blamed ("If it weren't for you . . ."); saved ("I'm only trying to help you . . ."); belittled ("My _____ is better than your _____"); or the object of revenge ("Now I've got you, you sonofabitch"). In another class of games the ulterior motive is to prove that you're wrong, and probably deserve sympathy. This can be achieved through put-down games ("Gee, I'm stupid"), or cop-out games ("Why does this always happen to me?"). While activities of this sort might gain the player some kind of support, we'll soon see that their costs outweigh their gains.

Sex Differences in Self-Disclosure

Are men and women equally willing to communicate in a disclosing way? Sidney Jourard was one of the first researchers to explore this question. Using his Self-Disclosure Questionnaire he found that females disclose more than males. He explained his results by discussing what he called the "lethal male role"—that is, males are socialized not to disclose and so build up more tension in their daily lives, which results in early death—and the notion that females are socialized to be open and self-disclosing.

More recent research isn't as certain: Some studies support Jourard's early findings, some indicate that there is no difference between the amount males and females disclose, and a few studies indicate that males disclose more (although these are fewest in number). It appears as if the relationship between sex and self-disclosure is not a simple, clear-cut one. For example, males disclose more about their family relationships, interests, and tastes. Also, males appear to disclose less negative and more neutral information about themselves than females.

In clarifying the relationship between sex and self-disclosure, Lawrence Rosenfeld, Jean Civikly, and Jane Herron found that the relationship is indeed a complex one,

Something there is that doesn't love a wall,
That sends the frozen-ground-swell under it,
And spills the upper boulders in the sun;
And makes gaps even two can pass abreast.

   . . . The gaps I mean,
No one has seen them made or heard them
   made,
But at spring mending-time we find them
   there.
I let my neighbor know beyond the hill;
And on a day we meet to walk the line
And set the wall between us once again.
We keep the wall between us as we go.
To each the boulders have fallen to each.

We wear our fingers rough with handling
   them.
Oh, just another kind of outdoor game,
One on a side. It comes to little more:

There where it is we do not need the wall:
He is all pine and I am apple orchard.
My apple trees will never get across
And eat the cones under his pines, I tell
   him.
He only says, 'Good fences make good
   neighbors.'

Spring is the mischief in me, and I wonder
If I could put a notion in his head:
'*Why* do they make good neighbors? Isn't it
Where there are cows? But here there are
   no cows.

Before I built a wall I'd ask to know
What I was walling in or walling out,
And to whom I was like to give offense.
Something there is that doesn't love a wall,
That wants it down.'

   . . . I see him there
Bringing a stone grasped firmly by the top
In each hand, like an old-stone savage armed.
He moves in darkness as it seems to me,
Not of woods only and the shade of trees.
He will not go behind his father's saying,
And he likes having thought of it so well
He says again, 'Good fences make good
   neighbors.'

Robert Frost
"Mending Wall"

calling for the consideration of a number of variables before any conclusions can be drawn. In general, they found that males disclose *more* to *strangers* than females, and are more willing to disclose *superficial* things about themselves, such as their work, attitudes, and opinions. Males are also less intimate and less personal than females.

When the target of disclosure is a friend and not a stranger it's very difficult to predict how either males or females will self-disclose. Is the revealer alone or in a group? Is the topic an intimate one, or one that is rather impersonal? At least these two questions must be answered before any predictions can be made.

Self-disclosure in families differs according to sex. A recent study by Victor Daluiso reported that daughters received the lion's share of disclosure from the parents and, probably as a consequence, had a more accurate perception of their parents. Sons received less disclosure than they gave, and they gave less than their sisters. This information suggests that the pattern for later life may be established in the family: Males have a tendency to disclose less intimate information about themselves than females.

Adrienne Abelman in a study she did for her doctoral dissertation uncovered some fascinating connections between self-disclosure and family relationships. Among her many conclusions were the following: (1) Mutual self-disclosure exists, but primarily between the parents and their children of the same sex; (2) A daughter's satisfaction with her family is related to her father's degree of self-disclosing to his wife; (3) Men seem to rely on self-disclosing with their wives to obtain family satisfaction, whereas women seem to rely on self-disclosing with their children in order to obtain the same thing (which may account for why a father's disclosure to his wife is a determinant of their daughter's satisfaction); (4) Information family members have about each other is related to the degree to which each family member self-discloses.

Men and women differ in their self-disclosing behaviors, but do they *avoid* opening up for the same or different reasons? Rosenfeld investigated this question in a recent study published in *Communication Monographs.* Men and women in beginning speech courses were asked to respond to reasons why people might avoid self-disclosure. Before reading the results of the survey you might want to complete the instrument for yourself. Simply indicate on a scale from 1 to 5 (1 = almost always; 2 = often; 3 = sometimes;

4 = rarely; and 5 = almost never) the extent to which you use each reason to avoid self-disclosing.

_____ 1. I can't find the opportunity to self-disclose with this person.

_____ 2. If I disclosed I might hurt the other person.

_____ 3. If I disclosed I might be evaluating or judging the other person.

_____ 4. I cannot think of topics that I would disclose.

_____ 5. Self-disclosure would give the other person information that he/she might use against me at some time.

_____ 6. If I self-disclose it might cause me to make personal changes.

_____ 7. Self-disclosure might threaten relationships I have with people other than the close acquaintance to whom I disclose.

_____ 8. Self-disclosure is a sign of weakness.

_____ 9. If I self-disclose, I might lose control over the other person.

_____ 10. If I self-disclose, I might discover I am less than I wish to be.

_____ 11. If I self-disclose, I might project an image I do not want to project.

_____ 12. If I self-disclose, the other person might not understand what I was saying.

_____ 13. If I self-disclose, the other person might evaluate me negatively.

_____ 14. Self-disclosure is a sign of some emotional disturbance.

_____ 15. Self-disclosure might hurt our relationship.

_____ 16. I am afraid that self-disclosure might lead to an intimate relationship with the other person.

_____ 17. Self-disclosure might threaten my physical safety.

_____ 18. If I self-disclose, I might give information that makes me appear inconsistent.

_____ 19. Any other reason: _____.

An analysis of responses to the questionnaire indicated that there is a great deal of similarity between why males and females avoid self-disclosure. The reason most commonly identified by both men and women was, "If I disclose I might project an image I do not want to project."

Important differences exist, too. For males, subsequent reasons (in order of importance) included: "If I self-disclose, I might give information that makes me appear inconsistent"; "If I self-disclose, I might lose control over the other person"; and "Self-disclosure might threaten relationships I have with people other than the close acquaintance to whom I disclose." Taken as a group, these reasons provide insight into the predominant reason why men avoid self-disclosure: "If I

disclose to you I might project an image I do not want to, which could make me look bad and cause me to lose control over you. This might go so far as to affect relationships I have with people other than you." *The object is to maintain control,* which may be hampered by self-disclosure.

For females, reasons in addition to, "If I disclose I might project an image I do not want to project" included (in order of importance): "Self-disclosure would give the other person information that he/she might use against me at some time"; "Self-disclosure is a sign of some emotional disturbance"; and "Self-disclosure might hurt our relationship." Taken as a group, these reasons add up to the following: "If I disclose to you I might project an image I do not want to, such as my being emotionally ill, which you might use against me and which might hurt our relationship." *The object is to avoid personal hurt and problems with the relationship,* both of which may result from self-disclosure.

The results of other analyses have supplemented these results. In general, it appears as if most males avoid self-disclosure to avoid loss of control, and to avoid having to face aspects about themselves which might force them to make changes. A fear of intimacy, and the fear of negative evaluations from others, supports the notion that males generally avoid self-disclosure because they are afraid of the other person. This may relate to the control issue: Males may perceive their relationships primarily as battles for control; hence, others are adversaries, people to fear.

Females, on the other hand, generally do not perceive control as the key issue in

their relationships. Rather, the issue is the avoidance of hurt, defined as poor interpersonal relationships or some threat to physical well-being.

Benefits of Self-Disclosure

So far we've talked about what self-disclosure is and who does it. But we haven't answered the most important question of all: Why self-disclose in the first place? Although the answers are all probably clear to most people who have opened themselves up to others, they are certainly worth describing here.

Better Relationships   Besides the general effects of self-disclosure on interpersonal relationships implied by the Johari Window, there are a number of other specific consequences. For example, as trust increases, self-disclosure increases. The process seems to work like this: In order to disclose something that is personal and intimate there must be a certain degree of trust for the other person. By disclosing, you are, in essence, telling the other person, ''I trust you.'' You have made yourself vulnerable, and the other person understands this. The response is logical: The other person relates something intimate involving self to you. You are now in a relationship where trust and intimacy are in operation. The next step is based on the first: The level of trust increases, and so does the level of intimacy, and as the level of intimacy increases, so does the level of trust. Initially, however, there had to be enough trust to begin the process.

Self-disclosure also leads to liking and often loving, important aspects of our better relationships. As Jourard writes:

. . . one who does not disclose himself truthfully and fully can never love another person nor can he be loved by another person. Effective loving calls for knowledge of the object. . . . How can I love a person whom I do not know? How can the other person love me if he does not know me? . . . A truly personal relationship between two people involves disclosure of oneself to the other in full and spontaneous honesty.

Self-disclosure may be taken as evidence for the depth of a given relationship, how close the friendship is. Part of how you evaluate others is according to how much they are willing to listen to what you have to say about yourself, whether they seem to care about what you have to say about yourself, whether they trust you enough to share their own secret thoughts and feelings with you. A deep friendship is one in which there is a great deal of mutual sharing of highly intimate information. The more information revealed, the deeper the relationship is and becomes.

Trust, attraction, liking, and loving are all inextricably bound up in self-disclosure. This is apparent in the family setting where self-disclosure implies a deep form of acceptance of the other person as well as a commitment to the relationship. A recent study by Ronald Burke and his associates found that self-disclosure correlates positively with marital satisfaction. Also, wives disclose more problems and tensions than husbands, although both disclose for the same reasons: to unburden themselves, to increase their spouse's understanding, to seek advice and solutions, and because they *valued their discussion* of their experiences and difficulties. The act of disclosing was valued in and of itself.

Mental Health   Besides being necessary for the success of interpersonal relationships, appropriate self-disclosure (we'll soon define appropriateness) promotes mental health.

O. H. Mowrer explains one way in which this is so. He argues that people are the sum of their contracts—the arrangements and agreements with others which define and order one's personal and social life. Some contracts are personal, such as marriage vows. Others are commercial, such as terms of employment. Many contracts are formal ones, signed and notarized. Others, however, are informal: "I'll do the dishes if you cook dinner." Some contracts are never even spoken about, though the partners still honor them. A typical unspoken agreement might be, "When I get mad at you about little things I'll hold my anger in. When we've built up a backlog of resentments we'll have a loud fight and say terrible things about each other. After a while, we'll have fun making up and then start the cycle over again."

Contracts have a way of going bad. Overcommitment, undercommitment, cheating, a change of interests or good-will—any of these reasons can lead to major changes in a relationship. The threat to mental health comes when one or both parties begin to *conceal*—from themselves and each other—the problems. Since this concealment usually makes the problem worse instead of solving it, the withholder feels more and more stressed, and emotional suffering increases.

i think of my poems as hands
and if i don't
hold them out to you
afraid that you might laugh
and spit on them
i find i won't be touched

if i keep them
in my pocket
i would never get to see you
seeing me
seeing you

and tho i know
from experience
many of you
for a myriad of reasons
will laugh
and spit
and walk away unmoved
still
to meet those of you who are
is well worth
the risk
the pain

so here are my hands
do what you will

Ric Masten

Jourard also discusses the link between nondisclosure and stress. He describes concealment as an energy drain, leading to loneliness, depression, physical and mental illness. Jourard summarizes the problem this way:

> **The dam was indeed broken, and I started pouring myself out with increasing frequency and ease to virtually all of my good friends. All were straight, as I expected; all were glad I had told them; and, some amusing awkwardness notwithstanding, all reacted well. Telling them made us closer friends. For my part, I was much more relaxed and happy, not having to think twice every time I opened my mouth. How refreshing to walk down the street with a straight friend, and, while he was nudging and leering about the approaching girl, nudge and leer right back about the approaching girl's date!**

John Reid
The Best Little Boy in the World

Every maladjusted person is a person who has not made himself known to another human being and in consequence does not know himself. Nor can he be himself. More than that, *he struggles actively to avoid becoming known by another human being.* . . . In the effort to avoid becoming known, a person provides for himself a cancerous kind of stress which is subtle and unrecognized, but none the less effective in producing not only the assorted patterns of unhealthy personality . . . but also the wide array of physical ills. . . .

Self-disclosure is a means of achieving a healthy personality. It eliminates stress and strain related to concealment, and offers the revealer the opportunity to learn about himself, to decrease the sense of *self-alienation* that comes from hiding.

Jourard argues that concealment and self-alienation are "normal" problems associated with living in our society. In his book *The Concept of Self* Kenneth Gergen elaborates on the problem by describing the conflicting demands of many social roles:

When a wife, children, car-pool cronies, secretary, boss, subordinates, office messenger, colleagues of equal rank, business and personal acquaintances who visit or call, bartender, waiter, newsstand manager, barber, drop-in or back fence neighbors, in-laws, Vladimir Nabokov, and Johnny Carson must all be catered to, grappled with, confronted, cajoled, influenced, loved, punished, taught, or escaped within one day . . .

The milieu is one that promotes self-alienation. The paradox, according to Gergen, is this: "to be maximally adaptive . . . is to be maximally vulnerable to experiences of self-alienation. . . . Self-alienation may be viewed as a necessary by-product of successful adaptation in a complex social world."
Is it worth the price?

Self-Concept Development   In Chapter 2 we talked about the need for effective communicators to have a changing, developing self-concept that reflects their true selves. Self-disclosure is one key to this change.

In order to change one's self-concept, three conditions must be met:

1. It's necessary to *experience a new environment.* As long as you deal with the same people in the same ways it's unlikely that you'll learn anything new about yourself.

2. You need to *share information about yourself* with others. By listening to yourself disclose you have the opportunity to learn who you are.

3. You need to *hear others share their perceptions of you.* Receiving feedback about yourself gives you the chance to test your own self-image with the way others view you.

These various views of yourself finally merge into a coherent whole, a reality-tested, reality-based self-concept.

Self-disclosure provides each of the three conditions necessary for changing your self-concept. For most people self-disclosure is a "new environment." It isn't often that the *subject* of conversation is "self," that the speaker is being honest, accurate, open, and revealing. The situation is a strange one, and this strangeness heightens your sense of awareness. Also, the second two conditions are met by definition: Self-disclosure is the process whereby you reveal yourself to others and they offer feedback.

Revealing yourself to others or discussing who you are increases your *self-knowledge* and, as discussed in Chapter 2, high self-knowledge gives you independence from the roles you're assumed to enact, as well as the images others have of you. *Knowing* who you are, *accepting* who you are, and, finally, *liking* who you are, assures that you are secure, supportive, optimistic, and flexible (able to change your ideas and opinions easily, and

accept ideas and opinions from others with as much ease). You are more likely to reach out to others and make them feel welcome and at ease, and be more accepting, warm, and involved with the people around you.

Why We Fear Self-Disclosure

The case for self-disclosure seems overwhelming. Why is it, then, such a small part of our total communication? Why do we have a problem doing it? As John Powell asks, "Why am I afraid to tell you who I am?"

Self-disclosing behavior, according to Paul Cozby in his excellent review of research in the area,

. . . may be seen as the product of two opposing forces, one operating to increase disclosure, the other operating to inhibit disclosure. The first force is the one studied most extensively by disclosure researchers. There are also factors which operate to inhibit disclosure. These might be termed discretion, or a need for privacy, and have been neglected in research on self-disclosure.

Though little empirical research has been done on self-disclosure avoidance, many good explanations have been offered.

Personal Reasons Focusing on interaction in the organizational setting, Fritz Steele discusses six overlapping causes of low disclosure (the motivation for each is practical):

> Sometimes a neighbor whom we have disliked for a lifetime for his arrogance and conceit lets fall a single commonplace remark that shows us another side, another man, really; a man uncertain, puzzled, and in the dark like ourselves.

Willa Cather

1. **Self-disclosure might lead to negative evaluations and rejection**, a loss of both self-esteem and esteem from those to whom the self-disclosures are made.

A: *I earned a C average last semester.*
B: *Really? You must be a real dummy!*

2. **If a particular self-disclosure alienates or angers the other person, it could lead to a decrease in the satisfaction that might be obtained from the relationship.**

A: *At the reunion I met someone, and we made love.*
B: *You have fifteen minutes to pack your bags and be out of here!*

3. **Self-disclosure might lead to a loss of control over some future situation.** Suppose, for instance, that in a moment of candor you confess to a friend that your critical sarcasm is often a way of hiding your feelings of inferiority to the object of your criticism. From that time on, you've sacrificed the usefulness of sarcasm as a way of fooling this person. Thus, your control over another's view of you has been diminished.

4. **A possible drawback of self-disclosure is the risk that your honesty might hurt another person.**

A: *Well, since you asked, I have been bored lately when we've been together.*
B: *I know. It's my fault. I don't see how you can stand me at all!*

5. **Self-disclosure might lead to the projection of a negative image.** You might look less "perfect" than you care to. Admitting that you've been unfair, acted foolishly, or are unsure of yourself might indicate that you're human, but in a world where a good public image seems important, revealing one's imperfections is often threatening.

6. **Lying often appears to have a greater benefit for the listener than does telling the truth.** Steele calls this the "Great Lie Theory." Statements such as "I'm not going to tell you because you'll be better off not knowing" fall into this category. Another example of avoiding self-disclosure to prevent pain is the "I love you" pledge uttered only to make the other person feel better. (Needless to say, confessions such as this have a way of creating much grief in the long run.) Of course, telling the truth usually does more to help the other person than does telling a lie. But this is not what most of us were taught. And that leads to several more reasons for avoiding self-disclosure.

Sociological Reasons   Gerard Egan, viewing self-disclosure from a sociological perspective, argues that there are two forces in our society that work against greater self-disclosure. The first is a kind of cultural ban against intimate self-disclosure based on a view that open sharing is a sign of weakness, exhibitionism, or mental illness. The second force is a societywide cultivation of the "lie" as a way of life. This force is related to the belief that misrepresentation is necessary to achieve or maintain power and wealth in our society. Unfortunately, the underlying justification for this reason is that how you present yourself to others must be different from how you really conceive of yourself because if your self-presentation was true to your self-conception, failure would surely result!

Paradoxical as it sounds, a third social force discouraging self-disclosure is precisely the fact that such open behavior does lead to increased awareness. Self-help books and human relations training notwithstanding, a society that uses advertising to promote appearance over reality and that equates material success with satisfaction can't stand too much self-examination and still survive. Thus, it's difficult to be open with one's self and others and "play the game" at the same time. As L. J. Sherrill put it, "The human organism seems capable of enduring anything in the universe except a clear, complete, fully conscious view of one's self as he actually is." Because self-disclosure leads to self-awareness and the revelation, in front of one or more others, that changes in behavior or goals are necessary, a commitment to *do something* becomes apparent. Self-disclosure demands a willingness to assume responsibility for making any changes revealed as important. The flight from this responsibility, which may appear both awesome and painful, is the avoidance of self-disclosure.

Another force acting against disclosure is the reluctance of many people in our society to truly communicate with others.

Which of us has known his brother?
Which of us has looked into his father's heart:
Which of us has not remained forever prison-bent?
Which of us is not forever a stranger and alone?

Thomas Wolfe

You may not fear getting in touch with yourself, yet you may fear letting *others* get in touch with *you*. As already mentioned, self-disclosure increases trust, liking, attraction, and may lead to an intimate relationship. Eric Berne's thesis in his book *Games People Play* is that intimacy frightens many people, which is why they play games. Games keep people apart and reduce the likelihood of intimate contact.

Reasons for avoiding self-disclosure may be best summarized by John Powell, who answers the question posed in the title of his book, *Why Am I Afraid to Tell You Who I Am?*, this way:

I am afraid to tell you who I am, because, if I tell you who I am, you may not like who I am, and it's all that I have.

Without your facade (that is, the mask others see, the mask that doesn't reflect the inner you), the risk of personal rejection is high indeed. And if you reveal your inner self, what excuses can you muster to overcome the rejection that might tear you apart? No, the risk is too great, so you

convince yourself that avoiding self-disclosure altogether is the best answer.

And the cycle begins: loneliness, depression, self-alienation, the loss of community. A high price to pay, but some—maybe you—perceive rejection an even higher price. If you don't share yourself with others, you stand little chance of establishing meaningful relationships with others. Without sharing yourself, it's difficult for others to help meet your basic social needs of belonging, being accepted, and being loved. Once you understand the connection between sharing knowledge of self and meaningful interpersonal relationships, it becomes apparent that you must take the risk that comes with self-disclosure. The question then becomes when to open up and when to remain quiet.

When to Self-Disclose?

One fear we've had while writing this chapter is that a few over-enthusiastic readers may throw down their books after reading half of what we've written and rush away to begin sharing every personal detail of their lives to whomever they can find. As you can imagine, this kind of behavior isn't an example of effective interpersonal communication.

Self-disclosure is a special kind of sharing, not appropriate for every situation. Let's take a look at some guidelines that can help you recognize how to express yourself in a way that's rewarding for you and the others involved.

1. Is the other person important to you? There are several ways in which someone might be important. Perhaps you have an ongoing relationship deep enough so that sharing significant parts of yourself justifies keeping your present level of togetherness intact. Or perhaps the person to whom you're considering disclosing is someone with whom you've previously related on a less personal level. But now you see a chance to grow closer, and disclosure may be the path toward developing that personal relationship.

There's still another category of "important person" to whom self-disclosure is sometimes appropriate: Strangers who are players in what has been called the "bus rider phenomenon." This occurs when we meet a total stranger whom we'll probably never see again (on a bus, plane, etc.) and reveal the most intimate parts of our lives. It's sometimes possible to call such strangers "important people" because they provide a safe outlet for expressing important feelings which otherwise would go unshared. A friend of ours tells the following story of how a total stranger can be a party to self-disclosure:

I was traveling with my husband (we had been married for two weeks) back east to have him meet all the relatives, especially my mother who couldn't make it out for the wedding. We sat three across on the plane; the third person was an old woman. I was very "into" being a new bride, and so did not notice that the woman made several attempts to talk to us. My husband noticed (thankfully!) and asked the usual question, "Where are you traveling?" She shared with us how her husband, who was back east, had just died there. She was going to take care of the necessary arrangements. It was a crisis unparalleled in her life. And she needed to tell someone, to have someone cry with her for a moment—even two strangers on a plane.

2. Is the risk of disclosing reasonable?
Take a realistic look at the potential risks of self-disclosure. Even if the probable benefits are great, opening yourself up to almost certain rejection may be asking for trouble. For instance, it might be foolhardy to share your important feelings with someone you know is likely to betray your confidences or ridicule them. On the other hand, knowing that your partner is trustworthy and supportive makes the prospect of speaking

out more reasonable. In anticipating risks, be sure that you are realistic. It's sometimes easy to indulge in catastrophic expectations, in which you begin to imagine all sorts of disastrous consequences of your opening up, when in fact such horrors are quite unlikely to occur.

3. Is the amount and type of disclosure appropriate?
A third point to realize is that there are degrees of self-disclosure, so that telling others about yourself isn't an all-or-nothing decision you must make. It's possible to share some facts, opinions, or feelings with one person while reserving riskier ones for others. In the same vein, before sharing important information with someone who does matter to you, you might consider testing their reactions by disclosing less personal data.

4. Is the disclosure relevant to the situation at hand?
Self-disclosure doesn't require long confessions about your past life or current thoughts unrelated to the now. On the contrary, it ought to be directly pertinent to your present conversation. It's ludicrous to picture the self-disclosing person as someone who blurts out intimate details of every past experience. Instead, our model is someone who, when the time is appropriate, trusts us enough to share the hidden parts of herself that affect our relationship.

Usually, then, the subject of appropriate self-disclosure involves the present, the "here and now" as opposed to "there and then." "How am I feeling now?" "How are we doing now?" These are appropriate

© United Features Syndicate, Inc.

topics for sharing personal thoughts and feelings. There are certainly times when it's relevant to bring up the past, but only as it relates to what's going on in the present.

5.   Is the disclosure reciprocated?
There's nothing quite as disconcerting as talking your heart out to someone only to discover that the other person has yet to say anything to you which is half as revealing as what you've been saying. And you think to yourself: "What am I doing?!" Unequal self-disclosure creates an imbalanced relationship, one doomed to fall apart.

There are few times when one-way disclosure is acceptable. Most of them involve formal, therapeutic relationships in which a client approaches a trained professional with the goal of resolving a problem. For instance, you wouldn't necessarily expect your physician to begin sharing his or her personal ailments with you during an office visit. Nonetheless, it's interesting to note that one frequently noted characteristic of effective psychotherapists, counselors, and teachers is a willingness to share their feelings about a relationship with their clients.

6.   Will the effect be constructive?
Self-disclosure can be a vicious tool if it's

"What is REAL?" asked the Rabbit one day, when they were lying side by side near the nursery fender, before Nana came to tidy the room.

"Does it mean having things buzz inside you and a stick-out handle?"

"Real isn't how you are made," said the Skin Horse, "it's a thing that happens to you. When a child loves you for a long, long time, not just to play with, but REALLY loves you, then you become Real."

"Does it hurt?" asked the Rabbit.

"Sometimes," said the Skin Horse, for he was always truthful. "When you are Real you don't mind being hurt."

"Does it happen all at once, like being wound up," he asked, "or bit by bit?"

"It doesn't happen all at once," said the Skin Horse. "You become. It takes a long time. That's why it doesn't often happen to people who break easily, or have sharp edges, or who have to be carefully kept. Generally, by the time you are Real, most of your hair has been loved off, and your eyes drop out and you get loose in the joints and very shabby. But these things don't matter at all, because when you are Real you can't be ugly, except to people who don't understand."

Margery Williams
The Velveteen Rabbit

not used carefully. Psychologist George Bach suggests that every person has a psychological "beltline." Below that beltline are areas about which the person is extremely sensitive. Bach says that jabbing at a "below the belt" area is a sure-fire way to disable another person, though usually at great cost to the relationship. It's important to consider the effects of your candor before opening up to others. Comments such as, "I've always thought you were pretty unintelligent" or, "Last year I made love to your best friend" *may* sometimes resolve old business and thus be constructive, but they also can be devastating— to the listener, to the relationship, and to your self-esteem.

7. Is the self-disclosure clear and understandable? When expressing yourself to others, it's important that you share yourself in a way that's intelligible. This means describing the *sources* of your message clearly. For instance, it's far better to describe another's behavior by saying, "When you don't answer my phone calls or drop by to visit anymore . . ." than to vaguely complain "When you avoid me . . ."

It's also vital to express your *thoughts* and *feelings* explicitly. "I feel worried because I'm afraid you don't care about me" is more understandable than "I don't like it . . ." We'll have more to say about thoughts and feelings in Chapter 5.

We hope these guidelines—and this chapter—have given you a better picture of the importance of self-disclosure in interpersonal communication. We've tried to acknowledge that self-disclosure is difficult and risky. Like you, we know that hiding from others is usually easier, and certainly less risky in the short run. But as our dreams of nakedness tell us, avoiding self-disclosure has consequences that can be more painful and risky than wearing masks.

Readings

Abelman, Adrienne K. "The Relationship Between Family Self-Disclosure, Adolescent Adjustment, Family Satisfaction, and Family Congruence." *Dissertation Abstracts International*, 36, (1976): 4248A.

Berne, Eric. *Games People Play*. New York: Grove Press, 1964.

Burke, Ronald J., Tamara Weir and Denise Harrison. "Disclosure of Problems and Tensions Experienced by Marital Partners." *Psychological Reports*, 38, (1976): 531–542.

Chelune, Gordon J., ed. *Self-Disclosure: Origins, Patterns and Implications for Openness in Interpersonal Communication*. San Francisco: Jossey-Bass, 1979.

Cozby, Paul C. "Self-Disclosure: A Literature Review." *Psychological Bulletin*, 79, (1973): 73–91.

Daluiso, Victor E. "Self-Disclosure and Perception of that Self-Disclosure Between Parents and Their Teen-Age Children." *Dissertation Abstracts International*, 33, (1972): 420B.

Derlega, Valerian J. and Alan L. Chaikin. "Privacy and Self-Disclosure in Social Relationships." *Journal of Social Issues*, 33, (1978): 102–115.

Derlega, Valerian J., and Alan L. Chaikin. *Sharing Intimacy: What We Reveal to Others and Why*. Englewood Cliffs, New Jersey: Prentice-Hall, 1975.

Derlega, Valerian J., Barbara Gockel, and David Sholis, "Sex Differences in Self-Disclosure: Effects of Topic Content, Friendships, and Partener's Sex." *Sex Roles,* in press.

Derlega, Valerian J., Midge Wilson and Alan L. Chaikin. "Friendship and Disclosure Reiprocity." *Journal of Personality and Social Psychology*, 34, (1976): 578–582.

Egan, Gerard. *Encounter: Group Processes for Interpersonal Growth*. Belmont, California: Brooks/Cole, 1970.

Gergen, Kenneth J. *The Concept of Self*. New York: Holt, Rinehart and Winston, 1971.

Giffin, Kim and Bobby R. Patton. *Personal Communication in Human Relations*. Columbus, Ohio: Charles E. Merrill, 1974.

Gilbert, Shirley J. "Self-Disclosure, Intimacy and Communication in Families." *Family Coordinator*, 25, (1976): 221–231.

Gilbert, Shirley J. and Gale G. Whiteneck. "Toward a Multidimensional Approach to the Study of Self-Disclosure." *Human Communication Research*, 2, (1976): 347–355.

Goodstein, Leonard D. and Virginia M. Reinecker. "Factors Affecting Self-Disclosure: A Review of the Literature." In *Progress in Experimental Personality Research,* VII, Brendan A. Maher, ed. New York: Academic Press, 1974.

Harris, Thomas A. *I'm O.K., You're O.K.* New York: Harper and Row, 1967.

Johnson, David W. *Reaching Out.* Englewood Cliffs, New Jersey: Prentice-Hall, 1972.

Jourard, Sidney M. *Disclosing Man to Himself.* Princeton, New Jersey: Van Nostrand, 1968.

Jourard, Sidney M. "Healthy Personality and Self-Disclosure." *Mental Hygiene,* 43, (1959): 499–507.

Jourard, Sidney M. *The Transparent Self,* 2nd Ed. Princeton, New Jersey: Van Nostrand, 1971.

Luft, Joseph. *Of Human Interaction.* Palo Alto, California: National Press Books, 1969.

Lyons, Arthur. "Personality of High and Low Self-Disclosers." *Journal of Humanistic Psychology,* 18, (1978): 83–86.

Moriwaki, Sharon Y. "Self-Disclosure, Significant Others and Psychological Well-Being in Old Age." *Journal of Health and Social Behavior,* 14, (1973): 226–232.

Mowrer, Orval Hobart. "Loss and Recovery of Community: A Guide to the Theory and Practice of Integrity Therapy." In *Innovations to Group Psychotherapy,* George M. Gazda, ed., Springfield, Illinois: Charles C. Thomas, 1968.

Pearce, W. Barnett, and Stewart M. Sharp. "Self-Disclosing Communication." *Journal of Communication,* 23, (1973): 409-425.

Powell, John. *Why Am I Afraid To Tell You Who I Am?* Niles, Illinois: Argus Communications, 1968.

Rosenfeld, Lawrence B. "Self-Disclosure Avoidance: Why Am I Afraid To Tell You Who I Am?" *Communication Monographs,* 46, (1979): 63–74.

Rosenfeld, Lawrence B., Jean M. Civikly and Jane R. Herron. "Anatomical Sex, Psychological Sex, and Self-Disclosure." In *Self-Disclosure: Origins, Patterns and Implications for Openness in Interpersonal Communication,* Gordon J. Chelune, ed., San Francisco: Jossey-Bass, 1979.

Rubin, Zick. "Lovers and Other Strangers: The Development of Intimacy in Encounters and Relationships." *American Scientist,* 62, (1974): 182–190.

Sherrill, L. J. *Guilt and Redemption.* Richard, Virginia: John Knox Press, 1945.

Steele, Fritz. *The Open Organization: The Impact of Secrecy and Disclosure on People and Organizations.* Reading, Massachusetts: Addison-Wesley, 1975.

Walker, Lilly S., and Paul H. Eright. "Self-Disclosure in Friendship." *Perceptual and Motor Skills,* 42, (1976): 735–742.

Wheeless, Lawrence R., and Janis Grotz. "The Measurement of Trust and Its Relationship to Self-Disclosure." *Human Communication Research,* 3, (1977): 250–257.

Williams, Margery. *The Velveteen Rabbit.*

Wood, John T. *What Are You Afraid Of?: A Guide to Dealing With Your Fears.* New York: Spectrum Books, 1976.

Perception  4

4 If you could choose one invention that would improve the human condition, what would it be? A cure for cancer? A system for producing plentiful, nutritious food for everyone? A nonpolluting energy source?

Our nomination for "best invention" would look like a two-person electric chair. The users would seat themselves and place electrically connected metallic caps on their heads. When the switch was thrown, each person would instantly experience the other's world. Each would see through the other's eyes, possess the other's memories, and in all other ways know what it felt to be the other person.

You can imagine how misunderstandings would disappear and tolerance would increase once everyone had used our invention. It's hard to dislike someone once you've been inside his or her skin.

Since our miracle chair doesn't exist, this chapter will have to attempt the same goal. In the following pages, we'll try to show you the many ways in which each of us experiences the world differently, and in so doing, hopefully show you how to experience the world as others do. In our survey we'll explore several areas: the physiological factors that shape our perceptions; the role culture plays in creating our world views; and, finally, how our personal needs, interests, and biases cause us to see things differently.

Physiological Influences

Visit a large camera store and you'll be confronted by an impressive array of equipment: everything from cheap pocket Brownies to sophisticated systems including lenses, filters, tripods, and timers. Some cameras can photograph miniature items at close range and others can capture distant objects clearly. With the right film, it's even possible to take pictures of objects invisible to the unaided eye. There's only one world "out there," but different equipment allows us to see different parts of it. In the same way, each person's perceptual equipment gives us a different image of the world. And sometimes these pictures are so unalike that it seems as if we're not talking about the same events at all.

Taste   The sense of taste depends on a chemical reaction for its information. Taste receptors (buds) located in pores in the mouth respond to food which enters each pore by sending a message to the brain. Although we may *think* there are an infinite variety of tastes (recall the last good meal you had), only four basic tastes exist: sweet, sour, salty, and bitter. Each part of the tongue is sensitive to only one of these tastes.

The degree to which each of us possesses the four different types of taste buds determines how foods taste. Not everyone tastes the same food in the same way. Older people, for example, taste a wide variety of things as predominantly bitter. This phenomenon happens because the taste buds for sweet, salty, and sour die off and are not as readily replaced, leaving the taste buds for bitter as the primary sources of taste information.

Differences are not merely a function of age; heredity also plays a role. You can test this fact by trying the following experiment. From your biology department or a chemical supply house, obtain strips of litmus paper treated with the chemical phenyl-thio-carbamide (PTC). (This litmus paper is quite inexpensive.) Give one strip to each member of your group, and have everyone taste their paper at the same time. Now immediately conduct a survey: "How many people found the paper salty? How many found it sweet? How many found it bitter? How many found no taste at all? Did anyone find a different taste?

Chances are that the paper tasted bitter to some people, while to others it was sweet, sour, or salty. Somewhat less than half your group probably didn't taste anything at all. If you've inherited a dominant "taster" gene from someone in your family, you'll get one taste or another. Otherwise, the treated paper won't seem any different from the untreated type.

The fact that the paper has different tastes for different people is interesting in itself, but it also has important implications for communication. You can imagine that something similar is true for our taste in foods. Do you remember having a conversation that went something like this:

Eat your liver, dear, it tastes so good.

But Ma! I hate liver! It tastes horrible!

Don't be foolish, dear. I spent a lot of time in the kitchen fixing it. It's delicious.

But every time I eat it, it makes me choke! I don't want any.

You listen to me. This is the best liver money can buy. Now be quiet and eat your dinner. All this 'not liking it' is just in your mind.

This kind of dialogue probably sounds familiar to you. In view of the PTC experiment, you can see its flaw: Mother and child are both arguing as if liver tastes the same to everyone. Either the food tastes good or it doesn't—so somebody's wrong. But when you think about the PTC experiment, you begin to get the idea that maybe liver just tastes *different* to different people.

What's your favorite food? When was the last time you told people they were crazy because they didn't like it? How did your remarks affect your communication?

Smell Located in the nostrils, the receptors for smell are also "triggered" by a chemical reaction. The sense of smell is extremely sensitive in that it takes little stimulus to activate the receptors and send a message to the brain (although if inundated with a particular smell, the receptors eventually "shut off").

Just as the ability to taste varies among people, so does the ability to smell. Some people are better at detecting odors than others, and the difference, as with most differences in taste, are inherited. The ability to smell is related to the yellow and brown pigments in the smell receptors— the darker the colors, the more sensitive the receptors. (Albino individuals have virtually no sense of smell.)

The ability to detect smells affects our interpersonal interactions. For example, R. A. Schneider reports that women are more sensitive to smells in the morning, whereas men are more sensitive to smells in the evening, and women are more sensitive to smells than men generally. To complicate the situation, male and female extroverts are more sensitive to smells than male and female introverts.

Putting all this information together may account for someone saying, "She's so sensitive" about a female extrovert in the morning who mentions a perfume she finds particularly offensive—a smell many others may not even detect to any significant degree! Also, this information may account for early morning interactions (when women and men differ the most in their ability to smell, with women far superior), such as:

Jane: *That coffee smells delicious!*
Tarzan: *Huh?*

A great many differences in the ability to detect odors and in preferences for odors exist. However, most people can easily agree about what odors they like least (burnt rubber or vomit, for example), and to a lesser degree, the ones they especially like (deep rose, fresh strawberries, honeysuckle), but there's no real consistency about whether most smells are "good" or "bad." For example, in one study people ranked their preferences among 132 different odors. Bay leaf (a spice commonly used in cooking) ranged from 9th to 98th; peppermint from 1st to 76th; and raw onion from 5th to 110th. Age and sex seem to play some part in people's odor preferences. Children and men generally like sweeter fruit odors, whereas women prefer odors less sweet; men ranked musky-smelling perfumes

higher than women did; and children tolerate unpleasant odors such as those from feces more than adults do.

Differences such as these demonstrate that smells or tastes pleasing to one person can be repulsive to somebody else. So whether it's your perfume, ladies, or your aftershave lotion, gentlemen, that provokes the comment, "What stinks?" don't be upset—the other person may only be perceiving the odor differently than you do.

Touch Sense organs located in the skin depend on physical contact for information about the environment. The amount of surface area that contains receptors amounts to about a million sensory fibers entering the spinal cord. And the amount of space taken up in the brain for processing tactile information is large (areas devoted to the lips, index finger, and thumb take up a disproportionately large portion of space in the brain). In light of these facts, the importance of environmental information received from our skin is clear.

Although touch may provide us with important information, it is not a very sensitive sense, especially when compared to the receptors in the nose. However, this "lack" is necessary for survival. If our sense of touch were highly sensitive, our own heartbeats would probably drive us crazy!

The role of touch in interpersonal communication is discussed at length in Chapter 9. Insofar as touch relates to perception, it is important to mention here that, as with the other senses, people differ in their touch sensitivity. It is possible, for example, to increase your ability to communicate tactilely by participating in sensitivity training. People who participate in groups of this type become more accurate in determining the intended meaning of the touch they receive.

Sensitivity to temperature is part of our sense of touch. Interestingly, we are sensitive to changes and contrasts in temperature, and not actual temperatures. We are able to detect changes as small as 1/100th of a degree every second! To test this sensitivity, try the following: Place your left hand in hot water, and your right hand in cold water, then place both hands in lukewarm water. To your right hand the lukewarm water most likely seemed hot, and to your left hand it seemed cold. It was the *change* that mattered, and not the temperature itself.

Like the other senses, sensitivity to temperature varies from person to person; forgetting this fact can block communication. For example, think of the times you've called someone "chicken" who thought the water was too cold for swimming or gotten angry at someone for turning the heat up or down when you were comfortable.

Again, the root of the problem may be biological. People's sensitivity to temperature varies greatly. Thus, if you're less sensitive to cold, it might be that 65° F to you feels like 55° F. to somebody else. If people could keep this in mind, they'd have less reason to disagree over who's right about the temperature. Rather than fighting, they could figure out alternative behaviors that would suit everyone involved. (That's why electric blankets with dual controls are so popular.)

Hearing Let's continue our study of the senses by examining hearing. We'll try to give you some feeling for how the world sounds to people who hear differently than you do (a normal person can distinguish 340,000 tones), and then we'll examine the implications this has for communication.

Suppose you have normal hearing. You can represent this visually by holding your book at arm's length and reading what's written below:

LOUDNESS

You should have no trouble reading this comfortably, just as the person with normal hearing has no difficulty understanding others in a conversation. However, it's possible to have a hearing loss without ever knowing it; in fact, it's likely that you know someone who does have a hearing loss. These people would have difficulty understanding the same sounds you hear so easily. You can represent how a person with the most common type of loss might hear a word by again holding your book at arm's length and reading this word:

LOU IIE! ;

You probably had to magnify these letters or move closer and also mentally fill in the blanks to understand the word. Likewise, hard-of-hearing people try to understand sounds by magnifying the volume (often with a hearing aid) or by getting closer to the source; they utilize clues in the situation and context to "fill in" sounds they can't hear or are unable to read on a speaker's lips.

The increased noise level of our civilization has caused permanent damage to the ears of many people, especially those who spend much of their time in noisy environments—factories, war zones, rock concerts, and so on. These people with hearing losses are usually the ones who may have to turn up the TV or radio to a volume that's uncomfortable for the rest of us.

Forgetting the difference between people's sensitivity to sound can lead to sad consequences. Audiologists and physicians report many cases of children being held back in school for being "slow learners" and punished at home for "not paying attention," when the real problem was that they simply couldn't hear what was going on. Whispering "sweet nothings" in your lover's ear may indeed turn out to be nothing!

Sight   We are a visual society. Rarely do you hear someone say, "Touch you later," "Hear you later," "Smell you later," or "Taste you later," even though any one of these may be as accurate a description as the everyday "See you later." Other common expressions show the importance of vision:

"Seeing is believing."

"You're a sight for sore eyes."

"I see what you mean."

"Look me up when you're in town."

"We don't see eye to eye."

It's logical that our language should stress visual images. Information received via sight is probably the most important information we receive, with sound—what we hear—second most important. The other three senses usually serve to "tone" and "integrate" the data we receive from our eyes and ears, as opposed to providing unique information on their own.

The normal eye can differentiate 7.5 million color shades, and make up 1 million discriminations each second. Most of this information is lost because the brain can only process it in limited amounts.

The part of the eye called the retina is crucial for gathering this sense data. The retina contains rods, which detect weak amounts of light, and cones, which detect high levels of illumination, distinguish points in space, discriminate fine details, and determine color. The cones contain three pigments, a red-sensitive one, a green-sensitive one, and a blue-sensitive one. Individuals vary in the degree to which they have sufficient amounts of each of the pigments, giving rise to the general term "color-blindness." A person labeled "color-blind" may be deficient in (or missing) one or two of the pigments, or, on rare occasions, all three (in which case the person can only see black and white). A common form of color-blindness is an absence (as opposed to a deficiency) of either the red-sensitive or blue-sensitive pigment. This problem, found in twice as many males as females, results in seeing reds and greens as yellows.

Consider selling color-blind people something to wear, or talking to them about a particular piece of art, or what color to paint the house. The number of problems in communication that may arise from color-blindness are numerous

More common perhaps than color-blindness is nearsightedness and farsightedness. It's obvious that people with uncorrected visual problems see differently than the rest of us, and that sometimes the corrections may not solve all the problems. Sherri Adler, Ron's wife, explains:

I started wearing glasses when I was eight years old, and my eyesight continued to deteriorate until I was about seventeen. So practically all my life I've had to account for communication difficulties because of my very poor vision. (In my last eye test I couldn't even read the big "E" at the top of the chart without my contact lenses!)

When I was young I went through the embarrassment of having "four eyes" and would only put my glasses on to sneak a look at the blackboard. Asking the teacher if I could sit closer to the front would have solved part of the problem, but also would have singled me out again as a glasses-wearer. I stayed quiet, and my grades declined.

Since I've known Ron we've had some experiences that have caused communication problems because of our differences in vision: He has perfect eyesight, and even when I'm wearing contacts, he can see better than I. I have to sit in the front half of a movie theater to be able to see well. Ron has adjusted to this, but he says he always sat in the back before he met me.

Sex   So far we've taken a look at how your five senses can make the world seem a different place to you and to other people. Now let's talk about another physiological factor that causes us to perceive things differently and show you how it can affect communication.

For some women, the menstrual cycle plays an important role in shaping feelings, and thus affects communication. But women aren't the only ones whose communication is affected by periodic changes in mood. Men, too, go through recognizable mood cycles, even though they aren't marked by obvious physical changes. Although they may not be aware of it, many men seem to go through biologically regulated periods of good spirits followed by equally predictable times of depression. The average length of this cycle is about five weeks, although in some cases it's as short as sixteen days or as long as two months. However long it may be, this cycle of ups and downs is quite regular.

If you were to ask most men why they were feeling so bad during the low part of their mood cycle, you'd get plenty of reasons: troubles with the family, troubles at work, the state of the economy, the "cussedness" of politicians, or a million other explanations. However reasonable these woes may sound, they're often not the real cause of the problem. Although extremely good or bad events can alter feelings, more often they're governed by the internal biological clock everyone carries around inside.

Although neither men nor women can change these emotional cycles, simply learning to expect them can be a big help in improving communication. When you understand that the cause of a bad mood is

During the preoperational stage, the child is also quite *egocentric*, meaning he is unable to take the viewpoint of other people. His ego seems to stand at the center of his world. To illustrate, show the child a two-sided mirror and then hold it between the two of you so the child can see himself in it. If you ask him what he thinks *you* can see, he imagines that you see *his* reflected image instead of your own. . . The concept of egocentrism helps us to understand why children can seem exasperatingly selfish or uncooperative at times. A child who blocks your view by standing in front of a television set assumes that you can see if he can. If you ask him to move so you can see, he may move so that he can see better!

Dennis Coon
Introduction to Psychology

predictable and caused by physiological factors, you can plan for it. You'll know that every few weeks your patience will be shorter, and you'll be less likely to blame your bad moods on innocent bystanders. The people around you can also learn to expect your periodic lows and attribute them to biology instead of getting angry at you.

Other Physiological Factors   So far we've only looked at the most obvious physical differences that influence our perception. Even a casual second look shows many other ways in which the state of our bodies determines how we perceive the world, and thus shapes the way we communicate.

Health   Recall the last time you came down with a cold, flu, or some other ailment. Do you remember how different you felt? You probably had much less energy. It's likely that you felt less sociable, and that your thinking was probably a bit slower than usual. It's easy to see that these

kinds of changes have a strong impact on how you relate to others. Obvious as this seems, it's easy to forget that someone else may be behaving differently due to illness. In the same way, it's important to let others know when you feel poorly so they can give you the understanding you need.

Fatigue   Just as being ill can affect your relationships, so too can being overly tired. Again we don't want to belabor an obvious point, but it's important to recognize the fact that you or someone else may behave differently when you're fatigued, and that trying to deal with important issues at such a time can get you into trouble.

Age   One reason older people view the world differently than younger ones is because of their generally greater scope and number of experiences. But there are also age-related physical differences that shape perceptions. Although none of the

"This is nothing. When I was your age the snow was so deep it came up to my chin!"

authors are exactly old geezers, each of us has had a share of troubles with our kids due to age. If you've been around children, you know that their energy level is quite high, to put it mildly. To us it often seems as if our children are superactive—"little maniacs," we sometimes call them. To the children, of course, adults must often seem like old bores. After all, what's wrong with someone who doesn't want to wrestle or play hide and seek five hours a day?

Height   To understand the role height plays in perception, imagine two people attending a parade—one six feet three inches tall and the other five feet two inches tall. Clearly what would be an enjoyable spectacle for the first person would probably be a frustrating jumble for the shorter companion. Countless other activities are affected by height, such as dancing, visiting the theater, and playing many sports. What does all this have to do with interpersonal communication? It's easy to see how failing to recognize the different worlds in which shorter and taller people live can lead to unnecessary frustration. Think, for instance, of the troubles children encounter in a world designed for people twice their size. Drinking from a fountain, climbing onto a chair, or even going to the bathroom can be chores. Parents would be wise to remember these difficulties before blaming kids for not being quick or tidy.

Hunger   This factor is an obvious one, at least once you consider it. People often get grumpy when they haven't eaten and sleepy after stuffing themselves. Yet how often do we forget these simple facts and try to conduct important business at times when our stomachs are running our lives?

Daily Cycles   Are you a "morning person" or a "night person?" Most of us can answer this question pretty easily, and there's a good physiological reason behind our answer. Each of us is in a daily cycle in which all sorts of changes constantly occur: body temperature, sexual drive, alertness, tolerance to stress, and mood. Most of these changes are due to hormonal cycles. For instance, adrenal hormones which affect feelings of stress are secreted at higher rates during some hours. In the same manner, the male and female sex hormones enter our systems at variable rates. We often aren't conscious of these changes, but they surely govern the way we relate towards each other. Once we're aware that our own cycles and those of others govern our feelings and behavior, it becomes possible to run our lives so that we deal with important issues at the most effective times.

Social Roles

So far you've seen how everyone's physiological makeup varies, and how these variations can block communication if people are not careful. But besides our physical makeup there's another set of perceptual factors that can lead to communication breakdowns. From almost the time we're born, each of us is indirectly taught a whole set of roles we're expected to play. In one sense this collection of prescribed parts is necessary because it enables a society to function smoothly and provides the security that comes from knowing what's expected of you. But in another way having roles defined in advance can lead to wide gaps in understanding. When roles become unquestioned and rigid, people tend to see the world from their own viewpoint, having no experiences to show them how other people view it. Naturally, in such a situation communication suffers.

Sex Roles   In every society one of the most important factors in determining roles is sex. How should a woman act? What kinds of behavior define being a man? Until recently most of us never questioned the answers our society gave to these questions. Boys are made of "snips and snails and puppy-dog tails" and grow up to be the breadwinners of families; little girls are "sugar and spice and everything nice," and their mothers are irrational, intuitive, and temperamental. Not everyone fits into these patterns, but in the past the patterns became well established and were mainly unquestioned by most people.

Research on male and female behavior in small group settings supports the stereotypes. As a group males appear more confident, dominant, achievement-oriented, and task-oriented than females, and females are more accommodating and social-oriented than males. In an analysis of male and female democratic leaders, Lawrence Rosenfeld and one of his colleagues, Gene Fowler, found that the personality variables that characterize democratic male leaders include the following: forcefulness, superior

Washing and ironing and cooking meals for me (yum yum)
Cleaning and sewing, she's busy as a bee (buzz buzz)
I want to help her in every single way
Because I love my mommy every day.

Working, he's working, he works so hard for us (work work)
Though he is tired he never makes a fuss (nay nay)
I want to help him in every single way
Because I love my daddy every day.

Preschool Song,
(overheard in 1979)

intellectual ability, being analytical of self and others, and being utilitarian. Democratic females were characterized as open-minded, helpful, affectionate, accepting of blame, and desirous of stability and unity.

In a follow-up study, Rosenfeld and Fowler observed the behavior of male and female democratic leaders. They found the communicative behavior of female democratic leaders to be predominantly socioemotional, expressing more friendly acts and agreement than male democratic leaders. The communicative behavior of male democratic leaders was concentrated in the task areas. For example, the male leaders offered more suggestions than female leaders, disagreed more, and performed more unfriendly acts.

These findings support the stereotyped sex-roles ascribed to males and females in our society. Males behave in independent, aggressive, competitive, risk-taking, and task-oriented ways, whereas females tend to be more noncompetitive, dependent, empathic, passive, fragile, interpersonally oriented, expressive, and cooperative.

What accounts for these differences? In an earlier time most people would have automatically assumed that *physical* differences between men and women cause them to think and act in distinct ways. More recently, however, social scientists and lay people have recognized that human behavior—male and female— is also influenced by *psychological* differences, brought about by the social environment in which each of us lives. One needn't be a social scientist to realize that the ways in which boys and girls are socialized differ in many ways. Boys are discouraged from behaving in "feminine" ways: playing with dolls, dressing up (except for a brief stint as Spiderman or the Incredible Hulk on Halloween). They're reinforced for playing in competitive sports. Girls, on the other hand, find that adults are more willing to accept cuddles, tears, and other overt emotional expressions from them. They don't receive much approval for assertive or aggressive acts.

J. M. Bardwick and E. Douvan point out another way in which the two sexes are socialized differently. They explain that male role behavior is more narrowly defined than female role behavior (young girls may behave in a moderatly masculine way as well as acting feminine, whereas young boys are firmly discouraged from behaving any way but extremely masculine), creating a situation in which males receive more punishment than females. Because early relationships for girls are rewarding, they tend toward being people- or relationship-oriented when they get older, and because early relationships for boys are generally punishing, they tend to seek satisfaction outside relationships with other people, and so become object-oriented as opposed to people-oriented.

The combination of social expectations, physiological differences, and personal characteristics has led Sandra Bem, one of the first researchers in the area of sociosexual behavior, to expand the traditional male-female dichotomy to eight categories:

1. **Masculine males**—males who rate high on masculine traits and low on feminine traits;
2. **Feminine males**—males who rate high on feminine traits and low on masculine traits;
3. **Androgynous males**—males who rate high on both masculine and feminine traits;
4. **Undifferentiated males**—males who rate low on both masculine and feminine traits;

5. **Feminine females**—females who rate high on feminine traits and low on masculine traits;
6. **Masculine females**—females who rate high on masculine traits and low on feminine traits;
7. **Androgynous females**—females who rate high on both masculine and feminine traits;
8. **Undifferentiated females**—females who rate low on both masculine and feminine traits.

In a series of studies designed to test whether psychological sex was a better predictor of behavior than anatomical sex, Bem observed the responses of psychological sex types to a variety of situations that called for independence, nurturance, and performance on sex-typed and nonsex-typed tasks. She found that only androgynous subjects (those who rate high on both masculine and feminine traits) display a high level of masculine independence as well as a high level of feminine nurturance. In general, research by Bem and others supports the conclusion that androgynous individuals are less restricted in their behaviors and are better able to adapt to situations that require characteristics presumed of men *or* women. This flexibility, this sex-role transcendence, may be the hallmark of mental health.

Masculine males and feminine females, the sex-typed individuals who most likely come to mind when we think of the words "male" and "female," experience more personality development problems, more marital problems, and more problem-solving difficulties than do androgynous males and females. Traditional sex-role stereotypes describe masculine males and feminine females fairly well.

What does this discussion of sexual stereotypes and attitudes have to do with perception and communication? A great deal. Each one of the eight psychological sex types, including the stereotyped masculine males and feminine females perceives the world differently. Given the traits describing each group, it's logical to assume that members of each group view interpersonal relationships differently. For example, masculine males probably see their interpersonal relationships as opportunities for competitive interaction, as opportunities to win something. Feminine females probably see their interpersonal relationships as opportunities to be nurturing, to express their feelings and emotions. Androgynous males and females, on the other hand, probably differ little in their perceptions of their interpersonal relationships.

Androgynous individuals probably see their relationships as opportunities to behave in a variety of ways, depending on the nature of the relationships themselves, the context in which a particular relation-ship takes place, and the myriad other variables affecting what might constitute appropriate behavior. These variables are usually ignored by the sex-typed masculine males and feminine females who have a smaller repertoire of behavior than the androgynous individuals.

Occupational Roles   The kind of work we do often governs our view of the world. Imagine five people taking a walk through the park. One, a botanist, is fascinated by the variety of trees and plants. The zoologist is on the lookout for interesting animals. The third, a meteorologist, keeps an eye on the sky, noticing changes in the weather. The fourth, a psychologist, is totally unaware of the goings-on of nature, concentrating instead on the interaction between the people in the park. The fifth, being a pickpocket, quickly takes advantage of the others' absorption to add to his collection of pocketbooks. There are two lessons in this little story. The first, of course, is to watch your wallet carefully. The second is that our occupational roles frequently govern our perceptions.

Even within the same occupational setting, the different roles of participants can affect their experience. Consider a typical college classroom, for example: the experiences of the instructor and students are often quite dissimilar. Having dedicated a large part of their lives to their work, most professors see their subject matter—whether French literature, physics, or speech communication—as vitally important. Students who are taking the course to satisfy a general education requirement may view the subject quite differently; maybe as one of many obstacles standing between them and a degree, or as a chance to meet new people.

Another difference centers on the amount of knowledge possessed by the parties. To an instructor who has taught the course many times, the material probably seems extremely simple; but to students encountering it for the first time it may seem strange and confusing. Toward the end of a semester or quarter the instructor

I have noticed
that men
somewhere around forty
tend to come in from the field
with a sigh
and removing their coat in the hall
call into the kitchen

> you were right
> grace
> it ain't out there
> just like you've always said

and she
with the children gone at last
breathless
puts her hat on her head

> the hell it ain't

coming and going
they pass
in the doorway

Ric Masten

might be pressing onward hurriedly to cover all the course material while the students are fatigued from their studies and ready to move more slowly. We don't need to spell out the interpersonal strains and stresses that come from such differing perceptions.

Even within occupational roles the different interests and personalities of each person can lead to differing perceptions. Some students, for instance, see the class as an extension of their home, a place to listen to "mom or dad" and do little thinking. Anxious-dependent students probably see the class as a place to look foolish, to lose part of their self-esteem. Independent students probably see it as a place to do well, to achieve important things. Attention-seekers see the class as a place to have some fun. Silent students find class a frustrating place, one in which they are torn between the desire to be accepted and the fear of being rejected.

The attitudes of instructors also govern their picture of a classroom. A teacher who takes on the role of expert probably sees the classroom as a place to display wisdom, to show off. Formal authorities most likely see the classroom as a place to play judge and jury, to represent the authority of the school, to wield power. Socializing agents see their students as children and see themselves as helpful fathers and mothers. Facilitators may see the classroom as a place to support egos, to help. Teachers who enact the role of ego ideal probably see the classroom as a place to obtain self-glorification, to be loved and admired. Other instructors see themselves as partners with their students in the learning process, cooperatively working with students whom they respect in the process of sharing new material. How would you characterize your instructors? Yourself as a student?

Perhaps the most dramatic illustration of how occupational roles shape perception occurred in 1971. Stanford psychologist Philip Zimbardo recruited a group of middle-class, well-educated young men, all white except for one Oriental. He randomly chose eleven to serve as "guards" in a mock prison set up in the basement of Stanford's psychology building. He issued the guards uniforms, handcuffs, whistles and billy clubs. The remaining ten subjects became "prisoners" and were placed in rooms with metal bars, bucket toilets, and cots.

Zimbardo let the guards establish their own rules for the experiment. The rules were tough: No talking during meals, rest periods, and after lights out. Head counts at 2:30 A.M. Troublemakers received short rations.

Faced with these conditions, the prisoners began to resist. Some barricaded their doors with beds. Others went on hunger strikes. Several ripped off their identifying number tags. The guards reacted to the rebellion by clamping down hard on protesters. Some turned sadistic, physically and verbally abusing the prisoners. They threw prisoners into solitary confinement.

Others forced prisoners to call each other names and clean out toilets with their bare hands.

Within a short time the experiment had become reality for both prisoners and guards. Several inmates experienced stomach cramps and lapsed into uncontrollable weeping. Others suffered from headaches, and one broke out in a head-to-toe rash after his request for early "parole" was denied by the guards.

The experiment was scheduled to go on for two weeks, but after six days Zimbardo realized that what had started as a simulation had become too intense. "I knew by then that they were thinking like prisoners and not like people," he said. "If we were able to demonstrate that pathological behavior could be produced in so short a time, think of what damage is being done in 'real' prisons . . ."

This dramatic exercise in which twenty-one well-educated, middle-class citizens turned almost overnight into sadistic bullies and demoralized victims tells us that how we think is a function of our roles in society. It seems that *what* we are is determined largely by the society's designation of *who* we are.

Cultural Factors

In addition to physiology and social roles, there's another kind of perceptual gap that often blocks communication—the gap between people from different backgrounds. Every culture has its own view, its own way of looking at the world, which is unique. When we remember these differing cultural perspectives, they can be a great way of learning more about both ourselves and others. But at times it's easy to forget that people everywhere don't see "reality" the way we do. For example, whereas most North Americans view spitting as a sign of disrespect or poor manners, to the Masai tribe of East Africa it symbolizes affection and blessing. And when done by an American Indian medicine man, spitting is a sign for healing.

In Athens, a pinch on the behind of a woman is an almost expected, if unappreciated behavior. In America, the same pinch is much more of an assault, likely to be met with a slap, a mean look, or even a call for a police officer.

One of our students provided us with the following example of cultural differences. He was visiting Lagos, Nigeria, and while walking down the street one afternoon he came upon two men, one a Nigerian and the other an American. The men were fighting wildly and cursing at each other, each in his own language. The police had come and seemed to be ready to take both fighters away when an English-speaking taxi driver saved the day.

After talking to both men, he explained the story: It seems that the American was hitchhiking through town, signaling for a ride the only way he knew—standing at the roadside with his thumb sticking out where the drivers could easily see it. Unfortunately for him, in Nigeria this gesture doesn't mean the same thing as in the United States. In fact, its closest equivalent in our terms is what we call

"the finger." So, although the American meant to politely ask for a ride, instead he had insulted the Nigerian's honor.

Thanks to the taxi driver (who ought to be working for the U.N.), the last time our student saw the two former enemies they were heading arm in arm into a bar. They'd learned by experience that to members of different cultures even little differences can have big consequences when you're not aware of them.

After looking at these examples, you can see that different cultures have customs that can cause trouble for the unaware foreigner. But you don't have to go this far from home to come across people with differing cultural perspectives. Within the United States there are many cultures, and the members of each one have backgrounds that cause them to see things in unique ways.

Probably the clearest example of these differing perceptions is the gap between white and black people in America. Even to people of goodwill it seems that there's a barrier that makes understanding difficult; there just seem to be too many different experiences that separate us.

John Howard Griffin found one way to bridge the gulf that separates whites and blacks. Realizing the impossibility of truly understanding the black experience by reading and talking about it he went one step further: Through a series of treatments that included doses of skin-darkening drugs, he transformed himself into a black man—or at least a man with black skin. And he traveled through the southern United States to get in touch with what it truly meant to be black in America. He was treated like a black, and eventually, to his own surprise, came to find himself

responding to white people's demands as if he were one. The insults, the prejudice, sickened him.

This experiment took place in the Deep South of 1959, and times have certainly changed since then. But to what extent is the world still a different place to contemporary whites and blacks? How about other groups—Hispanics, Orientals, Native Americans, old people, longhairs, military men and women. Do you ever find yourself prejudging or being prejudged before getting acquainted with someone from a different sector of society?

Perhaps by sharing the personal experiences of others in your group you can gain a more personal insight into how people from different subcultures view life in your community, not only in terms of discrimination, but also in terms of values, behavioral norms, and political and economic issues. How would life be different if you were of a different race or religion, social or economic class? See if you can imagine.

But talking can enable us to understand another person's viewpoint only to a certain degree. To comprehend what it's truly like to be someone else you have to almost become that person the way Griffin did. Have you ever read Mark Twain's famous novelette called *The Prince and the Pauper?* If you have, you'll remember what an education the young prince had when he was mistaken for a young peasant and treated accordingly. In the same way, think of the huge growth in tolerance that would result if the rich could become poor for a bit, if teachers could recall their student days, if whites could become black.

Total role reversals aren't likely to happen, but it's possible to create experiences that give a good picture of another's perspective. The story of one Iowa schoolteacher and her class illustrates the point. Shortly after Martin Luther King's assassination in 1968, Mrs. Jane Elliott wanted to make sure her third graders never became prone to the sickness that caused such events. But how could she do this? Everyone in the small town of Riceville was white, and most of her eight-year-olds had never really known blacks. How could she bring home to them the nature of prejudice?

Her solution was to divide the class into two groups, one containing all the children with blue eyes, and the other made up of the brown-eyed students. Then for the next few days she treated the brown-eyes as better people. They all sat in the front of the room, had second helpings at lunch, got five extra minutes of recess, and received extra praise for their work from Mrs. Elliott. At the same time the blue-eyes were the butt of both subtle and obvious discrimination. Besides the back-row seats, skimpy meals, and other such practices, the blue-eyes never received praise for their schoolwork from Mrs. Elliott, who seemed to find something wrong with everything they did. "What can you expect from a blue-eyed person?" was her attitude. The level of the blue-eyed children's schoolwork dropped almost immediately.

At first the children treated the experiment as a game. But shortly they changed from cooperative, thoughtful people into small but very prejudiced bigots. Classmates who had always been best friends stopped playing with each other and even quit walking to school together.

After the level of intolerance had grown painfully high, Mrs. Elliott changed the rules. Now the blue-eyed people were on top, and the brown-eyes were inferior. And soon the tables were turned, with children who had only days before been the object of discrimination now being bigots themselves.

Finally Mrs. Elliott ended the experiment. When she asked the children if they wanted to go back to the old days, where everyone was the same, the class answered with a resounding "Yes!" Now they really knew what discrimination was, and they didn't like it.

Psychological Processes

Physiological factors, social roles, and cultural differences offer three distinct consequences for our perception. They affect what we *select* to perceive, how we *organize* what we select to perceive, and how we *interpret* what we select to perceive.

Selective Perception To understand how selective perception works, think back to our discussion of self-concept. You'll remember we described the tendency people have to behave in ways that support the image they hold of themselves. If I see myself as a good student or musician, then an instructor who gives me a poor grade or a critic who doesn't appreciate my music *must* be wrong, and I'll find evidence to show it. If I've committed myself to support the government in what I believe is a moral cause, and someone tells me about illegal or immoral acts, I'll find a way to prove that no such event happened. If I want to think of myself as a good sport,

and someone shows me that the athletic team I've identified with all season plays dirty, I'll do everything I can to contradict this evidence.

As you can imagine, this tendency to protect our self-concept sometimes leads us to distort the facts. You only need recall the long list of defense mechanisms to see how inventive people can be when a threatened self-concept is at stake. And needless to say, when two or more people perceive the same event differently, communication between them suffers.

A classic illustration of selective perception in action began on a fall Saturday afternoon in 1951, when the Dartmouth and Princeton football teams met in the final game of the season. The game was important for both teams. Princeton was defending an unbeaten season, and Dartmouth hoped to beat their traditional rival. The game was rough. In the second quarter Princeton's star player left the field with a broken nose. Later a Dartmouth player suffered a broken leg. Dartmouth was penalized seventy yards, while Princeton (the home team) was penalized twenty-five yards. After the game (which Princeton won) the hostilities continued. The newspapers of both schools accused the others of dirty football and poor sportsmanship. Psychologists Albert Hastorf from Dartmouth and Hadley Cantril of Princeton decided that the contest offered a perfect chance to study selective perception. The researchers recruited students from both schools who knew the rules of football, had no personal friends on either team, and who were otherwise educationally, culturally, and economically similar. Equal numbers of both groups had attended the game or had seen films of it. The psychologists asked a series of questions designed to check the students' perception of the game.

For the most part we do not see first and then define; we define first and then see.

Walter Lippmann

Although predictable, the results were still dramatic. Nearly all the Princeton students (whose star player was sidelined by injuries) saw the game as "rough and dirty," and not a single one thought it was "clean and fair." By contrast, only 42 percent of the Dartmouth students agreed with the "rough and dirty" evaluation.

Princeton students saw the Dartmouth players make over twice as many infractions as their own team, whereas the Dartmouth students saw the number of infractions as about equal. Additionally, Dartmouth students saw their own team make only half the number of violations that the Princeton students saw them make.

Looking at these results, the researchers concluded that

. . . there is no such "'thing'" as a "'game'" existing "'out there'" in its own right, which people merely "'observe.'" Out of all the occurrences going on in the environment, a person selects those that have some significance for him from his own egocentric position. . . .

From this point of view it is inaccurate and misleading to say that different people have different " 'attitudes' " concerning the same " 'thing.' " For the " 'thing' " simply is *not* the same for different people whether the "'thing'" is a football game, a presidential candidate, Communism, or spinach.

As Hastorf and Cantril suggest, this kind of selective perception isn't limited to football. The same principle operates in other areas: criminal trials, where supposedly impartial eyewitness accounts can be distorted by the attitude of the witness toward the defendant; religious discussions, where each person chooses evidence to support one side and ignores information that argues against it; and, perhaps most commonly, in our personal evaluations of others. If, for instance, you describe an acquaintance of yours whom you'll soon be introducing to me by claiming that she is a terrific person, my expectations and my subsequent impression of her will probably be different than if you described the same person as an obnoxious fool.

Organization Besides selecting what information to consider, we must also organize that data in some meaningful way. To see how organizing operates, look at the picture of the woman.

Do you see a half view of an old woman with a big nose? Or do you see a young woman looking away from you to the left? If you can't see them both, let us help you.

A woman once said to me, "Do you know, when you were executing your dervish movements I understood the dance. You were a witch picking daisies in a field. I actually saw the daisies. That was it, wasn't it?" Now what could I say to this woman? If she thought I was picking daisies, well, all right. But I thought I was dancing.

Mary Wigman
Interview, *Boston Globe*
December 4, 1931

The long vertical line that makes up the old lady's nose is the cheek and jaw of the girl; the old woman's mouth is the girl's neckband, and her left eye is the girl's ear. Can you see them both now?

Illustrations like this one demonstrate that there are often many ways to organize a collection of perceptions. But what does this organization have to do with human relationships? To answer this question, think about all the ways we classify people: male or female; black, white, Hispanic, Oriental; young or old; stranger, acquaintance, or friend; economic status; education; political views; language; habits; musical taste . . . the list goes on and on.

Clearly, it makes a great difference which organizational scheme we use to recognize others. For instance, people who have classified themselves and others according to race have created everything from the Ku Klux Klan to ethnic studies programs to affirmative action. And what about those whose perceptual organizations run along sexual lines? They are concerned with issues such as the Equal Rights Amendment and all-male bars. And all of us have witnessed the fireworks that start when a person concerned with one organizational framework encounters someone who finds that system unimportant or foolish.

Interpretation   Once we selectively perceive and organize something, the final step is to interpret it. Our interpretations are affected by the context surrounding what we perceive. You can see this phenomenon by trying the following short experiment. Show the top figure to a group of people and ask them to write down what they see. Show the second figure to another group and ask them to do the same.

$$A \; B \; C$$
$$12 \; 13 \; 14$$

One group probably saw the top figure as A B C, and the other probably saw the bottom figure as 12 13 14. Interestingly, the middle figures, those interpreted as B and 13, are identical. The context affected the interpretation: It is as unlikely to find a 13 between an A and C as it is to find a B between a 12 and 14.

The role of interpretation in human communication starts to become clear when you try this simple experiment. Begin by describing the expression in each of the following faces:

A

B

You probably described Face *A* as *glum* and Face *B* as *happy*. Now, place the faces side by side and reinterpret the one you saw as happy.

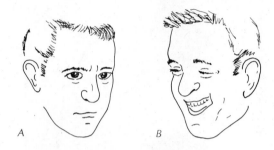

A   *B*

What happened? The once happy face now appears to be gloating, vicious, possibly the face of a bully. How did this change in interpretation take place? Again, the context affected your interpretation.

Context isn't all that affects how we interpret something. Our past experience, our assumptions, our expectations, and our knowledge, also determine how we interpret what we perceive. Let's see how these variables operate by considering a common experience and looking at two possible interpretations.

Imagine that a friend recently promised you that he would ask permission before smoking in the same room with you. Just a moment ago he lit up a cigarette without first asking. You could think to yourself, "John must have forgotten about our agreement that he wouldn't smoke without asking me first. I'm sure he's too considerate to go back on his word on something he knows I feel strongly about," or you could interpret the same behavior in an entirely different way: "John is a rude inconsiderate person. After promising not to smoke around me without asking, he's just deliberately done so. This shows that he cares only about himself. In fact, I bet he's deliberately doing this to drive me crazy!" What factors might lead you to choose one interpretation over the other? Perhaps one of the following:

1. **Context.** As we demonstrated, context might make the difference. What happenings were associated with the incident? Had you been fighting or were you getting along well? Has your friend been preoccupied and forgetful lately? Had you been discussing the issue of smoking?

2. **Past experience.** What has happened in the past? Is John the kind of person who has always kept promises in the past? Has he ever behaved spitefully before?

3. **Assumptions.** For instance, if you assume that unkept promises are a sign of dislike or anger, then you'll choose the less favorable interpretation. On the other hand, if you regard the issue as a small one that doesn't reflect on your whole relationship, then you'll be less concerned.

4. **Expectations.** If you had for some reason been anticipating hostility from John, then the smoking incident could confirm your prediction. If you'd been looking forward to a pleasant time together, then you might let the incident slide by without giving it a second thought.

5. **Knowledge.** You might have read somewhere that habitual cigarette smokers often are unaware of lighting up, in which case you'd be less likely to get angry at your friend.

In any case, it is essential to remember that interpretations are not always correct—assuming that you know someone else's motives you can get into real trouble. Whenever possible the wisest course is to consider your interpretations tentative until

you have somehow checked them for accuracy with the other person involved.

By now we hope you're aware of the need for the mindreading invention we described at the beginning of this chapter. With it we could experience the physical sensations of others, experience their social roles from the inside, understand their cultural backgrounds, and know with certainty what information they were selecting, organizing, and interpreting. With such an invention the behavior of others wouldn't be such a mystery.

Readings

Alpern, Mathew, Merle Lawrence and David Wolsk. *Sensory Processes.* Belmont, California: Brooks/Cole, 1967.

Alsbrook, Larry. "Marital Communication and Sexism." *Social Casework,* 57, (1976): 517-522.

Baird, John E., Jr. "Sex Differences in Group Communication: A Review of Relevant Research." *Quarterly Journal of Speech,* 62, (1976): 179-192.

Bardwick, J. M. and E. Douvan. "Ambivalence: The Socialization of Women." In *Women in Sexist Society,* V. Gornick and B. Moran, eds., New York: Basic Books, 1971.

Bem, Sandra L. "The Measurement of Psychological Androgyny." *Journal of Consulting and Clinical Psychology,* 42, (1974): 155-162.

———. "Sex Role Adaptability: One Consequence of Psychological Androgyny." *Journal of Personality and Social Psychology,* 31, (1975): 634-643.

———. "Probing the Promise of Androgyny." In *Beyond Sex-Role Stereotypes: Readings Toward a Psychology of Androgyny,* A. G. Kaplan and J. P. Bean, eds., Boston: Little Brown, 1976.

Bem, Sandra L. and E. Lenney. "Sex-Typing and the Avoidance of Cross-Sex Behavior." *Journal of Personality and Social Psychology,* 33, (1976): 48-54.

Bohannon, Laura. "Shakespeare in the Bush." *Natural History,* 75, (Aug.-Sept., 1966): 28-33.

Braga, Joseph L. "Teacher Role Perception." *Journal of Teacher Education,* 23, (1972): 53-57.

Buckhout, Robert. "Eyewitness Testimony." *Scientific American,* 231, (December, 1974): 6.

Burke, Kenneth, *Permanence and Change.* Indianapolis: Bobbs-Merrill, 1965.

Cline, M. "The Influence of Social Context on the Perception of Faces." *Journal of Personality,* 25, (1956): 142-158.

Dearborn, DeWitt C. and Herbert A. Simons. "Selective Perception: The Departmental Identifications of Executives." *Sociometry,* 21, (1958): 140-144.

Fowler, Gene and Lawrence B. Rosenfeld. "Sex Differences and Democratic Leadership Behavior." Paper presented at the Western Speech Communication Association Annual Convention, Los Angeles, February 1979.

Gorman, Alfred H. *Teachers and Learners,* 2nd Ed. Boston: Allyn and Bacon, 1974.

Hammer, Richard. "Role-Playing: A Judge is a Con, A Con is a Judge." *New York Magazine,* (September 14, 1969).

Hastrof, Albert, David Schneider and Judith Polefka. *Person Perception.* Reading, Mass.: Addison-Wesley, 1970.

Hastrof, Albert H. and Hadley Cantrill, "They Saw a Game: A Case Study." *Journal of Abnormal and Social Psychology,* 49, (1954): 129-134.

Hix, C. "Smelling Swell." *Gentlemen's Quarterly,* 44, (1974): 82.

Hoyle, Eric. *The Role of the Teacher.* New York: Humanities Press, 1969.

Ittelson, W. H. and F. P. Kilpatrick. "Experiments in Perception." *Scientific American,* (August 1951).

Leathers, Dale G. "The Tactile and Olfactory Communication Systems." In *Nonverbal Communication Systems.* Boston: Allyn and Bacon, 1976.

Moncrieff, R. W. *Odour Preferences.* New York: Wiley, 1966.

Montgomery, Charles L. and Michael Burgoon. "An Experimental Study of the Interactive Effects of Sex and Androgyny on Attitude Change." *Communication Monographs,* 44, (1977): 130-135.

Ramey, Estelle. "Men's Cycles." *Ms.* (Spring 1972): 10-14.

Ringwald, Barbara, Richard D. Mann, Robert Rosenwein and Wilbert J. McKeachie. "Conflict and Style in the College Classroom." *Psychology Today,* 4, (1971): 45-47, 76, 78-79.

Rosenfeld, Lawrence. B. and Jean M. Civikly. "Senses." In *With Words Unspoken: The Nonverbal Experience.* New York: Holt, Rinehart and Winston, 1976.

Rosenfeld, Lawrence B., Jean M. Civikly and Jane R. Herron. "Anatomical Sex, Psychological Sex, and Self-Disclosure." In *Self-Disclosure: Origins, Patterns, and Implications of Openness in Interpersonal Relationships,* Gordon J. Chelune, ed. San Francisco: Jossey-Bass, 1979.

Rosenfeld, Lawrence B. and Gene D. Fowler. "Personality, Sex, and Leadership Style." *Communication Monographs,* 43, (1976): 320-324.

Schneider, R. A. "The Sense of Smell and Human Sexuality" *Medical Aspects of Human Sexuality,* 5, (1971): 156-168.

Segall, M. H., D. T. Campbell and M. J. Herskovits. *The Influence of Culture on Visual Perception.* Indianapolis: Bobbs-Merrill, 1966.

Tyler, Leona. *The Psychology of Human Differences.* New York: Appleton-Century-Crofts, 1965.

Wilentz, Joan S. *The Senses of Man.* New York: Thomas Y. Crowell, 1968.

Emotions 5

5 At one time or another you've probably imagined how different life would be if you became disabled in some way. The thought of becoming blind, deaf, or immobile is certainly frightening, and though a bit morbid, it can remind you to appreciate the faculties you do have. But have you ever considered how life would be if you somehow lost your ability to experience emotions?

While life without feelings certainly wouldn't be as dramatic or crippling as other disabilities, consider its effect. Never again would you experience the excitement of Christmas or the first sunny day of spring. You would never enjoy a movie, book, or piece of art—or even find it interesting. Your life would be empty of chuckles, giggles, and smiles, not to mention belly laughs. Happiness, confidence, and love would be nothing but words to you. Of course, an emotionless life would also be free of boredom, frustration, fear, and loneliness, too— but most of us would agree that giving up pleasure is too steep a price to pay for freedom from pain.

This fantasy demonstrates the important role that emotions play in our relationships as well as in other parts of life. Because feelings play such a fundamental role in interpersonal communication, we will take a close look at them in this chapter. We'll explore exactly what feelings are, discuss the ways in which they are handled in contemporary society, and see how recognizing and expressing them can improve relationships. We'll explore a method for coping with troublesome,

debilitating feelings which can inhibit rather than help your communication. And finally, we'll look at some guidelines which should give you a clearer idea of when and how to express your emotions effectively.

What Are Emotions?

Suppose that a visitor from the planet Vulcan or Ork asked you to explain emotions. What would you say? You might start by saying that emotions are things that we feel. But this doesn't say much, since you would probably describe feelings as being synonymous with emotions. Social scientists who study the role of feelings generally agree that there are four components to our emotions.

Physiological Changes   When a person experiences strong emotions, many bodily changes occur. For example, the physical aspects of fear include an increased heartbeat, a rise in blood pressure, an increase in adrenaline secretions, an increase in blood sugar, a slowing of digestion, and a dilation of the pupils. Some of these changes are recognizable to the person experiencing them. These sensations are terms *proprioceptive stimuli,* meaning they are activated by movement of internal tissues. Proprioceptive messages can offer a significant clue to our emotions once we become aware of them. For instance, one woman we know began focusing on her internal messages and learned that every time she returned to the city from a vacation she felt an empty feeling in the pit of her stomach. From what she'd already learned about herself, she knew that this sensation always accompanied things she dreaded. She then realized she was much happier in the country. Now she is trying to find a way to make the move she knows is right for her.

Another friend of ours had always appeared easygoing and agreeable, even in the most frustrating circumstances. But after focusing on internal messages, he discovered his mild behavior contrasted strongly with the tense muscles and headaches that he got during trying times. This new awareness led him to realize that he did indeed experience frustration and anger—and that he somehow needed to deal with these feelings if he was going to feel truly comfortable.

Nonverbal Manifestations

A quick comparison between the emotionless Mr. Spock of *Star Trek* and full-blooded humans tells us that feelings show up in many nonverbal behaviors. Postures, gestures, facial expression, body positioning and distance, all provide clues suggesting our emotional state.

One of the first social scientists to explore the relationship between emotion and behavior was Charles Darwin. In 1872 Darwin published *The Expression of Emotion in Man and Animals,* which asserted that humans and certain other creatures seemed to behave in similar ways when enraged. Later researchers confirmed the premise that among humans, at least, the most basic emotional expressions are universal. A. G. Gitter and his colleagues found that people from a variety of cultures all agreed on the facial expressions that indicate emotions such as fear, sadness, happiness, and pain. (Chapter 9 discusses the value of observing nonverbal messages as clues to emotion.)

> **Half our mistakes in life arise from feeling where we ought to think, and thinking where we ought to feel.**
>
> John Churton Collins

Cognitive Interpretations

The physiological aspects of fear, such as a racing heart, perspiration, tense muscles, and a boost in blood pressure, are surprisingly similar to the physical changes that accompany excitement, joy, and other emotions. In other words, from measuring the physical condition of someone experiencing a strong emotion, it would be difficult to determine whether the person was trembling with fear or quivering with excitement. The recognition that the bodily components of most emotions are similar led Norman Schachter and some other psychologists to conclude that the experience of fright, joy, or anger comes primarily from the *label* that we give to the same physical symptoms. This cognitive explanation of emotion has been labeled *attribution theory.* Psychologist Philip Zimbardo offers a good example of attribution in action:

I notice I'm perspiring while lecturing. From that I infer I am feeling nervous. If it occurs often, I might even label myself a "nervous person." Once I have the label, the next question I must answer is "Why am I nervous?" Then I start to search for an appropriate explanation. I might notice some students leaving the room, or being inattentive. I am nervous because I'm not giving

affectionate
afraid
alarmed
alienated
alone
angry
anxious
apathetic
appreciated
attractive
awkward
beaten
beautiful
bewildered
brave
calm
caring
closed
comfortable
committed
compassionate
competent
concerned
confident
confused
contented
cowardly
creative
cruel
curious
cut off from others
defeated
defensive
dejected
dependent
depressed
deprived
desperate
disappointed
domineering
eager
easygoing
embarrassed

envious
evasive
evil
excited
exhilarated
fatalistic
fearful
feminine
flirtatious
friendly
frigid
frustrated
generous
genuine
gentle
giddy
glad
grateful
grudge-bearing
guilty
gutless
happy
hateful
homicidal
hopeful
hopeless
hostile
humorous
hurt
hyperactive
ignored
immobilized
impatient
inadequate
incompetent
indecisive
inferior
inhibited
insecure
insincere
involved
isolated
jealous

joyful
judgmental
lively
lonely
lovable
loved
loving
masculine
masked
masochistic
melancholy
misunderstood
needy
old
optimistic
out of control
overcontrolled
oversexed
paranoid
passionate
peaceful
persecuted
pessimistic
phoney
pitiful
playful
pleased
possessive
preoccupied
prejudiced
pressured
protective
proud
quiet
rejected
religious
remorseful
repelled
repulsive
restrained
sad
sadistic
secure

seductive
self-pitying
self-reliant
sexually aroused
shallow
shy
silly
sincere
sinful
sluggish
soft
sorry for self
stubborn
stupid
suicidal
superior to others
supported
supportive
suspicious
sympathetic
tender
terrified
threatened
tolerant
torn
touchy
triumphant
two-faced
ugly
unsure
understanding
unresponsive
uptight
useless
vindictive
violent
weary
weepy
wishy-washy
youthful

a good lecture. That makes me nervous. How do I know it's not good? Because I'm boring my audience. I am nervous because I am a boring lecturer and I want to be a good lecturer. I feel inadequate. Maybe I should open a delicatessen instead. Just then a student says, 'It's hot in here, I'm perspiring and it makes it tough to concentrate on your lecture.' Instantly, I'm no longer 'nervous' or 'boring.'

In his book *Shyness*, Zimbardo discusses the consequences of making inaccurate or exaggerated attributions. In a survey of more than 5,000 subjects, over 80 percent described themselves as having been shy at some time in their lives, while more than 40 percent considered themselves presently shy. Most significantly, these "not shy" people behaved in virtually the *same way* as their shy counterparts. They would blush, perspire, and feel their hearts pounding in certain social situations. The biggest difference between the two groups seemed to be the label with which they described themselves. This difference is significant. Someone who notices the symptoms we've described and thinks, "I'm such a shy person!" will most likely feel more uncomfortable and communicate less effectively than a person with the same symptoms who thinks, "Well, I'm a bit shaky here, but that's to be expected."

Verbal Expression The fourth component of emotion is verbal expression. As Gerard Egan points out, there are several ways to verbally express a feeling. The first is through single words: I'm angry, excited, depressed, curious, and so on. Many people are limited to these single word expressions, and suffer from impoverished emotional vocabularies. They have a hard time describing more than a few basic feelings, such as "good" or "bad," "terrible" or "great."

Another way of expressing feelings verbally is to use descriptive phrases: "I feel all jumbled up," "I'm on top of the world," and so on. As long as such phrases aren't too obscure—for example, "I feel somnolent"—they can effectively describe your emotional state.

It's also possible to express emotions by describing what you'd like to do: "I feel like singing"; "I'd like to cry"; "I feel like running away," etc. Often these expressions capture the emotion clearly, but in other cases they can be confusing. For instance, if somebody told you, "Every time I see you I want to laugh," you wouldn't know whether you were an object of enjoyment or ridicule.

The ability to verbally express emotions is crucial to effective communication. For example, notice the difference between

When you kiss me and nibble on my ear, I think you want to make love,

and

When you kiss me and nibble on my ear, I think you want to make love and I feel excited (or disgusted),

or between

Ever since we had our fight, I've been avoiding you,

and

Ever since our fight, I've been avoiding you because I've been so embarrassed (or so angry).

Many people think they're clearly expressing their feelings, when in fact their statements are emotionally counterfeit. For instance, it may sound emotionally revealing to say, "I feel like going to a show," or "I feel we've been seeing too much of each other." But neither of these statements actually exhibit emotional content. In the first sentence, the word "feel" really represents an intention: "I *want* to go to a show." In the second sentence, the "feeling" is really a *thought:* "I think we've been seeing too much of each other." The absence of emotion in each case becomes recognizable when you add a word with genuine feeling to the sentence. For instance, "I'm *bored* and I want to go to a show," or "I think we've been seeing too much of each other and I feel *confined.*"

Emotions in Contemporary Society

Once you can detect these kinds of counterfeit emotional statements, you notice that most people do very little sharing of their feelings. To verify this, try counting the number of genuine emotional expressions you hear over a two- or three-day period. You'll probably discover that emotional expressions are quite rare. People are generally comfortable making statements of fact and often delight in expressing their opinion, but they rarely disclose how they feel.

Why do people fail to express their feelings? There are several reasons.

Modeling and Instructions   Our society discourages the expression of most feelings. From the time children are old enough to understand language, they learn that the range of acceptable emotions is limited. Do these admonitions sound familiar to you?

"Don't get angry."
"There's nothing to worry about."
"That isn't funny."
"There's no reason to feel bad."
"Control yourself—don't get excited."
"For God's sake, don't cry!"

Notice how each of these messages denies its recipient the right to experience a certain feeling. Anger isn't legitimate, and neither is fear. There's something wrong with finding certain situations humorous. Feeling bad is considered silly. Excitement isn't desirable, so keep your emotions under control. And finally, don't make a scene by crying.

Often such parental admonitions are nothing more than a coded request for some peace and quiet. But when repeated often enough, the underlying instruction comes through loud and clear—only a narrow range of emotions is acceptable to share or experience.

In addition, the actions of most adults create a model suggesting that grownups shouldn't express too many feelings. Expressions of affection are fine within limits: A hug and kiss for Mother is all right, though a young man should shake hands with Dad. Affection toward friends becomes less and less frequent as we grow older, so that even a simple statement such as "I like you" is seldom heard between adults.

The Thinker

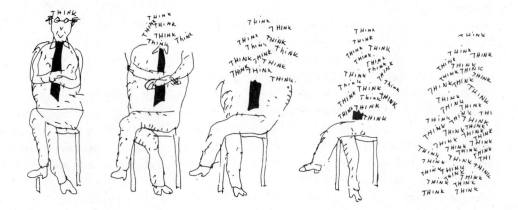

Social Roles Expression of emotions is further limited by the requirements of many social roles. Salespeople are taught to always smile at customers, no matter how obnoxious. Teachers are portrayed as paragons of rationality, supposedly representing their field of expertise and instructing their students with total impartiality. Students are rewarded for asking "acceptable" questions and otherwise being submissive creatures.

Furthermore, stereotyped sex roles discourage people from freely expressing certain emotions. The stereotype states that men don't cry and are rational creatures. They must be strong, emotionally and physically. Aggressiveness is a virtue ("the Marine Corps builds men"). Women, on the other hand, are socialized in a manner that allows them to express their emotions by crying. The stereotype states that women should be irrational and intuitive. A certain amount of female determination and assertiveness is appealing, but when faced with a man's resistance they ought to defer.

Inability to Recognize Emotions The result of all these restrictions is that many of us lose the ability to feel deeply. As a muscle withers away when it is unused, so our capacity to recognize and act on certain emotions reduces. It's hard to cry after spending most of one's life fulfilling the role society expects of a man, even when the tears are inside. After years of denying your anger, the ability to recognize that feeling takes real effort. For someone who has never acknowledged love for one's friends, accepting the emotion can be difficult indeed.

Fear of Self-Disclosure   In a society that discourages the expression of feelings, emotional self-disclosure can be risky. For a parent, boss, or teacher whose life has been built on the presumption of confidence and certainty, it may be frightening to say, "I'm sorry, I was wrong." A person who has made a life's work out of not relying on others has a hard time saying, "I'm lonesome. I want your friendship."

Moreover, one who musters up the courage to share feelings such as these still risks suffering unpleasant consequences. Others might misunderstand: An expression of affection might be construed as a romantic come-on, and a confession of uncertainty might appear to be a sign of weakness. Another risk is that emotional honesty might make others feel uncomfortable. Finally, there's always a chance that emotional candor could be used against you, either out of cruelty or thoughtlessness.

Benefits of Expressing Emotions

Given all the social conditioning and personal risks which discourage us from expressing feelings, it's understandable why so many people are emotionally uncommunicative. This is especially unfortunate when we look at the benefits that can flow from sharing feelings appropriately.

Physical Health   Sharing emotions is healthy. In fact, keeping your feelings pent up can lead to psychosomatic illnesses. We're not referring to hypochondria, where people believe they are ill but aren't, or malingering, where they pretend to be sick. A psychosomatic disease is real: It does not differ from an organically induced illness. What distinguishes a psychosomatic illness is its psychological basis. Whereas the pain comes from a physical condition, the problem has its origins in some aspect of the person's psychological functioning. Psychosomatic problems can grow out of the chronic stress that results when unexpressive people don't share their feelings. Remember the physiological changes that accompany strong emotions? (Digestion slows; heartbeat increases; adrenaline is secreted; and respiration grows quicker.) Whereas these conditions are short lived for people who can express their feelings, those who fail to act on these impulses develop a continual state of physiological tension. This tension damages the digestive tract, lungs, circulatory system, muscles, joints, and the body's ability to resist infections. It even hastens the process of aging.

These claims may sound preposterous, but a growing body of medical evidence points to their truth. For instance, S. W. Wolf found that the mucous lining protecting the inside of the stomach responds minute by minute to both conscious and unconscious emotions. When a person becomes angry, the lining becomes inflamed, producing excessive amounts of acids and gastric juices. In fact, ulcers have been produced experimentally in animals by subjecting them to stress. People who develop ulcers have stomachs that are almost constantly in this state of agitation, a condition often caused by a failure to appropriately express their feelings.

Hypertension, (high blood pressure) and heart trouble can also have their roots in chronic stress. Over a five-year period Flanders Dunbar studied a random sample of 1,600 cardiovascular patients at Columbia Presbyterian Medical Center in New York City. She found that four out of five patients shared common emotional characteristics, many of which were representative of either nonassertive or aggressive communicators. In fact, most of the patients were argumentative, had trouble expressing their feelings, and kept people at a distance. McQuade and Aikman describe other characteristics of cardiovascular sufferers: they are easily upset but unable to handle upsetting situations, anxious to please but longing to rebel, and alternately passive and irritable.

Evidence also suggests that nonassertive people are prone to yet another physical problem. The immunological system, which protects the body against infection, apparently functions less effectively when a person is under stress. The body doesn't always respond quickly enough to infection; and sometimes the body even responds incorrectly, as in the case of allergic reactions. Stress has even been diagnosed as one cause of the common cold. Stress or anxiety alone, however, are not sufficient to cause these disorders; a source of infection must also be present. But as research by Swiss physiologist Hans Selye suggests, persons subjected to stress have an increased chance of contracting infectious disease. Seyle states, "If a microbe is in or around us all the time and yet causes no disease until we are exposed to stress, what is the cause of our illness, the microbe or the stress?"

All this talk about psychosomatic illness is not intended to suggest that nonassertion automatically leads to ulcers and heart trouble, or perhaps worse. Obviously, many shy or aggressive people never suffer from such ailments and many assertive people do. There are also many other sources of stress in our society: financial pressures, the problems of people we care for, pollution, crime, and the nagging threat of war, to name a few. Nonetheless, an increasing amount of evidence suggests that the person who is not fully expressive increases the risk of developing physical disabilities. Just as nonsmokers are less likely to contract lung cancer than their pack-a-day counterparts, skillful communicators have a better chance of living a healthy life.

Increased Intimacy   Beyond the physio-logical benefits, another advantage of expressing emotions is the chance of reaching greater intimacy with others. A friend of ours, reflecting on his marriage, affirmed this point.

For the longest time I held back a lot of feelings from my wife which I thought would hurt her. I did spare her feelings, but by holding back I also felt more and more like a stranger to her. It finally got to the point where I was hiding so much of how I truly felt that instead of an honest, growing marriage, I felt like I was carrying on a charade. Finally I couldn't stand the experience of being isolated from the woman I was committed to spending my life with, and so I began to share the things that were going on inside me—the uncomfortable feelings as well as the pleasant ones. As we began to really talk about who we were again, we uncovered a lot of feelings which we had both been out of touch with. I won't say that this kind of sharing has made our life together easier—it's often hard for one of us to face how the other feels—but I can definitely say that we feel closer now than we have in a long time.*

Conflict Resolution   Although expressing feelings can sometimes lead to trouble, the consequences of not sharing them can be just as bad. When people don't communicate, boring marriages don't change, friendships continue in hurtful patterns, and job conditions stay unpleasant. How long can such destructive patterns go on? Surely there comes a time when it's necessary either to share emotions or to give up on the relationship. Moreover, research on conflict resolution conducted by David Johnson and others suggests that the skillful expression of emotions actually increases the quality of problem solving. After all, unresolved feelings can create obstacles that keep individuals and groups from dealing most effectively with their problems. On the other hand, once the participants in a conflict have expressed their feelings they're in a position to resolve the problems that led to them. Chapter 11 introduces several methods for handling interpersonal conflicts constructively.

Coping with Debilitative Feelings: A Cognitive Approach

At this point you may think that experiencing and expressing emotions is always beneficial. Actually, this position is extreme: Some feelings do little good for anyone. For instance, feeling dejected can sometimes provide a foundation upon which to grow (I'm so miserable now that I must do something to change"). More often, however, depression prevents people from acting effectively. The same point can be made about rage, terror, and jealousy: Most of the time these emotions do little to promote personal well-being or to improve relationships.

Debilitative vs. Facilitative Emotions   We need to make a distinction, then, between *facilitative* emotions, which contribute to effective functioning, and *debilitative* emotions, which hinder or prevent effective performance. The difference between facilitative and debilitative emotions isn't one of quality so much as degree. For instance, a certain amount of anger or irritation can be constructive, since it often stimulates a person to improve the unsatisfying conditions. Rage, on the other hand, usually makes matters worse, as will fear. A little bit of nervousness before an important athletic contest or job interview might boost you just enough to improve your performance (mellow athletes or actors usually don't do well). But total terror is something else. One big difference, then, between facilitative and debilitative emotions is their *intensity*.

As Gerald Kranzler points out, intense feelings of fear or rage cause trouble in two ways. First, the strong emotions keep you from thinking clearly. We've seen students in public speaking classes whose fear is so great that they can't even remember their

---

*A note of caution: Sharing every emotion you experience at the time is not always wise. When deciding whether to express a feeling that is difficult for you or another person to handle, read the guidelines for self-disclosure in Chapter 3.

name, let alone the subject of their speech. Second, intense feelings lead to an urge to act, to do *something, anything* to make the problem go away. And because a person who feels so strongly doesn't think clearly, the resulting action might cause more trouble. At one time or another we've all lashed out in anger, saying words we later regretted. A look at almost any newspaper provides a grim illustration of the injury and death that follow from the physical assaults of intensely angry assailants.

A second characteristic of debilitative feelings is their extended *duration*. Feeling depressed for a while after the breakup of a relationship or the loss of a job is natural. But spending the rest of one's life grieving over the loss accomplishes nothing. In the same way, staying angry at someone for a wrong inflicted long ago can be just as punishing to the grudge-holder as to the wrongdoer.

Thinking and Feeling   Our goal, then, is to find a method for getting rid of debilitative feelings while remaining sensitive to the more facilitative emotions. Fortunately, such a method was developed by cognitive psychologists such as Aaron Beck and Albert Ellis. This method is based on the idea that the key to changing feelings is to change unproductive thinking. Let's see how it works.

For most people, emotions seem to have a life of their own. People wish they could feel calm when approaching strangers, yet their voices quiver. They try to appear confident when asking for a raise, but their eyes twitch nervously. Many people would say that the strangers or the boss *make* them feel nervous, just as they would say that a bee sting causes them to feel pain.

> **What other dungeon is so dark as one's own heart! What jailer so inexorable as one's self!**
>
> Nathaniel Hawthorne

The connection apparent between physical and emotional discomfort becomes clear considered in the following way:

Activating Event	Causes	Consequences
bee sting	causes	physical pain
meeting strangers	causes	nervous feelings

When looking at emotions in this way, people may believe they have little control over how they feel. The causal relationship between physical pain and emotional discomfort (or pleasure) isn't, however, as great as it seems. Cognitive psychologists and therapists argue that it is not *events,* such as meeting strangers or being jilted by a lover, which cause people to feel poorly, but rather the *beliefs they hold* about these events.

Albert Ellis, who developed the cognitive approach called Rational-Emotive Therapy, tells a story that clarifies this point. Imagine yourself walking by a friend's house and seeing your friend stick his or her head out of a window and call you a string of vile names. (You supply the friend and the names.) Under these circumstances, it's likely that you would feel hurt and upset.

Now imagine that instead of walking by the house, you were passing a mental institution when the same friend, who was obviously a patient there, shouted the same offensive names at you. In this case, your reaction would probably be quite different; most likely, you'd feel sadness and pity.

A man is hurt not so much by what happens as by his opinion of what happens.

Montaigne

In this story the activating event—being called names—was the same in both cases, yet the emotional consequences were very different. The reason for the different feelings has to do with the pattern of thinking in each case. In the first instance you would most likely think that your friend was very angry with you, and imagine you must have done something terrible to deserve such a response. In the second case you would probably assume that your friend had experienced some psychological difficulty and would probably feel sympathetic.

This example illustrates that it is people's *interpretations* of events that determine their feelings. Thus, a more accurate model for emotions would look like this:

The key, then, to understanding and changing feelings lies in the pattern of thought. Consider the part of you that, like a little voice, whispers in your ear. Take a moment now and listen to what the voice is saying.

Did you hear the voice? It was quite possibly saying, "What little voice? I don't hear any voices!" This little voice talks to you almost constantly:

> "Better pick up a loaf of bread on the way home."
>
> "I wonder when he's going to stop talking."
>
> "It's sure cold today!"
>
> "Are there two or four cups in a quart?"

At work or at play, while reading the paper or brushing teeth, we all tend to think. This thinking voice rarely stops. It may fall silent for awhile when you're running, riding a bike, or meditating, but most of the time it rattles on.

Irrational Beliefs   This process of self-talk is essential to understanding debilitative feelings. Albert Ellis suggests that many debilitative feelings come from accepting a number of irrational beliefs—we'll call them fallacies here—that lead to illogical conclusions, and, in turn, to debilitating feelings.

Activating Event	Thought or Belief	Consequences
being called names	"I've done something wrong"	hurt, upset
being called names	"My friend must be sick"	concern, sympathy

The fallacy of perfection   People who accept this myth believe that a worthwhile communicator should be able to handle any situation with complete confidence and skill. Whereas such a standard of perfection might serve as a target and a source of inspiration (rather like making a hole in one for a golfer), it's totally unrealistic to expect that you can reach or maintain this level of behavior. The truth is, people simply aren't perfect. Perhaps the myth of the perfect communicator comes from believing too strongly in novels, TV or films. In these media perfect characters are often depicted, such as the perfect mate or child, the totally controlled and gregarious host, and the incredibly competent professional. While these images are certainly appealing, people will inevitably come up short when compared to these fabrications.

Once a person accepts the belief that it's desirable and possible to be a perfect communicator, they come to think that people won't appreciate them if they are imperfect. Admitting one's mistakes, saying "I don't know," or sharing feelings of uncertainty or discomfort thus become social defects. Given the desire to be valued and appreciated, these people are tempted to at least try to *appear* perfect. Thus, many people assemble a variety of social masks, hoping that if they can fool others into thinking that they are perfect, perhaps they'll find acceptance. The costs of such deception are high. If others ever detect that this veneer of confidence is a false one, then the person is considered a phony. Even if the unassertive person's role of confidence does go undetected, the performance consumes a great deal of psychological energy, and diminishes the rewards of approval.

The irony for these people is that their efforts are unnecessary. Research by Eliot Aronson and others suggests that the people we regard most favorably are those who are competent but not perfect. Why is this so? First, many people see the acts of would-be perfectionists as the desperate struggle that they are. It's obviously easier to like someone who is not trying to deceive you than someone who is. Second, most people become uncomfortable around a person regarded as perfect. Knowing they don't measure up to certain standards, most people are tempted to admire this super-human only from a distance.

> I never was what you would call a fancy skater—and while I seldom actually fell, it might have been more impressive if I had. A good resounding fall is no disgrace. It is the fantastic writhing to avoid a fall which destroys any illusion of being a gentleman. How like life that is, after all!

Robert Benchley

Not only can subscribing to the myth of perfection keep others from liking you, it also acts as a force to diminish self-esteem. How can you like yourself when you don't measure up to your own standards? You become more liberated each time you comfortably accept the idea that you are not perfect. For example:

1. Like everyone else, you sometimes have a hard time expressing yourself.
2. Like everyone else, you make mistakes from time to time, and there is no reason to hide this.
3. You are honestly doing the best you can to realize your potential, to become the best person you can be.

The fallacy of approval   This mistaken belief is based on the idea that it is vital—not just desirable—to obtain everyone's approval. Communicators who subscribe to this belief go to incredible lengths to seek acceptance from people who are significant to them, even to the extent of sacrificing their own principles and happiness. Adherence to this irrational myth can lead to some ludicrous situations.

For example:

1. Feeling nervous because people you really don't like seem to disapprove of you.
2. Feeling apologetic when others are at fault.
3. Feeling embarrassed after behaving unnaturally to gain another's approval.

The myth of acceptance is irrational because it implies that some people are more respectable and more likable because they go out of their way to please others. Often this simply isn't true. How respectable are people who have compromised important values simply to gain acceptance? Are people highly thought of who repeatedly deny their own needs as a means of buying approval? Genuine affection and respect are hardly due such characters. In addition, striving for universal acceptance is irrational because it is simply not possible. Sooner or later a conflict of expectations is bound to occur. One person approves of a certain kind of behavior, while another approves only the opposite course of action.

Don't misunderstand: Abandoning the fallacy of approval does not mean living a life of selfishness. It's still important to consider the needs of others and to meet them whenever possible. It's also pleasant—one might even say necessary—to strive for the respect of certain people. The point is that the price is too high when people must abandon their needs and principles in order to gain this acceptance.

The fallacy of shoulds   One huge source of unhappiness is the inability to distinguish between what *is* and what *should be*. For

instance, imagine a person who is full of complaints about the world:

"There should be no rain on weekends."

"People ought to live forever."

"Money should grow on trees."

"We should all be able to fly."

Beliefs such as these are obviously foolish. However pleasant such wishing may be, insisting that the unchangeable should be altered won't affect reality one bit. And yet many people torture themselves by engaging in this sort of irrational thinking: They confuse "is" with "ought." They say and think:

"That guy should drive better."

"She shouldn't be so inconsiderate."

"They ought to be more friendly."

"You should work harder."

In each of these cases the person *prefers* that people behave differently. Wishing that

things were better is perfectly legitimate, and trying to change them is, of course, a good idea; but it is unreasonable for people to *insist* that the world operate just as they want it to. Parents wish their children were always considerate and neat. Teachers wish that their students were totally fascinated with their subjects and willing to study diligently. Consumers wish that inflation wasn't such a problem. But, as the old saying goes, those wishes and a dime (now fifty cents) will get you a cup of coffee.

Becoming obsessed with shoulds yields three bad consequences.

1. This obsession leads to unnecessary unhappiness. People who are constantly dreaming about the ideal are seldom satisfied with what they have. For instance, partners in a marriage who focus on the ways in which their mate could be more considerate, sexy, or intelligent will have a hard time appreciating the strengths that drew them together in the first place.

2. This obsession keeps you from changing unsatisfying conditions. One instructor, for example, constantly complains about the problems at the university: The quality of teaching should be improved; pay ought to be higher; the facilities should be upgraded; and so on. This person could be using the same energy to improve these conditions. Of course, not all problems have solutions. But when they do, complaining is rarely the most producive method of improvement.

A man said to the universe:
"Sir, I exist!"
"However," replied the universe,
"The fact has not created in me
A sense of obligation."

Stephen Crane

---

3. This obsession tends to build a defensive climate in others. Imagine living around someone who insisted that people be more punctual, work harder, or refrain from using certain language. This kind of carping is obviously irritating. It's much easier to be around people who comment without preaching, such as asking, "Could you try to be more punctual?"

The fallacy of overgeneralization One type of overgeneralization occurs when a person bases a belief on a limited amount of evidence. Consider the following statements:

> "I'm so stupid! I can't understand how to do my income tax."

> "Some friend I am! I forgot my best friend's birthday."

In these cases people have focused on a limited shortcoming as if it represented everything. Sometimes people forget that, despite their difficulties, they solved tough problems, and that although they can be forgetful, they're often caring and thoughtful.

A second related category of overgeneralization occurs when we exaggerate shortcomings:

> "You *never* listen to me."

> "You're *always* late."

> "I can't think of *anything*."

Upon closer examination, such absolute statements are almost always false, and usually lead to discouragement or anger. It's better to replace overgeneralizations with more accurate messages:

> "You often don't listen to me."

> "You've been late three times this week."

> "I haven't had any ideas I like today."

The fallacy of causation People who live their lives in accordance with this myth believe they should do nothing that can hurt or in any way inconvenience others. This attitude often leads to guilty and resentful feelings, such as:

1. Visiting one's friends or family out of a sense of obligation rather than a genuine desire to see them.

2. Concealing an objection to another person's behavior that is in some way troublesome to you.

3. Pretending to be attentive to a speaker when one is already late for another engagement or is feeling ill.

4. Praising and reassuring others who ask for an opinion, although the honest response is a negative one.

A reluctance to speak out in situations like these often results from assuming that one person can cause another's emotions—that you hurt, confuse, or anger others. Acutally, this assumption is seldom correct. A person doesn't *cause* feelings in others; rather, others *respond* to your behavior with feelings of their own. Consider how strange it sounds to suggest that people make others fall in love with them. Such a statement simply doesn't make sense. It would be more correct to say that people first act in one way or another; then others may or may not fall in love as a result of these actions. In the same way, it's incorrect to say that people *make* others angry, upset, even happy. Behavior that upsets or pleases one person might not bring any reaction from another. More accurately people's responses are determined as much by their own psychological makeup as by other's behavior.

Restricting communication because of the myth of causation can produce three damaging consequences:

1. **People often will fail to meet your needs.** There's little likelihood that people will change their behavior unless they know that it affects you in a negative way.

2. **You are likely to begin resenting the person whose behavior you fail to complain about.** Although this reaction is illogical, as these feelings have never been made known, logic doesn't change the fact that burying the problem usually builds up hostility.

3. **Once people find out about your deceptive nature, they may find it difficult to determine when you are genuinely upset.** Even your most fervent assurances become suspect, as others can never be sure when you are concealing resentments. In many respects, assuming responsibility for others' feelings is not only irrational, it is counterproductive.

The fallacy of helplessness   This fallacy suggests that satisfaction in life is determined by forces beyond control. People with this outlook continuously see themselves as victims:

> "There's no way a woman can get ahead in this society. It's a man's world, and the best thing I can do is to accept it."

> "I was born with a shy personality. I'd like to be more outgoing, but there's nothing I can do about that."

> "I can't tell my boss that she is putting too many demands on me. If I did, I might lose my job."

The error in statements such as these becomes apparent once a person realizes that very few paths are completely closed. Most "can't" statements can, in fact, more correctly be rephrased in one of two ways.

The first is to say that you *won't* act in a certain way, that you *choose* not to do so. For instance, you may choose not to stand up for your rights or to follow unwanted requests, but it is usually inaccurate to claim that some outside force keeps you from doing so. The other way to rephrase a "can't" is to say that you *don't know how* to do something. Examples of this sort of situation include not knowing how to complain in a way that reduces defensiveness, or not being aware of how to best conduct a conversation. Many difficulties that a person claims can't be solved do have solutions: The task is to discover those solutions and to work diligently at applying them.

When viewed in this light, it's apparent that many "can'ts" are really rationalizations to justify not wanting to change. Once people persuade themselves that there's no hope, it's easy for them to give up trying. On the other hand, acknowledging that there is a way to change—even though it may be difficult—puts the responsibility for the predicament on your shoulders. Knowing that you can move closer to your goals makes it difficult to complain about the present situation. You *can* become a better communicator.

The fallacy of catastrophic failure Fearful people who adopt to this belief operate on the assumption that if something bad can happen, it probably will. These statements are typical of such an attitude:

"If I invite them to the party, they probably won't want to come."

"If I speak up in order to try and resolve a conflict, things will probably get worse."

"If I apply for the job I want, I probably won't be hired."

"If I tell them how I really feel, they'll probably laugh at me."

While it's undoubtedly naive to blithely assume that all of your interactions with others will meet with success, it's equally wrong to assume you will fail. One consequence of this attitude is that you'll be less likely to be expressive at important times. To carry the concept to its logical extreme, imagine people who fear *everything:* How can they live their lives? They wouldn't step outside in the morning to see what kind of day it is for fear they'll be struck by lightning or a falling airplane. They wouldn't drive a car for fear of a collision. They wouldn't engage in any exercise for fear the strain might cause a heart attack. Do these examples seem ridiculous? Consider if you have ever withdrawn from communicating because you were afraid of unlikely consequences. A certain amount of prudence is wise, but carrying caution too far can lead to a life of lost opportunities.

Even when one acts in spite of catastrophic fantasies, problems occur. One way to escape from the myth of cata-

strophic failure is to reassess the consequences that would follow even if
you fail in your efforts to communicate.
Failing in a given situation usually isn't as
bad as it seems. What if people do laugh?
Suppose you don't get the job? What if
others do get angry at certain remarks? Are
these matters really *that* serious?

A Rational-Emotive Approach   How can a
person overcome irrational thinking? Ellis
has developed a simple yet effective
approach that helps people cut down on
self-defeating thinking that leads to
debilitative emotions.

Monitor your emotional reactions   The
first step is to recognize debilitative
emotions. (Of course, it's also nice to be
aware of pleasant feelings when they
occur.) As suggested earlier, one way to
notice feelings is through proprioceptive
stimuli: butterflies in the stomach, racing
heart, hot flashes, and so on. While such
reactions may call for a trip to the
emergency room of the local hospital, more
often these feelings reflect strong emotion.
You can also recognize certain ways of
behaving that suggest a strong emotion,
such as stomping instead of normal walking, being unusually quiet, or speaking in a
sarcastic tone of voice.

Does it seem strange to suggest that you
look for emotions that should be immediately apparent? The fact is, people often
suffer from debilitating feelings for some
time without noticing them. For example,
at the end of a trying day you've probably
caught yourself frowning, only to realize
that you've been wearing that mask for
some time.

Note the activating event   Once you're
aware of how you're feeling, the next step
is to figure out what event activated the
response. Sometimes this activating event is
obvious. For instance, a common source of
anger is being accused unfairly (or fairly) of
behaving foolishly, or being rejected by
somebody personally important.

Other times there isn't a single activating
event, but a series of small incidents which
build toward a critical mass, later triggering
a debilitative feeling. This series of
incidents may happen when you're trying
to work or sleep and are continually
interrupted, or when you suffer a string of
small disappointments.

The best way to recognize activating
events is to notice the circumstances that
accompany debilitative feelings. Perhaps
they occur when you're around *specific
people*. In other cases you might be
bothered by certain *types of individuals,*
due to their age, role, background, and so
forth. Certain *settings* may also stimulate
unpleasant emotions: parties, work, or
school. In other cases, the *topic* of
conversation is the factor that sets you off,
whether it be politics, religion, sex, or some
other subject.

Record your self-talk   Now analyze the
thoughts that link the activating event to the
feeling. Let's look at a few examples to see
how the steps work in practice.

*Scott noticed that he became nervous
(emotional reaction) whenever he tried to
talk with an attractive woman he'd like to*

date (activating event). After some observation, he discovered that his self-talk included:

1. "I'm behaving like a fool."
2. "I don't know what to say to her."
3. "She'd never want to go out with me."
4. "I'm no good with women."

Brenda became infuriated at a friend whom she described as a "leech." This friend would call Brenda frequently, sometimes three or four times a day. She also dropped in for visits at awkward times without being invited. Brenda found that her self-talk focused on the statements:

1. "After all the hints I've dropped, she should get the idea and leave me alone."
2. "She's driving me crazy."
3. "I'm a coward for not speaking up and telling her to quit bothering me."
4. "If I do tell her, she'll be crushed."
5. "There's no solution to this mess. I'm damned if I tell her to leave me alone and damned if I don't."

Monitoring your self-talk might be difficult at first, but if you persevere, you'll soon be able to identify the thoughts that lead to your debilitative feelings. Once you habitually recognize the internal monologue, you'll identify your thoughts quickly and easily.

Dispute your irrational beliefs   This step is the key to success in the rational-emotive approach. Use the list of irrational beliefs on pages 119–124 to discover which of your internal statements are based on mistaken thinking.

You can see how this process works by looking at how Scott disputed his self-talk here instead of accepting his earlier beliefs. He examined each of his statements one at a time to discover which were reasonable.

1. "This is an exaggeration. I'm certainly not perfect, but I'm not a fool either. A fool would behave much worse than I do. It's more accurate to say that I'm behaving like a nervous guy around a pretty woman, which is exactly the case. There's nothing unusual about that."
2. "This is an accurate statement. I'm not sure what to say and so I'm searching for a good topic."
3. "This is an irrational, catastrophic belief. She may not want to go out, but on the other hand, she might want to. The only way I'll know is to ask her. In the meantime, it's foolish to expect the worst."
4. "This is an exaggeration. Based on my past experience I'd say that I have my strengths and weaknesses when it comes to dealing with women. My drawbacks are that I get nervous and tend to get a crush on lots of nice, beautiful women who I probably wouldn't get along with. On the other hand, I'm honest and kind, and I've had some good times with some fine women."

Brenda examined her self-talk in the same way.

1. "If she was perfect, then she would be more sensitive. But since she's an insensitive person, then she's behaving just like I'd expect her to do. I'd sure like her to be more considerate, but there's no rule that says she should be."

2. *"This is a bit melodramatic. I definitely don't like her interruptions, but there's a big difference between being irritated and going crazy. Besides, even if I was losing my mind, it wouldn't be accurate to say that she was driving me crazy, but rather that I'm letting her get to me. (But it is fun to feel sorry for myself though.)"*

3. *"This is an exaggeration. I am afraid to tell her, but that doesn't make me a coward. It makes me a less than totally self-assured person. This confirms my suspicion that I'm not perfect."*

4. *"There's a chance that she'll be disappointed if she knows that I've found her irritating. But I have to be careful not to catastrophize here. She would probably survive my comments and even appreciate my honesty once she gets over the shock. Besides, I'm not sure that I want to take the responsibility of keeping her happy if it leaves me feeling irritated. She's a big girl, and if she has a problem she can learn to deal with it."*

5. *"I'm playing helpless here. There must be a way I can tell her honestly while still being supportive."*

After reading about this method of dealing with unpleasant emotions, some readers have the following objections:

1. The rational-emotive approach sounds like nothing more than trying to talk yourself out of feeling bad. This accusation is totally correct: Cognitive therapists believe that it is possible to convince yourself to feel differently. After all, since we talk ourselves *into* debilitative emotions, what's wrong with talking ourselves *out* of them?

2. This kind of disputing sounds unnatural. "I don't talk to myself in sentences and paragraphs," many people say. There's no need to dispute your irrational beliefs in any particular literary style. You can be as colloquial as you want. The importance here is to clearly understand what thought led you into your debilitative feeling so you can clearly dispute them. When the technique is new for you, write or talk out your thoughts in order to make them clear. After you've had some practice, you will be able to do these steps in a quicker, less formal way.

There is nothing good or bad but thinking makes it so.

Shakespeare
Hamlet

---

3. Rational-emotive thinking seems to turn people into calculating, emotionless machines. This is simply not true. There's nothing wrong with having facilitative emotions: They are the stuff that makes life worth living. The goal of this approach is to get rid of the debilitative, harmful emotions that keep us from functioning well. Just as you remove weeds from a garden to let vegetables and flowers grow, so you can use rational thinking to weed out unproductive, harmful feelings to leave room for the productive, positive ones.

4. This technique appears to promise too much. It seems unrealistic to think that you could rid yourself of *all* unpleasant feelings. Rational-emotive thinking probably won't solve emotional problems *totally,* but what it *can* do is reduce the amount, intensity, and duration of debilitative feelings. This method is not the answer to all your problems, but it can make a significant difference, which is not a bad accomplishment.

Sharing Feelings: When and How?

Now that we've talked about how to deal with debilitative emotions, the question remains: How is it possible to best share facilitative feelings with others? It's obvious that indiscriminately sharing every feeling of boredom, fear, affection, irritation, etc. would often cause trouble. On the other hand, we can clearly strike a better balance between denying or downplaying feelings on the one hand and totally cutting loose with them on the other. The suggestions that follow are some guidelines on when and how to express emotions in a way that will give the best chances for improving your relationships.

Recognize Your Feelings   It's an obvious but important fact that you can best share your feelings when you're aware of what they are. As we've already said, there are a number of ways in which feelings can become evident. Physiological changes can clearly indicate emotions. Monitoring your nonverbal behaviours (facial expression, voice tone, posture, etc.) is

another excellent way to keep in touch with your feelings (See Chapter 9.) You can also recognize your feelings by monitoring your self-talk as well as the verbal messages you send to others. It's not far from the verbal statement "I hate this!" to the realization "I'm angry (or bored, or nervous, or embarrassed). Whether you recognize your feelings via any of these ways, the same point applies: it's important to know how you feel in order to tell others about those feelings.

Distinguish between Primary and Secondary Feelings   Many times the feeling we express isn't the only one we're experiencing. Consider the case of Heidi and Mike at a party. The subject of self-defense has come up, and Heidi recounts the time Mike drunkenly picked a fight in a bar, only to receive a sound beating from a rather short, elderly, pudgy customer. Later Mike confronts Heidi angrily, "How could you? That was a rotten thing to say. I'm furious at you." While Mike's anger may be justified, he failed to share with Heidi the emotion that preceded and in fact was responsible for his anger, namely the embarrassment when a secret he hoped to keep private was exposed to others. If he had shared this primary feeling, Heidi could have better understood his rage, and probably would have responded in a more constructive way. Anger often isn't the primary emotion, although it's the one we may express. In addition to embarrassment, it's often preceded by confusion, disappointment, frustration, or sadness. In each of these cases it's important to share the primary feeling as well as the anger that follows it.

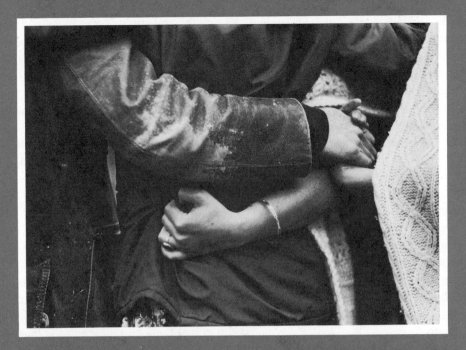

Recognize the Difference between Feeling and Acting   When children are infants, they often go through long spells of late night crying. Most parents experience moments in the wee hours of the morning when they are so tired that they feel like leaving home with all its noise and confusion. Needless to say, they rarely follow through on this impulse.

Of course most of us would like to be the kind of people who are totally patient, accepting, and rational, but we're not. While we don't always want to act on our immediate feelings, we also don't want to ignore them so that they'll build up inside and eventually consume us. For this reason we feel best when we can express what's happening, and then decide whether or not we'll act on it.

For instance, it may be appropriate to acknowledge nervousness in some new situations, even though you might not choose to show it. Likewise, you can acknowledge attraction to certain men or women even though you might not choose to act on these feelings. It's possible to get in touch with the boredom sometimes experienced in meetings and classes, even though you'll most likely resist falling asleep or walking out. In other words, just because you feel a certain way doesn't mean you must always act it out.

This distinction is extremely important, for it can liberate you from the fear that acknowledging and sharing a feeling will commit you to some disastrous course of action. If, for instance, you say to a friend, "I feel so angry that I could punch you in the nose," it becomes possible to explore exactly why you feel so furious and then to resolve the problem that led to the anger. Pretending that nothing is the matter, on the other hand, will do nothing to diminish resentful feelings, which can then go on to contaminate a relationship.

Accept Responsibility for Your Feelings
While you often experience a feeling in response to the behavior of others, it's important to understand that others don't *cause* your feelings. In other words, people don't make you sad, happy, and so on; *you* are responsible for the way you react. Look at it this way: It's obvious that people are more easily upset on some days than on others. Little things that usually don't bother you can suddenly bring on a burst of emotion. Since this is true, it isn't the things or people themselves that determine your reactions, but rather how you feel about them at a given time. If, for example, you're especially harassed due to the press of unfinished work, you may react angrily to a personal joke a friend has made. Was the friend responsible for this upset? No, it's more correct to say that the pressure of work—something within you—set off the anger. The same principle holds true for other emotions: Unrequited love doesn't break our hearts; we allow ourselves to feel hurt, or rather, we simply *are* hurt. A large dose of alcohol doesn't make us sad or happy; those emotions are already within us.

It's important to make sure that language reflects the fact of self-responsibility for feelings. Instead of "You're making me angry," say "I'm getting angry." Instead of "You hurt my feelings," say "I feel hurt when you do that." People don't make us like or dislike them, and pretending that they do denies the responsibility each of us has for our own emotions.

Choose the Best Time and Place to Express Your Feelings When you do choose to share your feelings with another person, it's important to pick a time and place that's appropriate. Often the first flush of a strong feeling is not the best time to speak out. If you're awakened by the racket caused by a noisy neighbor, by storming over to complain you might say things you'll regret later. In such a case it's probably wiser to wait until you have carefully thought out how you might express your feelings in a way that would most likely be heard.

Even after you've waited for the first flush of feeling to subside, it's still important to choose the time that's best suited to the message. Being rushed, or tired, or disturbed by some other matter are all good reasons for postponing the sharing of a feeling. Often, dealing with emotions can take a great amount of time and effort, and fatigue or distraction will make it difficult to devote enough energy to follow through on the matter you've started. In the same manner you ought to be sure that the recipient of your message is ready to listen before you begin sharing.

Share Your Feelings Clearly and Un-ambiguously Either out of confusion or discomfort we sometimes express emotions in an unclear way. Sometimes this entails using many words where one will do better. For example: "Uh, I guess what I'm trying to say is that I was pretty upset when I waited for you on the corner where we agreed to meet at 1:30 and you didn't show up until 3:00," would be better stated as, "I was angry when you were an hour and a half late." One key to making emotions clear is to realize that you most often can summarize a feeling in a single word: hurt, glad, confused, excited, resentful, and so on. In the same way, a little thought can probably provide brief reasons for feeling a certain way.

Another way the expression of a feeling may be confused is by discounting or qualifying it: "I'm a *little* unhappy"; "I'm *pretty* excited"; "I'm *sort* of confused." Of course, not all emotions are strong ones—we do experience degrees of sadness and joy—but some communicators have a tendency to discount almost every feeling. Do you?

Still another way the expression of an emotion becomes confused is when it is sent in a code. This most often happens when the sender is uncomfortable about sharing the feeling in question. Some codes are verbal ones, as when the sender hints more or less subtly at the message. For example, an indirect way to say, "I'm lonesome" might be, "I guess there isn't much happening this weekend, so if you're not busy why don't you drop by?" This indirect code does have its advantages: It allows the sender to avoid the self-disclosure of expressing an unhappy feeling, and it also serves as a safe-guard against the chance of being rejected outright. On the other hand, such a message is so indirect that the chances of the real feeling being recognized are reduced. For this reason people who send coded messages stand less of a chance of having their emotions understood and their needs met.

Finally, you can express yourself clearly by making sure that both you and your partner understand that your feeling is centered on a specific set of circumstances, rather than being indicative of the whole relationship. Instead of saying, "I resent you," say, "I resent you when you don't keep your promises." Rather than, "I'm bored with you," say, "I'm bored when you talk about your money." Be aware that, in the course of knowing anyone, you're bound to feel positive at some times and negative at others. By limiting comments to the specific situation, you can express a feeling directly without feeling that the relationship is jeopardized.

Readings

Adler, Ronald B. *Confidence in Communication; A Guide to Assertive and Social Skills.* New York: Holt, Rinehart and Winston, 1977.

Aronson, Eliot, *The Social Animal.* New York: Viking Press, 1972.

Beck, Aaron T. *Cognitive Therapy and the Emotional Disorders.* New York: International Universities Press, 1976.

Coon, Dennis. *Introduction to Psychology: Exploration and Application.* St. Paul, Minn.: West, 1977.

Dunbar, Flanders. *Mind and Body: Psychosomatic Medicine.* New York: Random House, 1947.

Egan, Gerard. *You and Me: The Skills of Communicating and Relating to Others.* Monterey, Calif.: Brooks/Cole, 1977.

Ellis, Albert. *A New Guide to Rational Living.* North Hollywood, Calif.: Wilshire Books, 1977.

Gitter, A. G., H. Block and D. Mostofsky. "Race and Sex in the Perception of Emotion." *Journal of Social Issues,* 170, (1972):63–78.

Johnson, David, "The Effects of Expressing Warmth and Anger upon the Actor and the Listener." *Journal of Counseling Psychology,* 18, (1971):571–78.

Kranzler, Gerald. *You Can Change How You Feel: A Rational-Emotive Approach.* Eugene, Ore.: RETC Press, 1974.

Jakubowski, Patricia and Arthur Lange. *The Assertive Option.* Champaign, Ill.: Research Press, 1978.

Lazarus, Arnold and Allen Fay. *I Can If I Want To.* New York: William Morrow, 1975.

McQuade, A. and A. Aikman. *Stress: What It Is and What It Does to You.* New York: E. P. Dutton, 1974.

Powell, John. *The Secret of Staying in Love.* Niles, Ill: Argus, 1974.

Selye, Hans. *The Stress of Life.* New York: McGraw-Hill, 1956.

Wolf, S. *The Stomach.* Oxford: Oxford University Press, 1965.

Wood, John T. *How Do You Feel?* Englewood Cliffs, N.J.: Prentice-Hall, 1974.

Zimbardo, Philip. *Shyness: What It Is, What to Do about It.* Reading, Mass.: Addison-Wesley, 1977.

Relationships

6 WANTED: A friend. Need to be considerate, intelligent, outgoing, and a good listener. Must like to watch Sunday football.

AVAILABLE: One older sister. I share my toys, keep the room clean, and can help you with your homework. Sometimes I get moody.

It pays to advertise. Sell a car. Buy a Siberian husky. Rent an apartment. Yet, we are a curious sort of people. For all the prominence that our culture gives to business enterprises and to personal relationships, the reaction to placing an ad in the paper "Friend Wanted" is one of suspicion, of thinking, "Hey, this person must be crazy!"

There are exceptions, though. Recently, a young man in New York had a poster made with his picture, a description of himself, and a note indicating his search for a female friend. The notice was placed in prominent locations throughout the city's subway labyrinth, and within a week, he had over 2,000 responses. Last heard, he was happily engaged.

This success story may have led people to place the following real newspaper ads:

SINCERE gentleman 40. Meet lady 30–40 for companionship. Would like long-term relationship if compatible. Call . . .

WOMAN. Young, intellectual, interested in warm, loving male companionship, also intellectual. Write with phone number to . . .

LOOKING FOR PERSON named Jay, male, black, drives green pickup truck. Reward. Call . . .

These advertisements and posters show that personal relationships *are* important. Although you may not have placed an ad for a particular relationship, you probably do have certain expectations and requirements of yourself and others if the relationship is to be successful.

In this chapter, we will look at the different *types* of relationships we share, the reasons for *why* we form them, and the *stages* in developing and ending relationships. After this survey we will take an in-depth look at one particular relationship: friendship.

Types of Relationships

Consider a typical day. With whom do you live, work, study, eat, sleep, party, play? Sometimes there is one person with whom you do all these things. But more commonly we have different relationships for each of our different activities. Let's take a look at three ways of categorizing these relationships.

Context The most obvious way of classifying relationships is to look at the contexts in which they occur. It's likely that your various relationships that take place in several different settings. For example, relationships can form at one's work site. (These usually take up a large amount of time.) Within any given job, there are many relationships existing in a variety of subcontexts. Some involve superiors, some are with subordinates, and still others occur with colleagues of equal status. In certain jobs interaction even takes place with people outside of the organization, as in sales or service positions in which there is continual contact with the public.

"Actually, I'm seeking a meaningless relationship."

Then there is the context of family. Here, of course, many relationships exist: between parents and children, between siblings, etc. Family relationships are the earliest type of interpersonal contact and often remain important into later life.

The social context is another that offers several kinds of relationships. Hopefully you're lucky enough to have a few very good, important friends. You certainly think of these people differently than more casual friends, whom you may see quite often but value in a different way. Included in the social context are new acquaintances, people you might meet in passing at a party or those you briefly chat with, such as neighbors.

In addition to the work, family, and social categories there are other contexts in which types of relationships can occur: therapeutic, for instance, such as with physicians or counselors; academic, such as are experienced at schools; religious, political, or recreational; random, such as relationships with total strangers—people whom you might chat with while waiting in a line, or those you approach while asking for directions or some other kind of assistance. Contextual categories are numerous.

Intimacy Important as they may be, contexts don't tell us everything about relationships. You can understand this point by trying a simple experiment. Make a list of all the contexts in which your relationships occur and then list all the people in each of these areas. Now review your list and place a star next to the name of each person with whom you feel close, and a circle next to those to whom you feel distant. It's likely that the context doesn't always determine closeness. You might, for example, feel much closer to one or two coworkers than you do some family members.

This difference brings us to the dimension of intimacy, which is the second way of looking at relationships. There are several kinds of intimacy: intellectual, emotional, and physical. It's possible to be intimate with someone in one of these ways and not in others. You may, for example, share a relationship in which you're not physically close with another person, but are highly intimate on an emotional or intellectual level.

One of the most prominent theories about how intimacy develops in relationships has been described by Irwin Altman and Dalmas Taylor in their book *Social Penetration: The Development of Interpersonal Relationships*. These authors suggest that relationships develop in increments, moving from superficial to more personal levels. As two people learn more about each other, primarily through the process of self-disclosure, the relationship gains importance. Depending on the *breadth* of the information shared (for example, the number of topics you discuss) and the *depth* of that information, a relationship can be defined as casual or intimate. In the case of a casual relationship, the breadth may be high, but not the depth. A more intimate relationship is likely to have high breadth and high depth. Altman and Taylor visualize these two factors as an image of concentric circles. Depth increases as you disclose information that is central to the relationship, information not available unless you provide it; for example, your

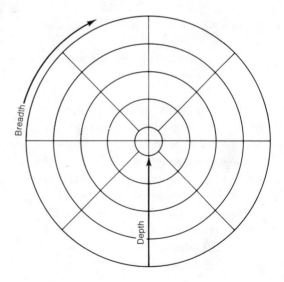

personal goals, fears, and self-images. Altman and Taylor see relationship development as a progression from the periphery to the center of the circle, a process that typically occurs over time.

Based on this theory of *social penetration,* you can visualize a diagram in which a husband's relationship with his wife has high breadth and high depth, his relationship with his friend has low breadth and high depth, and his relationship with his boss is one of low breadth-low depth. Imagine what your own relationship with various people would look like.

The Altman-Taylor model can be used to predict a variety of relationships. According to the theory, relationships proceeding rapidly to the central areas can be quite fragile. For example, an experience such as a "one-night stand" of sexual intimacy often lacks the accompanying transactions that build trust and understanding. When interpersonal conflict erupts, the relationship crumbles.

The model also explains the occurrence of situations known as the "stranger on the plane" phenomenon: You board a plane, ready to sleep or read a long-awaited novel, and within five minutes after take-off the person seated next to you begins a story of plight and personal feelings (high depth, and depending how many topics you cover, high breadth). As you will probably never see this person again, you are presumed to be a "safe stranger." Because the relationship is temporary, it can withstand the high-depth disclosures. If this becomes an ongoing relationship, it is likely to experience tensions.

Although Altman and Taylor do not deal extensively with relationship deterioration, the model would indicate that the de-

penetration process is similar, but in the reverse direction. Interactions experiencing depenetration move from the center to the periphery and decrease in breadth and depth. There are fewer topics of conversation, and each is more superficial than before. The relationship is being redefined as less intimate.

Time As our "stranger on the plane" and "one-night stand" examples suggested, time is another important way of looking at relationships. We've already seen that intimate relationships have a better chance of lasting if they develop slowly, but looking at the element of time can reveal other factors as well. For example, the amount of time a relationship has lasted can be one indicator of its importance. Everyone has heard the line "our friendship goes back a long way," and usually considers such statements as indicating how strong and valuable the relationship is. (Incidentally, the same principle holds true for enemies. The length of time a dispute lasts is one indicator of its importance.)

Of course some relationships can last for years but are still relatively unimportant (as, for example, neighbors who politely but superficially chat every once in a great while. Even in cases such as these, time can be an indicator of the relationship's strength or weakness. In such instances the amount of time we *choose* to spend with someone else indicates commitment to that relationship. You might work or even party with certain people out of duty, avoiding them whenever possible while seeking out

> In the local movie theatre, you can buy mint-flavored lozenges with the words: 'Will you marry me?' 'Do you love me?' written on them, together with the replies: 'This evening,' 'A lot,' etc. You pass them to the girl next to you, who replies in the same way. Lives become linked together by an exchange of mint lozenges.
>
> Albert Camus

other friends voluntarily. Think about the relational implications of the following statements: "I really hate to go. Let's get together soon." versus "Gee, I really don't have the time."

Now, as you might guess, the intimacy, context, and time dimensions of a relationship can form a lovely and complex (typically human) configuration, such that we come out with varied relationships; ones that are short-lived and highly intimate, and others that are long-term, casual acquaintances. If you think of a person with whom you share a special relationship, and a person whom you consider as a casual acquaintance, the differences become evident.

Why We Form Relationships

As the newspaper ads at the beginning of this chapter indicate, some people have extremely clear intentions when they look for relationships. What reasons do you have for interacting with others? You can find out by making a list of your relationships and then seeing which of the following explanations best fits each one:

1. "The other person and I are alike in many ways."
2. "I need things from the other person: guidance, support, information, money, status."
3. "The relationship is a good arrangement for both of us; I get what I'm looking for, and so does the other person."
4. "I care deeply for the other person; because of this caring, I feel glad when he or she is happy and I'm sad when he or she is troubled."
5. "The relationship just happened; we were thrown together and we're still together."

Each of these statements reflects a theory about why people form relationships. Let's take a look at each of these theories, and see which ones seem to best explain why you associate with the important people in your life.

1. **"The other person and I are alike in many ways."** Just what do you have in common with this person—similar attitudes, hobbies, what? Do you attend the same church? Eat at the same greasy spoon restaurants?

It's comforting to know someone who likes the things we like, who has similar values, and who may even be of the same race, economic class, or educational standing. This basis for the relationship is commonly and most appropriately known as the *similarity thesis*. There are at least two possible hypotheses to study in the dynamics of similarity and interpersonal attraction: (1) people with similar attitudes

are attracted to each other; and (2) people who are attracted to each other perceive themselves as similar, whether or not that's actually the case. Both of these ideas have been tested experimentally, and support for each has been demonstrated.

We like people who like what we like, and who dislike what we dislike. Several logical reasons exist for feeling this way. First of all, the other person serves as an external indication—a social validation—that we are not alone in our thinking, that we're not too "weird." Someone else *did* like the same controversial book as you. Thus, this other person offers good support for you, reinforcing your own sense of what is right.

Second, when someone is similar to you, you can make fairly accurate predictions about that person—whether he or she will want to eat at the Mexican restaurant or see the concert you're so excited about. This ability to make confident predictions reduces much uncertainty and anxiety that might otherwise exist.

There's a third explanation for the similarity thesis. It may be that when we learn that other people are similar to us, we assume they'll probably like us, and so, we in turn like them. The self-fulfilling prophecy creeps into the picture again.

These outcomes have been verified in a number of studies, most notably by Donn Byrne and his associates. These researchers told subjects they would be participating in a group discussion, and that some of the other participants (strangers) would have similar opinions to theirs, while others would not. As expected, students expressed more liking for people who supposedly had views similar to their own, and judged these strangers to be more intelligent, better informed, more moral, and better adjusted than those assumed to have dissimilar attitudes.

Research studies also support the second attraction-similarity relationship: When we like a person, we perceive that similarities exist with that individual. Studies by Byrne and Blaylock as well as by Levinger and Breedlove have found that the actual amount of similarity between husbands and wives is significantly less than the amount *assumed* to exist. In discussion of these findings, Ellen Berscheid and Elaine Walster speculate that couples deemphasize their disagreements in the interest of maintaining a harmonious relationship.

For either direction observed in this attraction-similarity relationship, the research indicates that specific aspects of similarity must be considered. For example, does it matter that the person is similar to you in attitudes, but not in personality (or the converse)? The answer is "Yes." *Attitude similarity* carries more weight than *personality similarity*. Does it matter that you and the other person are similar on a small number of issues of greater importance to you both, than on a large number of other issues of lesser significance? Again, "Yes." Finally, are there any limitations to the degree of similarity and attraction between two people? "Yes." A relationship can become *too* predictable, *too* patterned. This is the "I'm bored!" test of the relationship. It has also been found that people who are less anxious about whether or not others like them, will associate with people having different appearances, experiences, and attitudes.

2. "I need things from the other person . . ." In Chapter 1 we talked about how communication can satisfy human needs. We discussed Maslow's hierarchy of needs: physiological, safety, social, self-esteem, and self-actualization. We also looked at Schutz' theory of humans seeking inclusion, control, and affection. These theories reflect the need-fulfillment thesis: The idea that people seek out each other and establish certain types of relationships because of the needs they want fulfilled at that time in their lives.

This thesis of complementary need-fulfillment helps explain the times when you have looked at a couple and mumbled to yourself, "I don't know how they get along—they're so different." But think about it—often it's easier for a person who is very aggressive to live with someone more submissive, than for both to be so dominant. In such cases the partners probably serve important functions for each other. The competition of two perfectionists or the doldrum of two introverts can be dysfunctional to the relationship. Consider *The Odd Couple* characters sharing an apartment: Felix Unger compulsively neat and Oscar Madison compulsively sloppy. Although the two are constantly bickering, you get the idea that Felix enjoys taking care of Oscar, and Oscar likes to be the object of Felix's attention.

Need-fulfillment doesn't only work for opposites. It also explains how people with similar temperaments can serve valuable functions for each other. The mutual support might come in having a partner for playing tennis, discussing politics, sharing personal problems, or making love. In all these cases and many more, our relationships are based on having others do things for us which we can't do alone.

3. The relationship is a good arrangement for both of us . . ." This statement reflects one of the more developed theories about interpersonal relationships. The variations on this theory are known as *social exchange theory* and *reward-cost theory,* and its major proponents are psychologists John Thibaut and Harold Kelley, and sociologist George Homans.

These theorists suggest that we seek relationships from which we get *out* as much or more than what we put in. The rewards we get from a relationship (whether tangible or intangible) must outweigh the costs (again, tangible or intangible). Tangible outcomes might be money, property, and other material possessions. Intangibles include fame, status, respect, and support. In addition to costs and rewards, Thibaut and Kelley have identified each person as having a comparison level (CL), the minimum level set as necessary for positive outcomes. The CL is generally composed of *previous* relationships a person has experienced. A comparison level for alternatives (CL_{alt}) is the person's criterion for deciding whether to continue a relationship. The CL_{alt} is composed of other *possible* relationships. These comparison levels allow for four predictions about relationships:

a. **Stable-satisfactory relationship:** The reward in the current relationship is higher than the general comparison level and the comparison level for alternatives. For example, you perceive that the person you are dating is "better" than your previous dates (the CL) and is better than other possible dates you could have (the CL_{alt}).

b. **Unstable-satisfying relationship:** The reward in the current relationship is higher than the general comparison level, but lower than the comparison level for alternatives. For example, you perceive that the person you are dating is better than your previous dates (the CL), but is not better than other possible dates (the CL_{alt}).

c. **Stable-unsatisfactory relationship:** The reward in the current relationship is lower than the general comparison level, and higher than the comparison level for alternatives. For example, you perceive that the person you are dating is not better than your previous dates (the CL), but is better than your other possible choice (the CL_{alt}).

d. **Unstable-unsatisfactory relationship:** The reward in the current relationship is lower than the general comparison level and lower than the comparison level for alternatives. For example, you perceive that the person you are dating is not better than other previous dates (the CL) and is not better than other possible choices (the CL_{alt}).

Now, to give this theory some intrigue, keep in mind that the comparison levels change over *time* (with age and experience, for example), and can change as a *situation* changes and as the *people* available for comparison change. This is certainly true in the dating practices of many people, whose unstable-satisfying relationships only last until a better, more desirable partner comes along. The same principle also holds true in the business world, where both employers and employees will only maintain a relationship as long as it's rewarding to both parties.

4. "I care deeply for the other person . . ." In a recent article on friendship, Paul Wright takes issue with the reward-cost, grab-the-best-bargain, economic approach of social exchange theories. He suggests that they do not describe the depth, personal involvement, or continuity of many interpersonal relationships, and that a more appropriate concept would be an *investment thesis*. This thesis suggests that a person does more than calculate the rewards of particular relationships. The person also makes an investment of self—of interest, time, energy, and personal resources—to the other person and the relationship shared.

Unlike the social exchange theories, the investment thesis holds that the person looks for more than immediate or tangible rewards. The return on the investment of your self (Wright calls this the dividends) usually takes less concrete and observable forms: enhancement of your sense of individuality, confirmation of your self as a person, increased self-evaluation and self-growth. In Wright's view, a relationship forms and grows to the extent that the person makes a *commitment of self* to the other person and to the relationship.

This investment of self in a relationship is such that when the other person is satisfied or sad, you share in those feelings. A concept closely related to Wright's view of self-investment is that of interpersonal empathy: the ability to feel as another person does, to see what they see, to perceive and understand what they feel. If you have shared another person's joy as *he or she knows it,* or have felt the pain of that person's troubles *as he or she does,* you have experienced empathy with that person, and have made a self-investment in that relationship.

5. "The relationship just happened . . ." Some people see spontaneity and circumstance as the reason for certain relationships they share. There is no conscious design to develop a relationship—it just happens. Such events illustrate relationships based on the *proximity thesis:* The less physical distance there is between two people, the more likely it is that they will be attracted to each other. Consider people who are in close proximity to you: classmates, neighbors, office workers. Given your frequent interaction, it's likely that your relationships are stronger with many of these people than with more distant ones. The influence of proximity is strengthened by the fact that closeness is a kind of similarity, which adds to the attraction explained by that thesis.

The research studies supporting this proximity explanation include studies of integrated housing efforts, and even the arrangement of apartment dwellings. Each study indicates that physical location is important in the *initial* stages of an interaction, but that it is not a sufficient explanation for the *maintenance* of the relationship. So that choice apartment or favorite seat in class may function to set up the initial phases of a relationship by providing the opportunity for introductory interactions, but it is no guarantee of the development you may seek in the relationship or its subsequent outcomes.

The Stages of a Relationship

Although relationships come in many types and "sizes," social scientists have found that they all grow and dissolve by passing through similar phases. These phases can be broken into as few as three parts (initiation, maintenance, and dissolution), or as many as ten, which we'll now examine. These ten stages are outlined by Mark Knapp in his book *Social Intercourse: From Greeting to Goodbye.*

1. Initiation. This stage involves the initial making of contact with another person. Knapp restricts this stage to first impressions and conversation openers. A scene on a recent TV series illustrates this initial stage. Four male radio station

workers are at a local bar, where each tries his opening lines on Jennifer, the vivacious secretary:

Johnny Fever (the afternoon DJ who leaves his nursing home listeners in shock): "You're a Scorpio, aren't you?" (No-go, Johnny.)

Venus Flytrap (the nighttime Mr. Cool DJ): "Hey beautiful, can I buy you a drink?" (Sorry, Venus.)

Andy (the country-boy-made-good program manager): "Didn't I see you at Maxie's last Friday?" (Not a chance, Andy.)

Les (the middle-aged, ultra-conservative bumpkin news announcer): "Hi, I'm wealthy."

(In case you're wondering, money won out here!)

While an initial encounter *is* necessary to the succeeding interaction, its importance is overemphasized in books advising how to pick up men and women. These books suggest fail-proof openers ranging from, "Excuse me, I'm from out of town and I was wondering what people do around here at night?" to "How long do you cook a leg of lamb?" Whatever your preference for opening remarks, this stage is important because you are formulating your first impressions and presenting yourself as interested in the other person.

2. Experimenting. In this stage, the conversation develops as the people get acquainted by making "small talk." We ask: "Where are you from?"; "What do you do?"; "Do you know Josephine Mendoza? She lives in San Francisco too."

While small talk might seem meaningless, Knapp points out that it serves four purposes:

a. It is a useful process for uncovering integrating topics and openings for more penetrating conversation.

b. It can be an audition for a future friendship or a way of increasing the scope of a current relationship.

c. It provides a safe procedure for indicating who we are and how another can come to know us better (reduction of uncertainty).

d. It allows us to maintain a sense of community with our fellow human beings.

The relationship during this stage is generally pleasant and uncritical, and the commitments are minimal. Experimenting may last ten minutes or ten years.

3. Intensifying. In this phase (Knapp thinks most of our relationships don't get beyond experimenting) the relationship develops a character of its own indicated

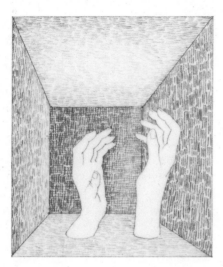

by a common identity: "*We* like to dance." You come to know the other person and develop accuracy in predicting the other's wants and whims. You are more accessible to that person and may use less formal terms, including nicknames and special terms of endearment. A truly *interpersonal* relationship begins on this level.

4. Integrating. At this point, the sense of union of the two people is heightened further—the interpersonal synchrony is high. You become identified by others as "a pair," "an item." This oneness may be accented by similar clothing styles, the similar phrasing of terms, and the designation of common property—for example, *our* song, *our* meeting time, or *our* project.

5. Bonding. When the relationship reaches this stage, it achieves some formal social recognition. This can take the form of a contract to be business partners, or a license to be married. During this stage,

more regulations for the interaction are established, and the participants may experience some disorientation and uneasiness until they adjust to the social formality and institutionalization of their relationship. Newlyweds, for example, may feel a need to rebel once the ceremony sanctions their relationship—the husband might take up car maintenance and spend all his free time in the garage, and the wife might work late.

6. Differentiating. Now that the two people have formed this commonality, they need to reestablish individual identities. How are we different? How am I unique? Former identifications as "we" now emphasize "I." Differentiation often first occurs when a relationship begins to experience the first, inevitable stress.

Whereas a happy employee might refer to "our company," the description might change to "their company" when a raise or some other request isn't forthcoming. We see this kind of differentiation when parents argue over the misbehavior of a child: "Did you see what *your* son just did?"

Differentiation can be positive too, for people need to be individuals as well as part of a relationship. The key to successful differentiation is the need to maintain commitment to a relationship while creating the space for members to be individuals as well.

7. Circumscribing. So far we have been looking at the growth of relationships. While some reach a plateau of development, going on successfully for as long as a lifetime, others pass through several stages of decline and dissolution. In

the circumscribing stage, communication between members decreases in quantity and quality. Restrictions and restraints characterize this stage, and dynamic communication becomes static. Rather than discuss a disagreement (which requires some degree of energy on both parts), members opt for withdrawal: Either mental (silence or daydreaming and fantasizing) or physical, where people spend less time together. Circumscribing doesn't involve total avoidance, which comes later. Rather, it entails a certain shrinking of interest and commitment.

8. Stagnation. If circumscribing continues, the relationship begins to stagnate. Members behave toward each other in old, familiar ways without much feeling. No growth occurs. The relationship is a hollow shell of its former self. We see stagnation in many workers who have lost enthusiasm for their job, yet who continue to go through the motions for years. The same sad event occurs for some couples

who unenthusiastically have the same conversations, see the same people, and follow the same routines without any sense of joy or novelty.

9. Avoiding. When stagnation becomes too unpleasant, parties in a relationship begin to create distance between each other. Sometimes this is done under the guise of excuses ("I've been sick lately and can't see you.") and sometimes it is done directly ("Please don't call me. I don't want to see you now."). In either case, by this point the handwriting about the relationship's future is clearly on the wall.

10. Termination. Characteristics of this final stage include summary dialogues of where the relationship has gone, and the desire to disassociate. The relationship may end with a cordial dinner, a note left on the kitchen table, a phone call, or a legal document stating the dissolution. Depending on each person's feelings, this stage can be quite short, or it may be drawn out over time, with bitter jabs at one another. In either case, termination doesn't have to be totally negative. Understanding one another's investments in the relationship and needs for personal growth may dilute the hard feelings.

Relational turnover is one of the most common yet least acknowledged experiences of contemporary living. We act toward our most intimate friends and lovers as if they will be with us always, yet there is a good chance they will not. We are taught in our early years how to make social ties, but the process of dissolving them is shrouded in mystery, hurt, and misunderstanding. In a study of friend-making and breaking, Jeff Bell and Ava Hadas found that first and third-graders knew how to make friends, but were at a loss about ending friendships. Common responses were that breaking a friendship was out of the child's control—it just happened. Two specific solutions voiced were to "wait until the end of school," or to "just punch him out." Unfortunately, as the years progress, the adult may see similar options as viable. The following accounts will probably sound familiar:

Two teenage sisters, Margaret S., thirteen, and Alice, fifteen, are being questioned about the death of their father Hugh. Police have reason to suspect that the sisters hired a "hit-man" to kill their father. The sisters were reported to be angry that their father would not let them stay out past midnight, and that they had made threats to take out a contract on him.

Robert J. was found dead today in his apartment at 713 Magnolia Blvd. He left a note indicating he was distraught about his relationship with an unidentified woman, and could not take the pressure any longer. Cause of death is listed as a drug overdose.

Of course not all relationships end so dramatically. But even in less notable cases the problem of how to part exists. Many marriages end with bitter recriminations, some jobs are terminated with bad feelings, and unhappy friends often drift apart without knowing how to end their relationships in a better way.

After outlining these ten steps, Knapp discusses several assumptions about his model. First, movement through the stages is generally sequential and systematic. We proceed at a steady pace and don't usually skip steps in the development. Second, movement can be forward or backward and there is movement within stages. A relationship, for example, may experience a setback—a lessening of intimacy, a redefining of the relationship. Two people may repeat certain stages, and although the stages are the same, each cycle is a new experience. It may also be the case that certain relationships will stabilize at a particular stage. Many relationships stabilize at the experimenting stage (friend and work relationships), some stabilize at the intensifying stage, and a few stabilize at the bonding stage. With these assumptions in mind, we can use Knapp's model as a set of developmental guidelines for movement within and between the stages of initiation and dissolution.

In a recent study which focused exclusively on children's perceptions of friendship, Robert and Anne Selman identified five overlapping stages through which children aged three to adolescence progress.

1. Momentary playmate (stage 0, ages 3 through 7). During this stage friends are valued for their material and physical offerings. A friend is identified as the person with the trampoline or the chocolate-chip cookie. At this stage, the child does not distinguish between her own viewpoint and that held by others.

2. One-way assistance (stage 1, ages 4 through 9). While the child still does not differentiate her own perspective from that held by others, and the "give and take" of friendship is not yet understood, a friend is identified as the person who does what the child wants.

3. Two-way fair weather cooperation (stage 2, ages 6 through 12). At this stage reciprocity enters into the relationship, so friendship includes a concern for what each person thinks about the other. However, a friend is still someone who serves *self-interests*.

4. Intimate, mutually shared relationship (stage 3, ages 9 through 15). This stage is marked by a significant change in perspective: Friendship is now defined as a collaboration with others for mutual and common interests (as opposed to self-interests). A friend is someone with whom to share secrets.

5. Autonomous interdependent friendship (stage 4, ages 12 and older). During this final stage there is a growing awareness that people have many needs and that relationships are complex. Friends are people who give emotional and psychological support to each other, *and* who allow each other to develop independent relationships. Support, trust, and the ability to "let go" of the other are distinguishing features of this stage.

Friendship: A Special Relationship

What Makes a Friend? You probably have a variety of friends. If you're lucky you have a few people whom you can count as special friends. It doesn't take any analysis to know that these people matter a great deal to you, and that your life is better for knowing them. But exactly what is it about these people that makes them special? Muriel James and Louis Savary attempted to answer this question by suggesting eight characteristics that most people commonly expect from this kind of relationship. As you read about these characteristics, see which ones are most important in your friendships.

Availability and *shared activities* are particularly important in the initial stages of a relationship. You expect to see the other person, spend time with him or her, get together to work on the term project, have lunch or dinner, or maybe sit and talk during TV commercials. If these expectations are not met, the relationship may never develop beyond an acquaintanceship. In most cases, being available presumes face-to-face interactions, but there are also times when availability happens through written letters or telephone calls, and you can use these techniques to reach others. When you're feeling down and depressed, you may surprise yourself by what you do. Sometimes, you may call someone you haven't spoken to in months, someone who may not even be a "close" friend, and other times you might write to someone who presumes you died or ran off for a tour of the world. No matter, the person is still available, and that's what is important.

Expectations common to the intermediate phases of relationships include *caring, honesty, confidentiality,* and *loyalty.* You expect these from the other person, and also expect to provide them yourself if the relationship is to be reciprocal. Sometimes, we forget that others expect the same treatment from us!

Although the degree of caring will vary with the type of relationship, James and Savary offer the following definition as a guide:

Caring is not the same as using the other person to satisfy one's own needs. Neither is it to be confused with such things as well-wishing, or simply having an interest in what happens to another. Caring is a process of helping others grow and actualize themselves. It is a transforming experience.

In like manner, honesty, confidentiality, and loyalty are expected in all types of relationships. Honesty in a relationship does not mean that you need to tell everything to the other person, but that you are honest about matters relevant to that relationship, while maintaining a respect for the other person's sense of privacy. Confidentiality and loyalty are two agreements made in relationships, at times in unstated and assumed ways, and sometimes in a quite formal (written) legal manner.

Understanding and *empathy* are the "bonuses" of a relationship. Many relationships can maintain themselves based on the other characteristics, but those that are particularly strong have a mutually high degree of understanding and empathy. Sue and Mary understand how each other work and think, and they can empathize with each other's feelings. It's not that they are so predictable as to be boring, but they do know each other's ways of thinking and feeling almost as well as they know their own. Usually, these features of a relationship take time to develop, and they require clear communication between the two people involved. Each must be willing to express needs, feelings, and wishes as

Caring is a process of helping others grow and actualize themselves. It is a transforming experience.

Muriel James and Louis M Savary
The Heart of Friendship

accurately as possible, and also must practice the skills of active listening for the other person.

These expectations for relationships have been noted in different ways by other psychologists, communication researchers, and even young children. In their ongoing research of children's imaginary playmates, John Caldeira, Jerome Singer, and Dorothy Singer found consistent evidence that children create playmates who are *always available, steadfast,* and *loyal.* These companions (usually male) talk with the child, and listen even more—the child perceives that they *care. The playmates give unfailing support,* and fill empty spaces in a child's life—times when the child is alone or perhaps without any playmates of the same age. Children who develop imaginary playmates have been found to be highly intelligent, less aggressive, and more cooperative than children without imaginary playmates. They smile more, show a greater ability to concentrate, are seldom bored, watch less TV, and have more advanced language skills. If these playmates do not become a crutch to the child, researchers view the invisible friends as providing an invaluable tool to the child. This tool allows children to rehearse themselves in different roles, to cope with problems that might otherwise produce overwhelming anxiety, and to test ways of mastering these problems.

Pressures on Friendships   Many times strong friendships wither away. Sad as this may be, it's not surprising, for there are both external and internal pressures on such friendships. The *external* pressures include physical circumstances, such as moving away from friends or changing jobs, and the existence of other competing people and relationships. Two people who have been friends throughout their school years, for example, may experience new tensions when one marries, or when other friends compete for one person's time and attentions. Friends usually come in pairs, and there's a good reason why that's so. In three-person interactions it is almost impossible for one participant to extend attention to both of the other two simultaneously. Unless each person is quite secure in the relationship and with self, most triadic arrangements cannot survive the tensions.

Internal factors can also pressure a friendship. One common internal pressure occurs when partners grow at different rates. For instance, a relationship that was born out of one person's dependency on the other loses its main reason for existing if the weaker partner becomes more self-reliant. Similarly, a friendship once based on agreement to avoid discussing any conflicts will be threatened if one person suddenly becomes willing to tackle

disputes directly. When such changes occur, the maintenance of the friendship depends on the ability of both persons to adapt to the new conditions. Thus, friendships lasting for long periods are often quite different now than they were at earlier times. The partners were wise enough to adapt to their personal changes rather than clinging to the old ways of relating which may have been comfortable and enjoyable, but are now gone.

Not all friendships can survive these pressures. It's important to realize that the end of a friendship does not always mean that the people have failed. Rather, it may simply reflect the fact that one or both partners has changed and now seeks a different (though not necessarily better) type of interaction. Of course, this kind of ending is easier to accept if both people have other relationships that can support their needs.

One way to avoid the brutal attacks on self (which can follow a separation) is to see the friendship not as a *fraction* of you, but as what James and Savary call an additional "third self." There's you, me, and *us*. And if the friendship changes or dissolves, the separate entities of you and me still exist intact and completely, and a new friendship will bring with it another third self.

Friendships for All Ages   In comparison to both job relationships and husband and wife relationships, a friendship has distinct advantages: There's no age limit to them. You don't have to wait until you're sixteen to get a license to acquire a friend. You had friends when you were two-years-old, and probably anticipate having friends for every day you are alive. Let's examine how a person's choice of friends and the qualities preferred in friends might change during a typical lifespan.

Observations of two-year-olds indicate that these youngsters engage in what is known as *parallel play*. A child may be in the same room with other children, but each is involved in his or her own activity. They do not interact *with* each other. It is not until the ages of three and four that a child develops a sense of cooperative play involving other children in such activities as playing school, playing house, or jumping rope.

If you have ever watched play between four- and eight-year-olds, you might have noticed a certain ease with which they establish relationships with strangers of similar ages. The range of behavior they find acceptable is extensive. As long as children of this age group do not get hit or have sand thrown in their faces, their relationships with other children are satisfactory. Racial background, social class, and level of intelligence generally do not matter in selecting a playmate. Of course, not all children make friends with ease. In a review of childhood friendships, James and Savary speculate on a strong relationship between childrearing behaviors and the child's companions. Children who are "unbefriended" at home may stand around at a playground or at school feeling awkward and excluded, not knowing what to do or say, or how to meet other children. On the other hand, youngsters whose parents spend more time with them are likely to learn how to form friendships and relate to others.

The time between eight and twelve years of age is known as the "chum" period. During these years, children typically select friends of the same sex, and enjoy a variety of activities: playing ball, riding bikes, learning games, and constructing various objects. Psychiatrist Harry Stack Sullivan's studies of children in this age range indicate that if the chum experience is missing, the child may not develop strong heterosexual attachments later.

At puberty, friendship patterns show other changes. For the first time, the emphasis is on opposite-sex friends. This period of adolescence intensifies pressures on the young adults for achievement (a concern of parents and teachers) and for acceptance (the child's concern). The pressures for acceptance in the social group are great, and often the demands for achievement take second place to the need to have friends. You probably can easily recall the parental arguing required to get you to come in the house and do your homework, and not stay out any longer with friends. James and Savary report this account of a fifteen-year-old boy:

You had to have a lot of friends. That was more important than anything else. My mother would say, "Are you going out to play now?" and I'd say, "No, I don't play. I want to be with my friends."

This emphasis on acceptance and friends is further intensified for adolescents who are somewhat shy. The fear of being rejected and not having friends can stay with them throughout adult life. And, although pressure to form relationships exists, there is little explanation of what to do when a relationship does not succeed. So, the shy adolescents are further intimidated when their first attempt doesn't work.

One of the least-studied periods of friendship are those that occur during the senior years of life. Just as in earlier years, friends are still important and serve a useful function to the aged. In a study of people over seventy years old, Zena Blau found that those belonging to friendship cliques were more apt to consider themselves as "middle-aged" than were those without such companions. Research indicates that elderly persons with confidants are better able to cope with the death of a spouse, are more apt to have good morale, and are less vulnerable to mental dysfunctions, such as senility and depression, than those without confidants.

From his observations of members of a senior citizen's center in Washington, D.C., Myron Brenton found that:

. . . some talk to no one, participate in no songfests, no card games, no activities with others. Yet day after day they show up and sit, . . . surrounded by people. They are like young children, who have not yet learned how to relate to other children; they do things by themselves, crocheting, perhaps, or playing solitaire—they are engaged in parallel play. At the Model Cities center a lady of about 75 comes in and follows the same routine everyday: She arrives sometime in midmorning, smiles at everyone, then sits by herself and refuses to say anything to anyone for the rest of the day. About the same time each day, an elderly gentleman shows up, sits down next to

her, and talks to her by the hour. She seems not to hear; he seems not to realize that she does not hear. Something, somehow is going on between them.

Brenton speculates that one reason why people are drawn to retirement communities is the fact that there are always new friends when old friends pass away: "The death of friends does not eliminate the need for friends." Reaching out to another person is a lifelong process.

Sex and Friendship Several studies have looked at friends selected by men and by women. Do men and women differ in their perceptions of friendship and choices of friends? In a survey of college students, Myron Brenton found that men place more value on friends who provide intellectual stimulation than do women. Traits such as honesty, trust, and acceptance were important to both men and women, but were more important to women. He observed that men and women use different techniques for meeting with friends of the same sex. Traditionally, men get together with their male friends to go fishing, play ball or poker, and to have a few drinks. Women get together with their female friends at volunteer organizations, book clubs, craftwork sessions and bridge games. For women, there has been a distinct absence of sports-based social activities. Caldwell and Peplau found that women see friendship as a means for sharing feelings, whereas men determine friends according to similar interests in physical activities.

In 1976, Gerald Phillips and Nancy Metzger published the results of an extensive investigation of friendship. College students completed a lengthy questionnaire called "The Friendship Protocol" which included questions about the subject's closest friend of the same sex, opinions about male-female relationships, and comments about friendship in general. Responses to the questionnaire provided the following differences.

Men tended to agree with these statements:

1. It is easy to make friends.
2. It is possible to size up a friend to see what the friend might provide.
3. Commitment to a friend should be made only when mutuality is proved.
4. If someone hurts you, it is all right to hurt back.
5. Commitment to friends should not interfere with commitment to yourself.

Women tended to agree with these statements:

1. Friendship should be spontaneous.
2. People should talk about the nature of their friendship.
3. Friend-making is a skill that can be learned.
4. I want to understand people.
5. It is possible to be friends with employees or students.

Based on responses to the inventory, Phillips and Metzger concluded that men are more approving of a planned and calculating relationship, whereas women are more concerned with the emotional aspects of the relationship and its spontaneity. Such differences may be the product of the socialization process for men and women. Messages to boys and girls about friends and friendship vary in subtle ways, such as in folktales and children's literature:

Then what a wonderful feast they had! All the boys did Indian dances and learned wild Indian chants, and Peter Pan was made a chief! Only Wendy had no fun at all, for she had to help the squaws carry firewood.

The Prince took Rapunzel to his kingdom where he was received with joy, and they lived long and happily together.

The importance of friendship for men and women, and the value of same-sex friendships is just being realized. Although few studies have gone beyond a philosophical analysis, a nationwide survey of opinions about friendship was recently reported in *Psychology Today*. A number of interesting findings were listed:

1. The qualities most valued in friendship are loyalty, warmth, and the ability to keep confidences. Qualities of less importance are age, income, and occupation.
2. One of the most important reasons for ending a friendship is feeling betrayed by the other person.
3. In a crisis situation, 51 percent of the sample indicated that they would seek the help of a friend before seeking the help of a family member.
4. A third of the respondents (male and female) indicated that they had had sexual relations with a friend during the past month.
5. About 29 percent of the sample indicated that they share a close friendship with a person who is homosexual.

6. About 38 percent indicated that they shared a close friendship with a person from a racial background different from their own.

7. A majority of male and female respondents (67 percent of each) indicated that they were lonely "sometimes" or "often."

8. Reports of what friends do together were remarkably similar for both male and female subjects. "Intimate talks" and "doing favors" were at the top of the list of each sex group, with "eating together in a restaurant," "asking favors," and "going out together"—to a movie, drinking, shopping—also ranking high.

Making Friendships Work Recently, Virginia Kidd published a study called, "Happily Ever After and Other Relationship Styles: Advance on Interpersonal Relations in Popular Magazines, 1951–1973." Her analysis of how magazines present relationship visions suggests two alternatives. First, there is a static vision: "Relationships don't change and people live happily ever after." Second, there is a more realistic vision that emphasizes the dynamic nature of communication. Individuals are constantly changing, and so too are the relationships they share. This second vision implies that we can improve our relationship effectiveness if we understand the transactional nature of the communication process and practice such communication skills as active listening, conflict management, and self-disclosure.

In accordance with Virginia Kidd's categories of relationships, William Wilmot discusses four aspects of his own relationship philosophy and vision. Rather than identify these aspects as "visions," they may be discussed in terms of *social realities*.

1. **Relationships do change.** Change is inevitable and relationships are no exception to the rule. Unfortunately, sometimes we do get stuck in our relationships. We stifle ourselves and others with expectations that each of us remain the same. *We impose the restrictions, and often fight to keep relationships from being redefined.* An extreme case of this can be observed in a parent who continues to treat a forty-six-year-old son as the baby, not as an adult and friend. Consider your own relationships. Do you accept the fact that your relationships will change?

2. **Relationships require attention.** As Wilmot notes, "Participants have to *keep working on their relationships until the day they die.*" He makes another comment: "If we all worked on our relationships as much as we did our jobs, we would have a richer emotional life." Work takes at least forty hours a week of your time. How much time do you devote to developing your close relationships?

3. **Good relationships meet the expectations of the participants.** Your satisfaction with a relationship is a function of how well that relationship meets *your* goals. For example, people get married for a variety of reasons: companionship, status, love, a good sex life, a name, money. So long as the two people sharing that relationship fulfill their expectations, the relationship is satisfying for them. The conflicts arise when the expectations differ and cannot be met with that relationship. *What expectations do you have? What do you want from your relationships?*

4. Relationships can be improved by dealing directly with relational issues. The nature of the relationship and its functions are defined by the people, not by some mystical outside force. Knowing how a relationship forms and how it can change should increase the quality of that relationship. *Rather than hoping problems won't occur and avoiding them when they do arise, do you use your best communication skills to prevent and confront your interpersonal problems?*

Write a few newspaper ads of your own. And then, ask yourself a tough question: Are you the kind of person you would choose for a friend? a lover? a boss? a parent?

WANTED: A good friend. Interested in meeting someone who is patient and loyal, who will keep my secrets and respect my privacy, as I will do for you. Should share many of my interests, especially dancing, occasionally acting foolish, and watching Bogart films. No guarantees, but seeking lasting relationship.

AVAILABLE: A parent who listens. Not a phony. You'll find me to be honest, even when it may hurt, and usually dependable. Right now, I'm practicing my ability to not be threatening and to allow others their separateness. Mixed references, but sincere desire to learn from past mistakes.

WANTED: Teacher who remembers what it was like to be a student: confused, tired, silly, sad, bored, determined. It will help if you take the time to answer our questions, even the "stupid" ones, and to let us explain what we think and how we feel. And, if *you're* tired or angry, or just not ready to work with us, let us know. Give us the chance to understand.

Readings

Altman, Irwin and Dalmas Taylor. *Social Penetration: The Development of Interpersonal Relationships.* New York: Holt, Rinehart, and Winston, 1973.

Bell, Jeff and Aza Hadas. "On Friendship." Paper presented to the WYOTANA Conference, University of Montana, June 1977.

Berscheid, E. and Walster, E. H. *Interpersonal Attraction.* Reading, Mass.: Addison-Wesley, 1969.

Brenton, Myron. *Friendship.* New York: Stein and Day, 1974.

Buley, Jerry L. *Relationships and Communication.* Dubuque: Kendall/Hunt, 1977.

Byrne, Donn. "Attitudes and Attraction." In *Advances in Experimental Social Psychology,* 4, L. Berkowitz, ed., New York: Academic Press, 1969.

Byrne, Donn and Barbara Blaylock. "Similarity and Assumed Similarity of Attitudes between Husbands and Wives." *Journal of Abnormal and Social Psychology,* 67, (1963):636–640.

Caldwell, Mayta Ann and Letitia A. Peplau. "Sex Differences in Friendship." Paper presented to the Western Psychological Association Convention, Seattle, Washington, April 1977.

Gillies, Jerry. *Friends: The Power and Potential of the Company You Keep.* New York: Coward, McCann and Geoghegan, Inc., 1976.

Homans, George C. *Social Behavior: Its Elementary Form.* New York: Harcourt, Brace, 1961.

James, Muriel and Louis M. Savary. *The Heart of Friendship.* New York: Harper and Row, 1976.

Johnson, David W. *Reaching Out: Interpersonal Effectiveness and Self-Actualization.* Englewood Cliffs, N.J.: Prentice-Hall, 1972.

Kidd, Virginia. "Happily Ever After and Other Relationship Styles: Advice on Interpersonal Relations in Popular Magazines, 1951–1973," *Quarterly Journal of Speech,* 61, (1975):31–39.

Knapp, Mark L. *Social Intercourse: From Greeting to Goodbye.* Boston: Allyn and Bacon, 1978.

Levinger, George and James Breedlove. "Interpersonal Attraction and Agreement." *Journal of Personality and Social Psychology,* 3, (1966):367–372.

Parlee, Mary Brown and the editors of *Psychology Today.* "The Friendship Bond: PT's Survey Report on Friendship in America." *Psychology Today,* 13, (October, 1979): 43–45, 49–50, 53–54, 113.

Phillips, Gerald M. and Nancy J. Metzger. *Intimate Communication.* Boston: Allyn and Bacon, 1976.

Pines, Maya. "Invisible Playmates," *Psychology Today,* 12, 38, (1978):41–2, 106.

Rogers, Carl. "The Characteristics of a Helping Relationship." In C. Rogers, *On Becoming a Person.* Boston: Houghton, Mifflin, 1961.

Rubin, Zick. *Liking and Loving.* New York: Holt, Rinehart and Winston, 1973.

Selman, Robert L. and Anne P. Selman. "Children's Ideas about Friendship: A New Theory." *Psychology Today,* 13 (October 1979): 71–72, 74, 79–80, 114.

Sullivan, Harry Stack. *The Interpersonal Theory of Psychiatry.* New York: Norton, 1953.

Swenson, Clifford H. *Introduction to Interpersonal Relations.* Glenview, Ill.: Scott, Foresman and Co., 1973.

Thibaut, John W. and Harold H. Kelley. *The Social Psychology of Groups.* New York: Wiley, 1959.

Villard, Kenneth L. and Leland J. Whipple. *Beginnings in Relational Communication.* New York: Wiley, 1976.

Wilmot, William W. *Dyadic Communication,* 2nd Ed. Reading, Mass.: Addison-Wesley, 1979.

Wright, Paul H. "Toward a Theory of Friendship Based on a Conception of Self," *Human Communication Research, 4,* (1978):196–207.

Communication Climate

7

7 How's the weather where you live?

We're not asking this question as a cliché, or even to be friendly. We want you to think about the effect that meteorological conditions have on your behavior. Take a minute to think about how the weather shapes the way you think, feel, and act. Do you behave differently when it's especially warm or cold? How does the humidity influence your moods? What about the length of daylight? The clarity or pollution of the air?

As we write these words we're sitting within a mile of the Pacific Ocean on a May afternoon. Late spring is the foggiest time of year along the West Coast, and the sky has been grey now for almost three weeks. Everybody knows that the sun will come out in another few weeks, but this doesn't change the mood now. And just like this foggy California spring, warm summers bring about their own feelings, as does briskness of autumn days and the cold, rainy darkness of winter.

What Is Communication Climate?

Just as physical locations have their own meteorological characteristics, interpersonal relationships have unique climates too. You can't measure the interpersonal climate by looking at a thermometer or glancing at the sky, but it's there nonetheless. Think about a relationship in which you're presently involved. How would you describe the climate between you and the other person or people? Fair and warm? Stormy? Cold? Hot? Almost everybody who tries this simple exercise immediately recognizes that their relationships *do* have a feeling, a pervasive mood that colors the goings-on of the participants. And it's this feeling we call a *communication climate*.

Social scientists define communication climates as the social/psychological context in which a relationship functions. The key word in this definition is *context*. A climate doesn't refer so much to specific activities as to the emotional backdrop against which those activities are carried out. For example, as professors we've taught courses in interpersonal communication for several years. During this time, some of our classes have been exciting, friendly ones, while others (thankfully not too many) have been dull, uncomfortable experiences. In other words, the content of the courses has remained basically the same, but the climates have varied.

What creates a positive or negative climate? There are two answers to this question. One concerns the sending behavior of the people involved. As you'll read later in this chapter, there are a number of behaviors likely to create positive, supportive climates and others almost certain to stimulate negative, defensive feelings. You'll see that criticism, secrecy, and indifference, for example, are almost certain to pollute the emotional climate of a relationship.

But climates aren't created solely by senders. Receivers play a strong role by interpreting messages in ways that leave them feeling better or worse about the communication environment. Imagine, for instance, that your boss mentions that he or she wants to see you first thing Monday morning. As you read in Chapter 5, this kind of activating event can lead to at least two interpretations. You might think, "Here comes trouble. I must have done something wrong. I know I've made a few mistakes lately, but I've also worked especially hard. It's not fair!" Needless to say, this self-talk leads to feelings of apprehension and defensiveness, which would probably affect your personal and working behavior and would show up in your meeting. On the other hand, you could interpret the request for a meeting in an entirely different way, thinking, "The boss mentioned last week that some people around here were working much harder than others— probably wants to give me some praise for putting out so much. It's nice to be appreciated!" Again, this interpretation would obviously affect your behavior, in the meeting with your boss as well as with others.

Because communication is a process, the thoughts and actions of senders and receivers affect each other, so that a shared climate begins to evolve. Such situations develop at home when one person becomes quiet. The other might interpret the silence as anger and react by either retreating or becoming defensive. This response in turn is likely to cause the first person to ask, "What's the matter with you?" By this time it's easy to imagine how an uncomfortable climate can evolve from a simple, innocuous event. Of course, positive climates also develop from the interaction of two or more persons. Warmth and supportiveness beget the same behavior in others, and a reciprocal spiral of positive feelings begins to grow as the participants build off each other's behavior.

Characteristics of Positive and Negative Climates

What makes some communication climates positive and others negative? A short but accurate answer is that *communication climate is determined by the degree to which people see themselves as valued.* Communicators who perceive others in a relationship as being concerned about their welfare feel positive, while those who feel unimportant or abused bring negative attitudes to the relationship.

Two researchers in the field of organizational communication, Robert R. Blake and Jane S. Mouton, have created a graphic demonstration of how interpersonal concern operates in a business setting. Their "Managerial Grid" consists of a two-dimensional model (See Fig. 7–1). The horizontal axis describes the manager's concern for *production.* This involves a focus on accomplishing the organizational task, with efficiency being the main concern. The vertical axis measures the manager's concern for *people,* for their feelings and needs.

Blake and Mouton suggest that it is possible to identify a manager's style by plotting his or her behavior on a graph. For example, a 1,1 manager has minimum concern for both production and people. The resultant climate is one of indifference, insensitivity, and inefficiency. A 9,1 style focuses on high concern about getting the job done, while paying little attention to the human needs of the workers. In such cases, the organizational climate is resentful

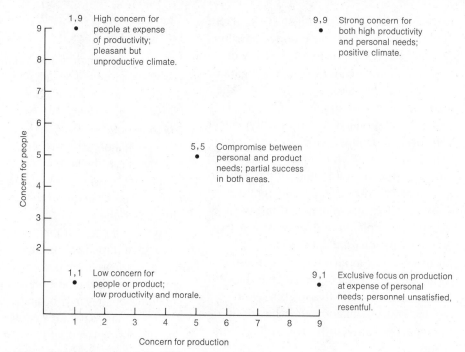

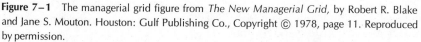

Figure 7–1 The managerial grid figure from *The New Managerial Grid,* by Robert R. Blake and Jane S. Mouton. Houston: Gulf Publishing Co., Copyright © 1978, page 11. Reproduced by permission.

and fearful. By contrast, a 1,9 leader views the needs of the employees as of utmost importance, while disregarding the task of the organization. Although personnel here may feel safe, there is often a lack of respect for managers who don't seem to be doing their jobs successfully.

A 5,5 "middle of the road" manager has a moderate concern with both people and productivity. Managers of this type frequently compromise in search of harmony. As its position on the graph implies, this management style only goes part way in achieving personal and task needs. As such, members of the organization may feel only partially

satisfied with their situation. Finally, the 9,9 manager has a high concern with both the personal concerns of employees and with the mission of the organization. Managers with a 9,9 rating stress cooperative problem solving with their staffs, not only for the sake of good feelings, but also to achieve productive goals. As we might expect, the climate in this sort of organization is generally more positive than in other groups.

This concern for people as well as products determines climate in all situations, not just in organizational settings. If you examine your experiences in school you will almost certainly see that when teachers and students respect each other the climate is positive, and when this interpersonal regard is missing, the mood is one of dissatisfaction. The same principle applies in personal relationships. With both families and friends, the mood at any given time is generally a function of the regard participants hold for each other.

But words like "regard" and "respect" are vague. Exactly what *behaviors* characterize positive and negative climates?

Disconfirming Responses Evelyn Sieburg and Carl Larson outline one set of behaviors that express an uncaring attitude called *disconfirming responses*. A disconfirming response is one in which the speaker ignores some important part of another person's message. This is, of course, a severe blow to the other's self-concept. To be told that an aspect of your self-concept is "wrong"—not in line with reality—at least leaves some room for argument. You can acknowledge the attack on a specific self-perception and talk about it. But a disconfirming response does not attack an aspect of your self-concept, it denies all of it.

Sieburg and Larson discuss seven disconfirming responses, communicative behaviors which indicate to the other person that he or she does not exist.

1. **Impervious response.** This type of message fails to acknowledge the other person's communicative attempt, either verbally or nonverbally. The other person is ignored, disregarded. Children seem to master this behavior early. Almost everyone can remember times—especially as children—when others acted as if we weren't present. At times such as this, we want to shout "Notice me! I'm here, and I have something to say!"

2. **Interrupting response.** This kind of behavior commonly occurs when one person begins to speak before the other is through making a point. Disconfirming interruptions do not include short interjections that acknowledge the other person's immediate remark, such as an, "I understand," or when two people begin at the same time and one stops or defers to the other by saying, "It's okay, I'll talk after you."

3. **Irrelevant response.** This involves comments totally unrelated to what the other person was just saying. An irrelevant response can introduce a new topic (without warning, of course) or return to an earlier conversation without any acknowledgment of what went on since.

4. **Tangential response.** Unlike the three behaviors just discussed, a tangential comment does acknowledge the other person's communication. However, the acknowledgment is used to steer the conversation in another direction. Tangents can come in two forms: (1) The tangential "shift," which is an abrupt change in conversation; and (2) the tangential "drift," which makes a token connection with what the other person is saying, but slowly moves the conversation in another direction entirely.

Consider the following situation: A student rushes up to the teacher at the end of the class to discuss the grade on a recent exam.

Student: *Dr. Jones, I'd like to talk about my grade on the exam.*
Dr. Jones: *Fine. But you'd better hurry along so you're not late for your next class.*

This response is a tangential shift, executed rather adroitly by Jones. An acknowledgment was made of the student's remark ("fine"), and an abrupt change in direction was also made ("hurry along . . ."). Following is an example of a tangential drift (which the professor could have used).

Dr. Jones: *Fine. We'll have to discuss the test. I also used to be concerned with understanding things I got wrong on tests. Of course, I was also concerned with punctuality! You'd better hurry along now so you're not late for the next class.*

In this case, Jones indicated readiness to discuss the examination, but went on to talk about something unrelated. A tangential response, if done well, can keep the other person guessing about how the change in the conversation's direction was accomplished.

5. Impersonal response. In this kind of message the speaker conducts a monologue filled with impersonal, intellectualized, and generalized statements. The speaker never really interacts with the other on a personal level.

Employee: *I've been having some personal problems lately and I'd like to take off early a couple of afternoons to clear them up.*
Boss: *Ah, yes. We all have personal problems. It seems to be a sign of the times.*

6. Ambiguous response. This communication contains a message with more than one meaning. The words are highly abstract or have meanings private to the speaker alone.

A: *I'd like to get together with you soon. How about Tuesday?*
B: *Uh, maybe so. Anyhow, see you later.*
A: *How can I be sure you mean it?*
B: *Who knows what they mean?*

7. Incongruous response. An incongruous response is one containing two messages that seem to deny or contradict each other, one at the verbal level and the other at the nonverbal level.

He: *Darling, I love you!*
She: *I love you too. (giggles)*

Teacher: *Did you enjoy the class?*
Student: *Yes. (yawns).*

Attacking and Supportive Behaviors

Nothing creates a poor communication climate more than defensiveness. In an attempt to explore the causes of defensiveness, Jack Gibb spent eight years observing groups and noting what behaviors seemed to provoke defensive reactions. He found six types of behaviors that have a strong likelihood of being perceived as attacks, thus polluting the communication climate. By contrast, he also discovered six contrasting behaviors that seemed to reduce the level of threat and defensiveness, thereby improving the interpersonal climate. He classified these latter ways of responding as *supportive behaviors*.

In the next few sections we will discuss six pairs of contrasting behaviors that Gibb developed. Each set describes the way people act to cause defensiveness, and the behavior that tends to reduce it. As you read, keep two points in mind: First, none of the following behaviors will bring on defensive reactions unless the receiver perceives them as threatening. Insecure receivers may be threatened by almost anything that's said to them, but more secure people are much less easily threatened. You probably know people who seem to take everything in stride. Would you say they tend to be rather secure individuals? Second, even though we're talking about these behaviors as if they were distinct from one another, in actuality you may run into them in various combinations. The six-part division is made for clarity, but don't be misled by it.

1. Evaluation vs. description. The first type of defense-provoking behavior Gibb noted was *evaluation*. Most people become irritated at judgmental statements, which they are likely to interpret as indicating a lack of regard. Evaluative language has often been described as "you" language, since most such statements contain an accusatory use of that word. For example:

You don't know what you're talking about.
You're not doing your best.
You smoke too much.

The Gibb Categories of Defensive and Supportive Behaviors

Defensive Behaviors	Supportive Behaviors
1 Evaluation	1 Description
2 Control	2 Problem orientation
3 Strategy	3 Spontaneity
4 Neutrality	4 Empathy
5 Superiority	5 Equality
6 Certainty	6 Provisionalism

Not all evaluative statements provoke defensiveness. Positive judgments, although judgmental, are usually received warmly, and even some criticisms have no negative impact on the interpersonal climate. We'll explain the reason for this apparent disparity between theory and practice shortly. But for now, we can clarify Gibb's formulation by stating that evaluations with which the receiver disagrees almost always arouse defensiveness.

In contrast to evaluative "you" language is what Gibb calls *descriptive* communication, or "I" language. Instead of putting the emphasis on judging another's behavior, the descriptive speaker simply explains the personal effect of the other's action. For instance, instead of saying, "'you talk too much," a descriptive communicator would say, "When you don't give me a chance to say what's on my mind, I get frustrated." Notice that statements such as this include an account of the other person's behavior, plus an explanation of their effects on the speaker and a description of the speaker's feelings.

2. **Control vs. problem orientation.** A second defense-provoking message involves some attempt to *control* another. This controlling occurs when a sender seems to be imposing a solution on the receiver with little regard for the receiver's needs or interests. The object of controls can range from where to eat dinner or what TV show to watch all the way to whether to remain in a relationship or how to spend a large sum of money. Whatever the situation, people who act in controlling ways create a defensive climate. None of us likes to feel that our ideas are worthless, and that nothing we say will change other people's determination to have their way—yet this is precisely the attitude a controller communicates. Whether done with words, gestures, tone of voice, or through some other channel; whether control is accomplished through status, insistence on obscure or irrelevant rules, or physical power, the controller generates hostility wherever he or she goes. The unspoken message controller behavior communicates is, "I know what's best for you, and if you do as I say we'll get along."

By contrast, *problem-oriented* communicators focus on finding a solution that satisfies both their needs and those of the others involved. The goal here isn't to "win" at the expense of your partner, but to work out some arrangement in which everybody feels like a winner. (Chapter 11 has a great deal to say about "no-lose" problem solving as a way to find problem-oriented solutions.)

3. **Strategy vs. spontaneity.** The third communication behavior that Gibb identified as creating a poor communication climate involves the use of *strategy* or manipulation. One of the surest ways to make people defensive is to get caught trying to manipulate them into doing something for you. The fact that you tried to trick them instead of just asking for what you wanted is enough to build mistrust. Nobody likes to be a guinea pig or a sucker, and even well-meant manipulation can cause bad feelings.

A teenager reported that her dad was tricky. It seems that whenever the father wanted to criticize the young woman he'd always say something nice first, and then somewhere along the way let the axe fall. "He would then conclude with another positive remark. This strategem has been referred to as the "psychological sandwich," two pieces of praise with criticism between.

It didn't take too many repeats of this strategy before the daughter cringed every time she heard praise from her father because she learned it was only given to soften criticism. Probably it would have been better for the relationship if the daughter had received honest praise or honest criticism rather than a strategy that seemed a dishonest mixture of both.

Another person had an irritating strategy for getting favors. He would call a friend's house and chat for about fifteen minutes then say goodbye. About three days later,

he'd call again with about five minutes of chit-chat followed by a request. If the favor were a really big one, it was preceded by two fifteen-minute calls consisting of only chit-chat. After the favor was done, it could be weeks or months before there was another call and the pattern repeated itself.

Spontaneity is the behavior that contrasts with strategy. Spontaneity simply means being honest, reporting what you're feeling right now rather than planning your words to get the best response. Often spontaneity won't get what you want, but in the long run it's usually better to be candid and perhaps miss out on some small goal than to say all the right things and become a fraud. More than once we've heard people say, "I didn't like what he said, but at least I know he was being honest."

Although it sounds paradoxical at first, spontaneity can be a strategy too. Sometimes you'll see people using honesty in a calculating way, being just frank enough to win someone's trust or sympathy. This "leveling" is probably the most defense-arousing strategy of all because once we've learned someone is using frankness as a manipulation there's almost no chance we'll ever trust that person again.

You may be getting the idea that using supportive behaviors such as description, problem orientation, empathy, and so on, is a great way to manipulate others. Before going any further we want to say loudly and clearly that if you ever act supportively without being sincere in what you're saying, you've misunderstood the idea behind this chapter, and you're running a risk of causing even more defensiveness than before. None of the ideas we present in this book can go into a "bag of tricks" that can be used to control others: If you ever find yourself using them this way, beware!

4. Neutrality vs empathy. Gibb used the term *neutrality* to describe a fourth behavior that arouses defensiveness. Probably a better descriptive word would be *indifference*. Acting with a neutral attitude communicates a lack of concern for the welfare of another, and implies that the other person isn't very important to you. This perceived indifference is likely to promote defensiveness because people do not like to think of themselves as worthless, and they'll protect a self-concept that pictures themselves as worthwhile.

The small child who has urgent things to tell a parent but is met with indifference may be expected to become upset. The physician who seems clinical and detached to his patients may wonder why they look for another doctor.

The poor effects of neutrality become apparent when you consider the hostility that most people have for the large, impersonal organizations with which they have to deal: "They think of me as a number instead of a person."; "I felt as if I was being handled by computers and not human beings." These are two common statements that reflect feelings of being handled in an indifferent way.

Gibb has found that *empathy* helps rid communication of the quality of indifference. When people show that they care for the feelings of another there's little chance that a self-concept will be threatened. Empathy means accepting another's feelings, putting yourself in another's place. This doesn't mean you need to agree with that person. By simply letting someone know about your care and respect, you'll be acting in a supportive way.

Gibb noted the importance of nonverbal messages in communicating empathy. He found that facial and bodily expressions of concern are often more important to the receiver than the words used.

5. Superiority vs. equality. A fifth behavior creating a defensive climate involves *superiority*. How many interpersonal relationships have you dropped because you couldn't stand the superiority that the other person projected? Like the other behaviors we've talked about, an individual who communicates superiority arouses feelings of inadequacy in the recipients. We're not particular as to the type of superiority presented to us; we just become defensive. Money, power, intellectual ability, physical appearance, and athletic prowess are all areas our culture stresses. Consequently, we often feel a need to express our superiority along these lines.

The individual who acts superior communicates that he or she doesn't want to relate on equal terms with others in the relationship. Furthermore, people like this seem to imply that they don't want feedback nor need help because that feedback or help would be coming from someone "inferior." This message of superiority alerts the listener to be on guard because the sender is likely to attempt to reduce the receiver's worth, power, or status to maintain or advance self superiority.

Perhaps you've had professors who continually reminded students of their superior intellectual ability and position. Remember how delighted you were when you or a classmate caught one of these superior types making a mistake? Why do you suppose that was so satisfying? Some might argue that this is a good strategy to keep students awake, but in reality much of students effort is directed to defending self-worth rather than pursuing the objectives of the course.

The worst sin towards our fellow creatures is not to hate them, but to be indifferent to them; that's the essence of inhumanity.

George Bernard Shaw

When we detect people communicating superiority we usually react defensively. We "turn them off," justify ourselves, or argue with them in our minds. Sometimes we choose to change the subject verbally or even walk away. Of course there is always the counterattack, which includes an attempt to belittle the senders of the superiority message. We'll go to great lengths "to cut them down to size." All these defensive reactions to projected superiority are destructive to an interpersonal climate.

Many times in our lives we are in a relationship with individuals who possess talents greater than ours. But is it necessary for these people to project superiority? Your own experiences will tell you that it isn't.

Gibb has found ample evidence that many who possess superior skills and talents are capable of projecting feelings of *equality* rather than superiority. Such people communicate that although they may have greater talent in certain areas, they see others as having just as much worth as human beings.

6. Certainty vs. provisionalism. Have you ever run into people who are positive they're right, who know that theirs is the only or proper way of doing something, who insist that they have all the facts and need no additional information? If you have, you've met individuals who project the defense-arousing behavior Gibb calls *certainty*.

How do you react when you're the target of such certainty? Do you suddenly find your energy directed to proving the dogmatic individual wrong? If you do, you're reacting normally, if not very constructively.

The need to be right—the sign of a vulgar mind.

Albert Camus

Communicators who regard their own opinions with certainty while disregarding the ideas of others demonstrate a rather clear lack of regard for the thoughts others hold to be important. As such, it's likely that the receiver will take the certainty as a personal affront, and react defensively.

In contrast to dogmatic communicators are those *provisional* people who may have strong opinions but who are willing to acknowledge that they don't have a corner on the truth, and who will change their stand if another position seems more reasonable.

An Anatomy of Defensiveness

What Is Defensiveness? The word "defensiveness" suggests defending or protecting one's self from attack, but what kind of attack? Surely, very few if any of the times you become defensive involve a threat to your physical safety; so if you're not threatened by bodily injury, what can it be that you *are* guarding against? To answer this question we need to talk more about the notion of the self-concept.

You'll recall that the self-concept consists of perceptions of self, including physical characteristics, personality traits, strengths and weaknesses, and a large number of other characteristics and beliefs you see yourself as possessing. As we mentioned earlier, this self-concept is nothing less than the sum of your personal identity, and as such it is extremely important. Of course, not all parts of your self-concept are equally significant to you. For example, the fact that you consider yourself a resident of a particular state is probably less important than your identity as a female or male or the kind of friend you are.

Imagine what might happen if someone attacked a part of your self-concept that was of particular value to you. Suppose, for instance, that:

1. An instructor labeled you as an idiot when you regard yourself as reasonably bright.

2. An acquaintance accused you of being snobbish when you believe you are friendly.

3. An employer called you lazy, when you see yourself as a hard worker.

What are your choices in such situations? One alternative would be to accept the new information and change your self-concept accordingly, relabeling yourself as stupid, snobbish, or lazy. On the other hand, given the human tendency to perpetuate an existing self-concept, a more likely reaction would be to discount the critical information in some way in order to maintain the old picture of yourself. You might do so by ignoring this dissonant information (pretending you didn't hear it, forgetting it, avoiding the critic, and so on), or by disputing it (offering evidence to the contrary or counterattacking the critic). In any case, the main point here is that we often act to protect a threatened self-concept.

So far, then, we've said that people become defensive when they perceive others attacking their self-concepts. While this statement explains much defensive behavior, it doesn't account for every case. Frequently, others offer an evaluation that coincides with your self-concept, and yet you *still* become defensive. For example, consider the many times you failed to meet obligations, so that, at the last moment, you had to rush to get the job done. Certainly, like most people, you would probably admit to including the word *procrastinator* in your self-concept. When confronted with this failure to meet deadlines, however, you might not willingly admit this habit of stalling, making instead all sorts of excuses to justify your tardiness. In the same way

there are probably other parts of your self-concept that you might not readily own up to when others point them out— perhaps the telling of an occasional lie, a periodic streak of unreasonableness, or tendencies toward selfishness.

To understand what's going on here we need to recognize the existence of two selves in every person: one public and the other private. The public self is the face shown to the world; the private self is one seen in moments of self-honesty. These two selves are similar. For instance, you might see yourself as a perfectionist or a person who dislikes opera and be perfectly willing to express these attitudes publicly. On the other hand, there are some cases in which the face displayed to the world is quite different from the one seen when you stare at yourself in the mirror. Perhaps you sometimes feel insecure but try to act confidently. Maybe you find yourself feeling angry when you want to appear calm and happy. Or perhaps you sometimes feel stupid but try to appear bright in the eyes of others.

The image presented to the world—the public self—is something most of us believe is necessary in order to survive. We tend to think that if we present the private self we would look foolish, or possibly be offensive, or we think that others would find out something about us which we prefer to keep hidden, something about which we are embarrassed or ashamed. From the time most of us are quite young we're taught that certain kinds of behavior are the only way to gain acceptance. In such environments perfection is the model: One should always act in a pleasant manner, be reasonable, selfless, and kind. This stress on perfection is carried on in most forms of entertainment, where the models are characters who are always self-assured, knowledgeable, and socially talented. The message here is that the kind of person who gains the approval of others is *perfect*. Of course, privately each of us knows that we're not perfect, so we are faced with the choices of sharing our private self and risking rejection or putting on a public mask and gaining what we think will be social rewards.

John Powell speaks to the problem of fear and defensiveness with a question that also serves as the title to his book *Why Am I Afraid to Tell You Who I Am?* One of the answers he recorded from an actual conversation says ". . . if I tell you who I am, you may not like who I am, and it is all that I have." So one reason we wear masks is to show the world an acceptable public or "ideal" self, trying to be the kind of person others think we should be instead of the person we truly are.

With this explanation it becomes easy to see why, at times, we get defensive when a critic makes an evaluation that does match our private image: The concept that we

most strongly defend is our public one. Thus, we can finally say that *defensiveness is the attempt to protect a public image that we perceive is being attacked.*

Defense Mechanisms   Now you recognize that defensiveness occurs when you try to protect a public (usually ideal) image that you perceive to be under attack. Before going any further it's important to point out that there's usually an element of self-deception in such mask-wearing. Much of the time we're misrepresenting ourselves to others, we also want desperately to believe the act we're putting on. It's unpleasant to admit that you're not the person you'd like to be (even if your ideal image is totally unrealistic). Faced with a situation where the truth might hurt, it's tempting to convince yourself that you do fit the superhuman image you've constructed for others.

How do we manage these attempts at deception? In the following pages you'll find a number of devices, generally called *defense mechanisms,* that enable people to avoid admitting an unpleasant part of the self-concept to themselves and others. Just as the two methods of protecting yourself from physical attack are to flee or to fight, the mechanisms for defensive communication fall into the two categories of avoidance and attack. In general, each defense mechanism defines a particular way in which individuals *distort* reality so that their world will look the way they want it to be. The fact that these mechanisms become habits we perform unconsciously makes them difficult to recognize, especially in ourselves. Consequently, we don't recognize that we're distorting the reality that makes up our

lives, and our communication with others suffers because we're not allowing ourselves to be aware of what's actually happening.

We don't want to suggest that defense mechanisms are always undesirable. There are times when these techniques of protecting your private self are desirable, particularly when such disclosure would be treated cruelly by others. Also, confronting too many unpleasant truths or perceptions of one's self too quickly can be unmanageable, and thus these mechanisms serve as a safety valve for handling the process of self-discovery at a safe rate. However, your own experience will show that, most often, acting in the following defensive ways can damage your relationships with others. We therefore believe that acquainting you with some of the most common defense mechanisms—with the hope of reducing them in your life—is a valuable step in helping you become a better communicator.

Rationalization   One of the most common ways of avoiding a threat to our self-concept is to *rationalize;* that is, to think up a logical but untrue explanation that protects the unrealistic picture we hold of ourselves.

Have you ever justified cheating in school by saying the information you were tested on wasn't important anyway or that everybody cheats a little? Were those your real reasons, or just excuses? Have you ever shrugged off hurting people's feelings by saying they'll soon forget what you've done? In cases like these it's often tempting to explain behavior you feel guilty about by justifying it in terms that fit your self-concept.

Compensation   This is another technique people use for avoiding what they think is a personal shortcoming. Rather than face a problem head on, compensators stress a strength in some other area of their personality, hoping that it will camouflage what they feel is their fault.

A good example of compensation is the man whose home life is unhappy but refuses to do anything about it; instead, he puts all his energy into becoming successful in his business. Another example, is the woman who can't make friends with other women and compensates by attracting as many boyfriends as she can, rather than working on the real problem.

There are many instances when people try to compensate for the lack of good interpersonal relationships with material things. Parents in broken families may attempt to replace their missing relationships with their children by loading them up with toys, sporting equipment, clothes, and so on. This solution is hardly helpful to either the child or parent.

Reaction formation   People who use reaction formation as a defense mechanism are avoiding facing a problem by acting in a way that is an exaggerated opposite of how they truly feel. For example, have you ever known somebody who acts like the life of the party, always laughing and making jokes? In reality this person may be unhappy, but covers this feeling by acting just the opposite.

A classic example of the reaction formation is the "Don Juan," a person who is insecure about being attractive to members of the opposite sex. Don Juans hide this feeling by collecting as many dates and sexual conquests as possible.

Projection   In projection you avoid an unpleasant part of yourself by disowning that part and attributing it to others. For instance, on the days when as instructors we aren't as prepared for class as we might be, it's tempting to claim that the hour hasn't gone well because the students didn't do *their* homework. Similarly, you may have found yourself accusing others of being dishonest, lazy, or inconsiderate when in fact such descriptions fit your behavior quite well. In all of these cases we project an unpleasant trait of our own onto another, and in so doing we avoid facing it in ourselves. It doesn't matter whether the accusation you make about others is true or not: In projection the important point is that you are escaping from having to face the truth about yourself.

The mechanism of projection explains the common experience of taking an instant dislike to someone you've just met and realizing later that the traits you found so distasteful in that person are precisely those you dislike in yourself. By criticizing the new acquaintance you can put the undesirable characteristic "out there," and not have to admit it belongs to you.

A surefire test to determine whether you are using projection to fool yourself is to take every attack you make on others and substitute "I" for the words you use to identify the other person. For example, "He talks too much" becomes "I talk too much," or "They're being unfair" is instead

"I'm being unfair." When you try this simple experiment and your accusation of another seems to be true of you, you are projecting.

Identification   Sometimes when we're unsure or don't like ourselves, we hide our feelings by imitating someone we admire. The problem with identification of this sort is that it's artificial. We get so involved in "being like" another person that we can't respond to a situation genuinely; instead, we react as we think our "hero" would, often denying our own feelings in the process. Thus, when we use the mechanism of identification, our life becomes an act.

Many families only relate to each other in artificial ways. Without being conscious of it they pick up a mental picture of the "ideal, trouble-free family" from TV shows. Then when real problems occur—as they're bound to do—nobody is willing to admit it for fear that something is wrong with them. Instead, everyone goes on acting a role, while the problem usually grows because of neglect.

Fantasy   When our desires or ambitions are frustrated, we often resort to a fantasy world to satisfy them. We daydream ourselves out of our "real" world into one that is more satisfying. A good example of this is the young career woman who finds herself bored with her dull life as a typist. To insulate herself from this unbearable existence she escapes into the excitement of her own fantasies. She becomes the leading lady in the romance magazine stories, the television dramas, and the movies she frequents. No matter how exciting and glamorous these fantasies are,

they're not connected to the problem of her reality and therefore can't help her make changes to improve her life.

There is much to be said for the short daydream that lifts the boredom of an unpleasant task, or the fantasies that can be creative tools to help us think up new solutions to problems. But as with all defense mechanisms, the danger of fantasizing is that it keeps us from dealing squarely with what's bothering us by providing a temporary escape which doesn't really solve the problem.

It is in the ability to deceive oneself that the greatest talent is shown.

Anatole France

Repression   Sometimes rather than facing up to an unpleasant situation and trying to deal with it, we protect ourselves by denying its existence. Quite simply, we "forget" what would otherwise be painful. Take a couple, for example, who can't seem to agree about how to handle their finances. One partner thinks that money is meant to be spent, while the other believes that it's important to save for the future. Rather than working to solve this important problem, the husband and wife pretend nothing is wrong. This charade may work for a while, but as time goes by each partner will probably begin to feel more and more uncomfortable and will likely begin to build up resentments about the way the other one uses their common money. Eventually these resentments are almost sure to leak into other areas of the marriage.

In the same way, we've seen families with serious problems—an alcoholic parent, a teenager into drugs, a conflict between members—try to pretend that everything is perfectly all right, as if acting that way will make it so. Of course, it's unlikely that they'll solve these problems without admitting that they exist.

Dependency or regression   Sometimes rather than admit *we don't want* to do something, we convince ourselves that we *can't* do it. We resort to behavior that is more characteristic of an earlier age, an age when we were more helpless. This behavior is known as *regression* or *dependency*.

The person who says, "Gee, I'd really like to have a relationship with you, but I'm not ready" might really be hiding the truth: that he or she simply doesn't care enough about the relationship to make it grow. The pitiful soul who says, "I'd really like to improve my life, but I can't" could be hiding from the fact that he or she isn't willing to put in the work necessary to change the present situation.

Emotional insulation and apathy   Often, rather than face an unpleasant situation, people will avoid hurt by not getting involved or pretending they don't care. Probably the most common example of *emotional insulation* is the person who develops a strong attachment to someone

only to have the relationship break up. The pain is so great that the sufferer refuses to become involved like this again. At other times people who are hurt in this way defend their feeling of self-worth by becoming *apathetic,* by saying they don't care about whoever hurt them.

The sad thing about emotional insulation and apathy is that they prevent the person who uses them from doing anything about dealing with the cause of the defensiveness. As long as I say I don't care about dating when I really do, I can't go out with anyone because this would be inconsistent with my artificial self-concept. As long as I don't admit that I care about you, our relationship has little chance of growing.

Displacement   This occurs when we vent aggressive or hostile feelings against people or objects that are seen as less dangerous than the person or persons who caused the feelings originally. Children who are reminded that they have to clean up their rooms before they can play may get rid of some of their hostility by slamming the door or beating up a younger brother or sister. They know it might cause more pain if they expressed this hostility against their parents.

A clerk gets angry because the boss puts on some pressure. Not wanting to risk getting fired, the clerk takes it out on family or friends.

Have you ever had the experience of being in a bad mood or feeling mean? Have you noticed how difficult it seems to get along with others during these times? Chances are something has happened that hasn't been to your liking, and the feelings generated by that "something" are being displaced upon whomever comes along.

Undoing   In undoing we make up for an act that doesn't fit with our ideal self-concept by offering a symbolic token of apology, usually to the person we've hurt. For example, a young man who is constantly late picking up his date may bring her gifts to show that he's not so bad after all. Parents who punish their child and then feel guilty may be "extra" nice to the child for a while to raise their own self-esteem.

We should point out that symbolic gestures that really *do* signal a change in behavior aren't undoing. But these gestures become defense mechanisms when we use them to fool ourselves into thinking we've turned over a new leaf when we really haven't.

Verbal aggression   Sometimes, when we can get away with it, the easiest way to avoid facing criticism is to drown it out. Verbal aggression illustrates the old saying, "The best defense is a good offense." Counterattacking somebody who threatens our self-concept tends to relieve tension and helps the defensive person feel better because fireworks probably cover up whatever it was in the original remark that was threatening.

A good example of verbal aggression is the "so are you" defensive maneuver. When people say something we feel is too critical, we counterattack by telling them all their faults. Our remarks may be true, but they don't answer the criticism and only wind up making people more defensive. Temper tantrums, hitting below the belt, and bringing up past grievances are some other types of verbal aggression.

> **Most of our faults are more pardonable than the means we use to conceal them.**
>
> Francois de la Rochefoucauld

Now that you've had a look at several ways people defend an unrealistic self-concept, we hope you'll be able to detect the role defense mechanisms play in your life. We want to repeat that these mechanisms aren't usually destructive unless they're practiced to the point where an individual's view of reality becomes distorted. We also hope that you don't instantly become a self-appointed psychiatrist, analyzing the defense mechanisms in others. Rarely will you find an individual's behavior so transparent and uncomplicated that it can be diagnosed from casual observation. What appears on the surface as a defense mechanism in operation may be authentic, honest behavior. Our hope is that you can look at *yourself* with a little more knowledge of how you operate when you detect a threat to your self-concept.

Finally, you'll find defensive mechanisms don't usually appear as simple, clear-cut behaviors. We usually use them in combination because it's only natural to protect one's self in as many ways as possible.

Creating Positive Communication Climates

If you weren't already convinced, the last few pages should have clearly demonstrated the unpleasant consequences of a negative communication climate, both for the defensive sender and everyone else. The question then becomes how to avoid this type of destructive communication and instead how to develop feelings of supportiveness.

Initiating and Maintaining a Positive Climate   Your best chances for having a supportive relationship occur either when a relationship is just beginning or when it has a positive history. In either of these cases there's no backlog of hostility or defensiveness to overcome. But even in the absence of any negative factors, a relationship needs certain stimuli to remain healthy and grow stronger. Here are several important ones:

Trust   Two types of trust contribute to a supportive atmosphere. The first is *task-related*. Your relationship will grow if others know they can depend on you to carry out your share of whatever tasks you work on together. In a personal relationship this can involve small but important jobs such as doing the dishes when it's your turn or arriving at meeting places on time. In school or work-related settings, you can develop task-related trust by carrying out your part of a job without requiring others to check up on you.

The second type of trust, *interpersonal* trust, is another strong element of a positive climate. We value people on whom we can depend—to keep a secret, to support us when we're feeling down, and to defend us against the unfair attacks of others.

Honesty   This trait is so fundamental to positive relationships that it needs little amplification here. It's sufficient to remind you about the effects of another person's dishonesty on your relationship, and to point out that one of the most valued parts of your strong relationships has probably been the truthfulness of the person. Of course, we're not talking about the kind of brutal honesty that can be used as a weapon to hurt someone; but rather a supportive candor by which another person expresses the idea that you are important enough to know the truth.

Participative decision making   This technical-sounding term comes from a study of organizational communication, where it is used to describe a management style in which leaders involve their subordinates' help in deciding issues that affect their own welfare. In his survey *Communication within the Organization,* W. Charles Redding explains that in most cases participative decision making contributes strongly to a positive communication climate. Employees whose managers consult them feel important and valued and develop much stronger positive feelings about the organization.

This same principle holds true in interpersonal relationships. As Gibb pointed out in describing problem orientation, supportive climates develop when you

work *with* others to find mutually satisfying solutions to problems instead of *against* them as if you were adversaries.

Concern for the other's welfare   Relationships grow when people care about each other, and they wither away with a lack of concern. There are two elements comprising personal concern. The first is *empathy* (discussed on p. 168). We know that communication climate is a function of interpersonal regard, and the ability to recognize how another feels is one way of showing that regard. Beyond the important element of caring about another is a second dimension of interpersonal concern: *the taking of an active role in improving another's welfare.* Your personal experience should prove that the climate improves when others do favors for you, such as helping you to find a job or to do better in school, lending you help in completing a task, arranging for you to meet new people, and so on. However you show concern, you can improve the climate of your relationships by helping others.

Validating the other's assets   While all of the above categories imply valuing the other person, explicitly affirming the ways in which you appreciate another person will give a strong lift to the climate of your relationship. It's often a sad fact that we begin to take the good qualities of others for granted while continuing to mention their shortcomings. Besides seeming to be intrinsically wrong, this kind of behavior has undesirable consequences. As psy-

chologist B. F. Skinner and other behaviorists have clearly demonstrated, positive reinforcement leads to increased frequency of a behavior, while ignoring that behavior leads to its extinction. The effects of this principle in interpersonal relationships can be profound. The simple statement "I appreciate you," whether for looking attractive, offering help, being good natured, or any other valued behavior, is one of the surest ways to keep that behavior coming.

To test the validity of this principle, try a simple experiment. Take a moment now and write a brief, sincere note to somebody you care about. Tell him or her what it is you appreciate. When the time seems right, deliver the message and notice the positive effect on the communication climate. Having observed the results, ask yourself why you waited so long to do such a simple and yet significant act.

Transforming Negative Climates: Coping with Criticism   In the last few pages we've talked about how to build a positive communication climate at the beginning of a relationship and how to keep a positive climate going once it's started. But what about cases in which negative feelings exist? Changing the climate in these cases is like slowing down a runaway horse: You have to stop the animal before you can begin to move toward your destination.

One of the biggest barriers to overcoming poor climates is the torrent of negative criticism characterizing so many of them. Because the problem of handling criticism is so difficult and important, we'll devote the rest of this chapter to it. When you're finished reading, you should have acquired

some workable skills to help you in these difficult cases.

In order to handle criticism constructively you need to have available honest, nonmanipulative ways of dealing with criticism without feeling the need to justify yourself or to counterattack. There are two such methods, each of which at first appears to be almost childishly simple, yet in practice has proved over and over to be among the most valuable assertive skills many communicators have learned.

When Criticized, Seek More Information
This response makes good sense when you realize that it's foolish to respond to a critical attack until you understand what the other person has said. Even comments that upon first consideration appear to be totally unjustified or foolish often prove to contain at least a grain of truth, and sometimes much more.

Many readers object to the idea of asking for details when they are criticized. Their resistance grows from confusing the act of *listening open-mindedly* to a speaker's comments with *accepting* them. Once you realize that you can listen to, understand, and even acknowledge the most hostile comments without necessarily accepting them, it becomes much easier to hear another person out. If you disagree with a speaker's objections, you will be in a much

> **Love your enemies, for they tell you your faults.**
>
> Benjamin Franklin

better position to explain yourself once you understand the critic. On the other hand, after carefully listening to the other's remarks, you might just see that they are valid, in which case you have learned some valuable information about yourself. In either case you have everything to gain and nothing to lose by hearing the critic out.

Of course, after years of instinctively resisting criticism, this habit of hearing the other person out will take some practice. To make matters more clear, here are several ways in which you can seek additional information from your critics.

Ask for specifics Often the vague attack of a critic is practically useless, even if you sincerely want to change. Abstract accusations such as, "You're being unfair" or "You never help out" can be difficult to understand. In such cases it is a good idea to request more specific information from the sender. "What do I *do* that's unfair?" is an important question to ask before you can judge whether the accusation is correct. "When haven't I helped out?" you might ask prior to agreeing with or disputing the accusation.

If you already solicit specifics by using questions and are still accused of reacting defensively the problem may be in the *way* you ask. Your tone of voice and facial expression, posture, or other nonverbal clues can give the same words radically different connotations. For example, think of how you could use the words, "Exactly what are you talking about?" to communicate either a genuine desire to know or your belief that the speaker is crazy. It's important to request specific information only when you genuinely want to learn more from the speaker, for asking under any other circumstances will only make matters worse.

Guess about specifics On some occasions even your sincere and well-phrased requests for specific details of another's criticism won't meet with success. Sometimes your critics won't be able to define precisely the behavior they find offensive. In these instances you'll hear such comments as, "I can't tell you exactly what's wrong with your sense of humor— all I can say is that I don't like it." In other cases your critics may know the exact behaviors they don't like but for some reason they seem to get a perverse satisfaction out of making you struggle to figure it out. At times like this you hear such comments as, "Well, if you don't know what you did to hurt my feelings, I'm certainly not going to tell you!"

Needless to say, failing to learn the details of another's criticism when you genuinely want to know them can be a frustrating experience. In instances like these you can often learn more clearly what is bothering your critic by *guessing* at the specifics of a complaint. In a sense you become both detective and suspect, with the goal being to figure out exactly what "crime" you have committed. Like the technique of asking for specifics, guessing must be done with goodwill if it's to produce satisfying results. You need to convey to the critic that for both of your sakes you're truly interested in finding out what is the matter. Once you have communicated this intention, the emotional climate generally becomes more comfortable, since in effect both you and the critic are seeking the same goal.

Here are some typical questions you might hear from someone guessing about the details of another's criticism:

1. "So you object to the language I used in writing the paper. Was my language too formal?"
2. "O.K. I understand that you think the outfit looks funny. What is it that's so bad? Is it the color? Does it have something to do with the fit? The fabric?"
3. "When you say that I'm not doing my share around the house, do you mean that I haven't been helping enough with the cleaning?"

Paraphrase the speaker's ideas Another strategy for learning more about criticism is to draw out confused or reluctant speakers by paraphrasing their thoughts and feelings. You'll learn more about this technique when we discuss active listening in Chapter 8. You'll see that paraphrasing is especially good at helping others solve their problems; and since people generally criticize you because your behavior creates some problem for them, the method is especially appropriate for such times.

One advantage of paraphrasing is that you don't have to come up with any guesses about the specifics of your behavior that might be offensive. By clarifying or amplifying what you understand critics to

be saying, you'll learn more about their objections. A brief dialogue between a disgruntled customer and an especially talented store manager using paraphrasing might sound like this:

Customer: *The way you people run this store is disgusting! I just want to tell you that I'll never shop here again.*
Manager: (reflecting the customer's feeling) *It seems that you're quite upset. Can you tell me your problem?*
Customer: *It isn't my problem, it's the problem your salespeople have. They seem to think it's a great inconvenience to help a customer find anything around here.*
Manager: *So you didn't get enough help locating the items you were looking for, is that it?*
Customer: *Help!? I spent twenty minutes looking around in here before I even talked to a clerk. All I can say is that it's a hell of a way to run a store.*
Manager: *So what you're saying is that the clerks seemed to be ignoring the customers?*
Customer: *No. They were all busy with other people. It just seems to me that you ought to have enough help around to handle the crowds that come in at this hour.*
Manager: *I understand now. What frustrated you the most was the fact that we didn't have enough staff to serve you promptly.*

Customer: *That's right. I have no complaint with the service I get once I'm waited on, and I've always thought you had a good selection here. It's just that I'm too busy to wait so long for help.*

Manager: *Well, I'm glad you brought this to my attention. We certainly don't want loyal customers going away mad. I'll try to see that it doesn't happen again.*

This conversation illustrates two advantages of paraphrasing. First, the critic often reduces the intensity of the attack once it is realized that the complaint is being heard. Often criticism grows from the frustration of unmet needs—which in this case was partly a lack of attention. As soon as the manager genuinely demonstrated interest in the customer's plight, the customer began to feel better, and was able to leave the store relatively calm. Of course this sort of active listening won't always mollify your critic, but even when it doesn't, there's still another benefit that makes the technique worthwhile. In the sample conversation, for instance, the manager learned some valuable information by taking time to understand the customer. The manager discovered that there were certain times when the number of employees was insufficient to help the crowd of shoppers, and also learned that the delays at these times seriously annoyed at least some shoppers, thus threatening a loss in business. This knowledge is certainly important, and by reacting defensively to the customer's complaint the manager would not have learned from it. As you read earlier, even apparently outlandish criticism

often contains at least a grain of truth, and thus a person who is genuinely interested in improving would be wise to hear it out.

Ask about the consequences of your behavior As a rule people complain about your actions only when some need of theirs is not being met. One way to respond to this kind of criticism is to find out exactly what troublesome consequences your behavior has for them. You'll often find that actions that seem perfectly legitimate to you cause some difficulty for your critic; once you have understood this, comments that previously sounded foolish take on a new meaning.

A: *You say that I ought to have my cat neutered. Why is that important to you?*

B: *Because at night he picks fights with my cat, and I'm tired of paying the vet's bills.*

C: *Why do you care whether I'm late to work?*

D: *Because when the boss asks where you are, I feel obligated to make up some story so you won't get in trouble, and I don't like to lie.*

E: *Why does it bother you when I lose money at poker? You know I never gamble more than I can afford.*

F: *It's not the cash itself. It's that when you lose you're in a grumpy mood for two or three days, and that's no fun for me.*

Solicit additional complaints Although the idea might at first sound outlandish, once you've understood one complaint it's often beneficial to see if there is anything else about your behavior that bothers your critic. Soliciting additional complaints can be a good idea for the simple reason that if you can learn one valuable lesson from a single criticism, you ought to double your knowledge by hearing two.

Of course, it isn't always wise to seek additional gripes, at least not immediately. You should be sure that you understand the first complaint before tackling another one in the same sitting. Resolving the complaint sometimes means agreeing to the other's demands for change, but in other circumstances it can mean hearing out the other's request and promising to think about it. In still other instances the critic really doesn't expect you to change; in such cases resolution can simply mean that you've taken the time and spent the effort to truly understand the criticism.

You can see how solicitation of additional criticism works by returning to the conversation between the store manager and a disgruntled customer.

M: *I can promise you that I'll see what I can do about having more employees on hand during busy periods. While you're here, I'd like to know if you can think of any other ways we could improve our operation.*
C: *What? You really want to know what else I think you're doing wrong?*
M: *Sure. If we're not aware of ways we could do better, we'll never change.*
C: *Well, the only other thing I can think of is the parking situation. A lot of times I'll come by and have to wait several minutes for a delivery truck to unload before I can get into the lot from the south side. I wish you could have the trucks park somewhere else or unload at a quieter hour.*
M: *That's a good point. We can't always control when the drivers from other companies will show up, but I can sure*

> To avoid criticism, do nothing, say nothing, be nothing.
>
> Elbert Hubbard

give their dispatchers a call and see what can be done. I want to say that I appreciate your thoughts. Even when we have our bad days around here, it's important to us that we do everything we can to make this a good place to shop.

Sometimes soliciting and understanding more information from a critic isn't enough. What do you do, for instance, when you fully understand the other person's objections and still feel a defensive response on the tip of your tongue? You know that if you try to protect yourself, you'll wind up in an argument; on the other hand, you simply can't accept what the other person is saying about you. The solution to such a dilemma is outrageously simple, and is discussed in the following section.

When Criticized, Agree with the Speaker
But, you protest, how can you honestly agree with comments that you don't believe are true? The following pages will answer this question by showing that there's virtually no situation in which you can't honestly accept the other person's point of view and still maintain your position. To see how this can be so, you need to realize that there are four different types of agreement, each of which you can express in different circumstances.

Agree with the truth   This is the easiest type of agreement to understand, though not always to practice. You agree with the truth when another person's criticism is factually correct:

1.   "You're right, I am angry."
2.   "I suppose I was being defensive."
3.   "Now that you mention it, I did get pretty sarcastic."

Agreeing with the facts seems quite sensible when you realize that certain matters are indisputable. If you agree to be somewhere at 4:00 and don't show up until 5:00, you *are* late, no matter how good your explanation for tardiness is. If you've broken a borrowed object, run out of gas, or failed to finish a job you started, there's no point in denying the fact. In the same way, if you're honest you will have to agree with many interpretations of your behavior, even when they're not flattering. You do get angry, act foolishly, fail to listen, and behave inconsiderately. Once you rid yourself of the myth of perfection, it's much easier to acknowledge these truths.

But if it's so obvious that the descriptions others give of your behaviors are often accurate, why is it so difficult to accept them without being defensive? The answer to this question lies in a confusion between agreeing with the *facts* and accepting the *judgment* that so often accompanies them. Most critics don't merely describe the action that offends them, they also evaluate it, and it's this evaluation that we resist:

1.   It's silly to be angry."
2.   "You have no reason for being defensive."
3.   "You were wrong to be so sarcastic.

It's judgments like these that we resent. By realizing that you can agree with—and even learn from—the descriptive part of many criticisms and still not accept the accompanying evaluations, you'll often have a response that is both honest and nondefensive. A conversation between a teacher and a student illustrates this point.

Teacher: *Look at this paper! It's only two pages long and it contains twelve mis-spelled words. I'm afraid you have a real problem with your writing.*
Student: *You're right. I know I don't spell well at all.*
T: *I don't know what's happening in the lower grades. They just don't seem to be turning out people who can write a simple, declarative sentence.*
S: *You're not the first person I've heard say that.*
T: *I should think you'd be upset by the fact that after so much time in English composition classes you haven't mastered the basics of spelling.*
S: *You're right. It does bother me.*

Notice that in agreeing with the teacher's comments the student did not in any way demean herself. Even though there might have been extenuating circumstances to account for her lack of skill, the student didn't find it necessary to justify her errors because she wasn't saddled with the burden of pretending to be perfect. By simply agreeing with the facts she was able to maintain her dignity and avoid an unproductive argument.

Of course, in order to reduce defensiveness it's important that your agreements with the facts are honest ones admitted without malice. It's humiliating to accept descriptions that aren't accurate, and maliciously pretending to agree with these only lead to trouble. You can imagine how unproductive the above conversation would have been if the student had spoken the same words in a sarcastic tone. Only agree with the facts when you can do so sincerely. While this won't always be possible, you'll be surprised at how often you can use this simple response.

At this point you might accept the idea that agreeing with criticism is fine, but insisting that it is so by itself isn't an adequate response to your critic. For instance, once you've admitted to another that you are defensive, habitually late, or sarcastic, you can expect the other to ask what you intend to do about this behavior.

Questions like these are fair ones. In most cases it would be a mistake simply to understand another's criticism, to agree with the accusations, and then to go on behaving precisely as before. Such behavior makes it clear that you have no concern for the speaker. The message that comes through is, "Sure, now I understand what I've done to bother you. You're right, I have been doing it and I'll probably keep on doing it. If you don't like the way I've been behaving, that's tough!" Such a response might be appropriate for dealing with people you genuinely don't care about—manipulative solicitors, abusive strangers, and so on—but it is clearly not suitable for people who matter to you.

Before reading on, then, understand that responding nondefensively to criticism is only the *first step* in resolving the conflicts that usually prompt another's attack. Because it is such an important step it's worthy of an extended treatment here; but by itself it won't help you satisfactorily manage many of the interpersonal problems you face. In order to fully manage your conflicts, you'll need to learn the skills described in Chapter 11. For now, it's sufficient to practice the coping skills of questioning and agreeing with criticism.

Agree with the odds   Sometimes a critic will point out possible unpleasant consequences of your behavior:

1.   "If you don't talk to more people, they'll think you're a snob."
2.   "If you don't exercise more, you'll wind up having a heart attack one of these days."
3.   "If you run around with that crowd, you'll probably be sorry."

Often comments such as these are genuinely helpful suggestions that others offer for your own good. In other cases, however, they are really devices for manipulating you into behaving the way your critic wants you to. For instance, "If we go to the football game, you might catch cold" could mean, "I don't want to go to the football game." "You'll probably be exhausted tomorrow if you stay up late" could be translated as, "I want you to go to bed early." Chapter 11 will have more to say about such methods of indirect aggression, but for now it is sufficient to state that such warnings often generate defensiveness. A mother-son argument shows this:

Mother: *I don't see why you want to ride that motorcycle. You could wind up in an accident so easily.* (Stating the odds for an accident)

S: *Oh, don't be silly. I'm a careful driver, and besides you know that I never take my bike on the freeway.* (Denying the odds)

M: *Yes, but every time I pick up the paper I read about someone being hurt or killed. There's always a danger that some crazy driver will miss seeing you and run you off the road.* (States the odds for an injury)

S: *Oh, you worry too much. I always look out for the other driver. And besides, you have a lot better maneuverability on a motorcycle than in a car.* (Denies the odds for an injury)

M: *I know you're careful, but all it takes is one mistake and you could be killed.* (States the odds for being killed)

S: *Somebody is killed shaving or taking a shower every day, but you don't want me to stop doing those things, do you? You're just exaggerating the whole thing.* (Denies the odds for being killed)

From this example you can see that it's usually counterproductive to deny another's predictions. You don't convince the critic, and your mind stays unchanged as well. Notice the difference when you agree with the odds (though not the demands) of the critic.

M: *I don't see why you want to drive that motorcycle. You could wind up in an accident so easily.* (States the odds for an accident)

S: *I suppose there is a chance of that.* (AGREES with the odds)

M: *You're darned right. Every time I pick up the newspaper I read about someone being hurt or killed. There's always a danger that some crazy driver will miss seeing you and run you off the road.* (States the odds for an injury)

S: *You're right, that could happen* (AGREES with the odds), *but I don't think the risk is great enough to keep me off the bike.*

M: *That's easy for you to say now. Some day you could be sorry you didn't listen to me.*

S: *That's true. I really might regret driving the bike some day.* (AGREES with the odds)

Notice how the son simply considers his mother's predictions and realistically acknowledges the chance that they might come true. While responses such as this might at first seem indifferent and callous, they can help the son to avoid the pitfall of indirect manipulation. Suppose the conversation was a straightforward one in which the mother was simply pointing out the danger of motorcycle riding to her son. He acknowledged that he understood her concern and even agreed with the possibility that her prediction could come true. If, however, her prediction was really an indirect way of saying, "I don't want you to ride anymore," then the son's response would force her into making her demand clear, thus allowing him to deal with it openly. At this point they might be able to figure out a solution that lets the son satisfy his need for transportation and excitement and at the same time allows the mother to alleviate her concern.

In addition to bringing hidden agendas into the open for resolution, agreeing with the odds has the added advantage of helping you become aware of some possible consequences of your actions that you might not have previously considered. Instead of blindly denying the chance that your behavior is inappropriate, agreeing with the odds will help you take an objective look at whether your course of action is in fact the best one. After such a look you might agree with your critic that the odds are such that you really should change your behavior.

Agree in principle   Often criticism comes in the form of abstract ideals against which you're unfavorably compared:

1. "I wish you wouldn't spend so much time on your work. Relaxation is important too, you know."
2. "You shouldn't expect so much from your kids. Nobody's perfect."
3. "What do you mean, you're not voting? The government is only going to get better when people like you take more of an interest in it."
4. "You mean you're still upset by that remark? You ought to learn how to take a joke better."

In such instances it's entirely possible for you to accept the principle upon which the criticism is based and still continue to behave as you have been doing. This apparent inconsistency is reasonable for two reasons. First, no abstract statement applies to every instance of human behavior. For instance, while relaxation is important, there are occasions where it is appropriate to throw yourself totally into your work for a period of time. While it is unfair to put excessive demands on one's children, in some cases it becomes necessary for them to behave in an exceptional manner. As the *Bible* says, there is a time for every purpose, and what might usually be right isn't always so.

A second reason why you might agree in principle with a criticism but not change your behavior is precisely because people *are* inconsistent. Not being totally rational, we often do things that aren't in our best interests or those of another person. Again the myth of perfection needs debunking: Since you're not a saint, it's unrealistic to expect that you'll always behave like one. As authors and teachers of assertive communication, we can relate to this principle. There are occasions when we find ourselves behaving in a very unassertive manner: Failing to define our problems and goals behaviorally, expecting ourselves to improve in some way all at once instead of changing in gradual steps, and (ironically enough) becoming defensive in the face of criticism. In the face of such situations our inner dialogues often go something like this:

Top dog: *Boy, are you a hypocrite. Here you are, the expert on assertiveness, and you can't even take a little criticism yourself. Do as I say, not as I do, eh?*

Under dog: (whining) *Well, it's not just my fault, you know. I do the best I can, but sometimes other people are so obnoxious that . . . Wait a second. You're right. (Agreeing with the principle.) I probably ought to be able to accept criticism better, but I guess I still haven't managed to totally master everything I teach. Maybe after a little longer I'll get better. I sure hope so for everybody's sake!*

Agree with the critic's perception   What about times when there seems to be no basis whatsoever for agreeing with your critic? You've listened carefully and asked questions to make sure you understand the objections, but the more you listen, the more positive you are that they are totally out of line: There is no truth to the criticism, you can't agree with the odds, and you can't even accept the principle the critic puts forward. Even in these cases there's a way of agreeing—this time not with the critics' conclusions, but with their right to perceive things their way.

A: *I don't believe you've been all the places you were just describing. You're probably just making all this up so we'll think you're hot stuff.*
B: *Well, I can see how you might think that. I've known people who lie to get approval.*
C: *I want to let you know right from the start that I was against hiring you for the job. I think the reason you got it was because you're a woman.*
D: *I can understand why you'd believe that with all the antidiscrimination laws on*

the books. I hope that after I've been here for a while you'll change your mind.
E: *I don't think you're being totally honest about your reasons for wanting to stay home. You say that it's because you have a headache, but I think you're avoiding Mary and Walt.*
F: *I can see why that would make sense to you since Mary and I got into an argument the last time we were together. All I can say is that I do have a headache.*

Responses such as these tell critics that you're acknowledging the reasonableness of their perception, even though you don't choose to accept it yourself or change your behavior. This coping style is a valuable one, for it lets you avoid the debates over who is right and who is wrong, which can turn an exchange of ideas into an argument. Note the difference in the following scenes between Amy and Bob.

Disputing the Perception:

Amy: *I don't see how you can stand to be around Josh. The guy is so crude that he gives me the creeps.*
Bob: *What do you mean, crude? He's a really nice guy. I think you're just touchy.*
A: *Touchy! If it's touchy to be offended by disgusting behavior, then I'm guilty.*
B: *You're not guilty about anything. It's just that you're too sensitive when people kid around.*
A: *Too sensitive, huh? I don't know what's happened to you. You used to have such good judgment about people. . . .*

Agreeing with the Perception:

A: *I don't see how you can stand to be around Josh. The guy is so crude that he gives me the creeps.*

B: *Well, I enjoy being around him, but I guess I can see how his jokes would be offensive to some people.*

A: *You're damn right. I don't see how you can put up with him.*

B: *Yeah. I guess if you didn't appreciate his humor, you wouldn't want to have much to do with him.*

Notice how in the second exchange Bob was able to maintain his own position without attacking Amy's in the least. This acceptance is the key ingredient for successfully agreeing with your critics' perceptions: When it is present, you make it clear that in no way are you disputing their views of the matter. And since you have no intention of attacking your critics' views, they are less likely to be defensive.

Readings

Adler, Ronald B. *Confidence in Communication: A Guide to Assertive and Social Skills*. New York: Holt, Rinehart and Winston, 1977.

Blake, Robert R. and Jane S. Mouton. *The Managerial Grid*. Houston: Gulf Publishing Co., 1964.

Deutsch, Morton A. "Trust and Suspicion." *Journal of Conflict Resolution*, 2, (1958): 265–279.

Gibb, Jack R. "Defensive Communication." *Journal of Communication*, 11, (September 1961):141–148.

Hays, Ellis R. "Ego-Threatening Classroom Communication: A Factor Analysis of Student Perceptions." *Speech Teacher*, 19, (1970): 43–48.

Horney, Karen. *Our Inner Conflicts: A Constructive Theory of Neurosis*. New York: Norton, 1945.

Kelman, Herbert C. "Compliance, Identification, and Internalization." *Journal of Conflict Resolution*, 2, (1958):51–60.

McGregor, Douglas. *Human Side of Enterprise*. New York: McGraw-Hill, 1960.

Powell, John. *Why Am I Afraid to Tell You Who I Am?* Chicago: Argus Communications, 1969.

Redding, W. Charles. *Communication Within The Organization*. New York: Industrial Communication Council, 1972.

Rokeach, Milton. *The Open and Closed Mind*. New York: Basic Books, 1960.

Sieburg, Evelyn and Carl Larson. "Dimensions of Interpersonal Response." Paper presented to the International Communication Association, Phoenix, Arizona, 1971.

Shostrom, Everett L. *Man, The Manipulator*. New York: Basic Books, 1960.

Smith, Manuel. *When I Say No, I Feel Guilty*. New York: Bantam Books, 1975.

8 In a world where almost everyone acknowledges the importance of better communication, the experience of not being listened to is all too common. The problem is especially bad when you realize that listening is the most frequent type of communication behavior. This fact was established as early as 1926 when Paul Rankin surveyed a group of businesspersons, asking them to record the percentage of time they spent speaking, reading, writing, and listening. Rankin found that his subjects spent more time listening than in any other communication activity, devoting 42 percent of their time to it.

Fifty years later, Rudolph Verderber, Ann Elder, and Ernest Weiler discovered that the frequency of time spent listening is, if anything, higher now than it was in the past. These researchers surveyed a number of college students, asking them to record their various communication interactions for several days. The students proved to spend almost 61 percent of their waking hours communicating, with 63 percent of that time devoted to some type of listening to others.

Listening, then, is one of the most frequent activities in which we engage. Despite this fact, our experience shows that much of the listening we and others do is not at all effective. We misunderstand others and are misunderstood in return. We become bored and feign attention while our minds wander. We engage in a battle of interruptions where each person fights to speak without hearing the other's ideas.

As you'll soon read, some of this poor listening is inevitable. But in other cases we can be better receivers by learning a few basic listening skills. The purpose of this chapter is to help you become a better listener by teaching you some important information about the subject. We'll talk about some common misconceptions concerning listening and show you what really happens when listening takes place. We'll discuss some poor listening habits and explain why they occur. Finally, we'll introduce you to some more effective alternatives, both to increase your own understanding and to help others.

Myths about Listening

In spite of its importance, listening is misunderstood by most people. Since these misunderstandings so greatly affect our communication, let's take a look at three common misconceptions that many communicators hold.

1. **Listening and hearing are the same thing.** *Hearing* is the process wherein sound waves strike the eardrum and cause vibrations that are transmitted to the brain. *Listening* occurs when the brain reconstructs these electrochemical impulses into a representation of the original sound, and then gives them meaning. Barring illness, injury, or cotton plugs, hearing cannot be stopped. Your ears will pick up sound waves and transmit them to your brain whether you want them to or not.

Listening, however, is not so automatic. Many times we hear but do not listen. Sometimes we deliberately do not listen. Instead of paying attention to words or other sounds, we avoid them. This most often occurs when we block irritating sounds, such as a neighbor's power lawnmower or the roar of nearby traffic. We also stop listening when we find a subject unimportant or uninteresting. Boring stories, TV commercials, and nagging complaints are common examples of messages we avoid.

There are also cases when we honestly believe we're listening although we're merely hearing. For example, recall times when you think you've "heard it all before." It's likely that in these situations you might claim you were listening when in fact you had closed your mental doors to new information.

People who confuse listening with hearing often fool themselves into thinking that they're really understanding others when in fact they're simply receiving sounds. As you'll see by reading this chapter, true listening involves much more than the passive act of hearing.

2. **Listening is a natural process.** Another common myth is that listening is like breathing: a natural activity that people do well. "After all," this common belief goes, "I've been listening since I was a child. Why should I have to study the subject in school?"

This attitude is understandable considering the lack of attention most schools devote to listening in comparison with other communication skills. From kindergarten to college most students receive almost constant training in reading and writing. Every year the exposure to literature continues, from Dick and Jane through Dostoyevsky. Likewise, the emphasis on writing continues without break. You could probably retire if you had a dollar for every composition, essay, research paper,

and bluebook you have written since the first grade. Even spoken communication gets some attention in the curriculum. It's likely that you had a chance to take a public speaking class in high school and another one in college.

Compare all this training in reading, writing, and speaking with the almost total lack of instruction in listening. Even in college, there are few courses devoted exclusively to the subject. This state of affairs is especially ironic when you consider the fact that over 60 percent of our communication involves listening.

The truth is that listening is a skill much like speaking: Virtually everyone listens, though few people do it well. Your own experience should prove that communication often suffers due to poor listening. How many times have others misunderstood directions or explanations because they didn't seem to be receiving your ideas clearly? And how often have you failed to accurately understand others because you weren't receiving their thoughts accurately? The answers to these questions demonstrate the need for effective training in listening.

3. **All listeners receive the same message.** When two or more people are listening to a speaker, we tend to assume that they are each hearing and understanding the same message. In fact, such uniform comprehension isn't the case. Communication is *proactive:* Each person involved in a transaction of ideas or feelings responds uniquely. Recall our discussion of perception in Chapter 4, where we pointed

out the many factors that cause each of us to perceive an event in a different manner. Physiological factors, social roles, cultural background, personal interests, and needs all shape and distort the raw data we hear into uniquely different messages.

Components of Listening

In this book *Listening Behavior,* Larry Barker describes the process of listening as having four components: hearing, attending, understanding, and remembering.

1. **Hearing.** As we already discussed, *hearing* is the physiological aspect of listening. It is the nonselective process of sound waves impinging on the ear and, insofar as these waves range between approximately 125 and 8,000 cycles per second (frequency) and 55 to 85 decibels (loudness), the ear can respond. Hearing is also influenced by background noise. If a background noise is the same frequency as the speech sound, then the speech sound is said to be masked; however, if the background noise is of a different frequency than speech, it is called "white noise," and may or may not detract greatly from our ability to hear. Hearing is also affected by auditory fatigue, a temporary loss of hearing caused by continuous exposure to the same tone or loudness. People who spend an evening in a discotheque may

experience auditory fatigue and, if they are exposed often enough, permanent hearing loss may result.

2. Attending. After the sounds are converted into electrochemical impulses and transmitted to the brain, a decision—often unconscious—is made whether to focus on what was heard. While the listening process started as a physiological one, it quickly became a psychological one. An individual's needs, wants, desires, and interests determine what is *attended to.* If you're hungry, you are more likely to attend to the message about restaurants in the neighborhood from the person next to you than the competing message on the importance of communication from the speaker in front of the room.

3. Understanding. The component of understanding is composed of several elements. First, understanding a message involves some recognition of the grammatical rules used to create that message. We find the children's books by Dr. Seuss amusing because he breaks the rules of grammar and spelling in interesting ways, and we are familiar enough with the rules to recognize this. Second, understanding depends upon our knowledge about the source of the message—whether the person is sincere, prone to lie, friendly, an adversary, and so on. Third, there is the *social context.* The time and place, for example, helps us decide whether to take a friend's insults seriously or as a joke. Understanding depends, generally, upon sharing common assumptions about the world. Consider the following two sentences (used by Jerrold Katz and Jerry Foder):

a. I bought alligator shoes.
b. I bought horse shoes.

Both sentences can be interpreted the same way since they have the same grammatical structure, and may be uttered by the same person (the first two components of understanding). Both could indicate that a person bought two pairs of shoes, one made from alligator, the other from horse, or that two pairs of shoes were purchased, one for an alligator, the other for a horse. However, because of the common assumptions we share about the world, we understand that the first sentence refers to shoes made *from* alligator hides, and that the second refers either to shoes *for* horses (or for playing a game).

Finally, understanding often depends on the ability to organize the information we hear into recognizable form. As early as 1948, Ralph Nichols related successful understanding to a large number of factors, most prominent among which were verbal ability, intelligence, and motivation.

A more recent investigation completed in 1979 by Lawrence Rosenfeld and Tim Plax examined the relationship of a large number of ability, personality, and motivational variables to the comprehension of organized and disorganized messages. They found that people who were successful at comprehending organized spoken messages were generally less intelligent, yet more secure, more sensitive to others, and more willing to try to understand them. People who were successful at comprehending disorganized spoken messages proved to be insightful and versatile in their thinking, yet somewhat unchanging and inflexible in their view of themselves. People who were not successful at comprehending disorganized spoken messages were flexible, comfortable in unfamiliar situations, and of average or less than average intelligence.

While it is difficult to draw all these diverse results into a neat package, it seems reasonable to conclude that people who are good listeners are generally more intelligent and less flexible than those who are not good listeners. Also, people who are not good listeners are more comfortable with new situations and more willing to work to understand other people than are good listeners.

It may seem odd that inflexibility is associated with successful listening, at least listening for information. However, most of the research done on the characteristics of good listeners (as little as there is) has used students as subjects. Once we realize that intelligence in students is often measured by the ability to absorb, memorize, and repeat information, then the connection between "inflexibility" and "successful *student* listening" becomes clearer. Students are trained to listen for the information most likely to appear on comprehension tests. There is little emphasis on the student critically analyzing that information.

4. Remembering. The ability to recall information once we've understood it is a function of several factors: The number of times the information is heard or repeated; how much information there is to store in the brain; and whether the information may be "rehearsed" or not.

Research conducted during the 1950s revealed that people remember only about half of what they hear *immediately after* hearing it. This is true even if people work hard at listening. This situation would probably not be too bad if the half remembered right after was retained, but it isn't. Within two months, half of the half is forgotten, bringing what we remember down to about 25 percent of the original message. This loss, however, doesn't take two months: People start forgetting immediately (within eight hours the 50 percent remembered drops to about 35 percent). Given the amount of information we process every day—from teachers, friends, the radio, TV, and other sources— the *residual message* (what we remember) is a small fraction of what we hear.

Functions of Listening

"All right," you might respond. "So I don't listen to everything I hear, I don't understand everything I listen to, and I don't remember everything I understand. I still seem to get along well enough. Why should I worry about becoming a better listener?" Author Rob Anderson suggests four benefits that can come from improving your listening skills.

1. Information reception. People who can understand and retain more information have a greater chance of becoming successful, however you define that term. In school the advantages of listening effectively are obvious. Along with the skills of effective writing and reading, the ability to receive and understand the spoken word is a major key to academic success. The same holds true in the business and professional worlds. Understanding the instructions and advice of superiors and colleagues, learning about the needs and reactions of subordinates, and discovering the concerns of clients and other members of the public are important in virtually every job.

Even in one's personal life, the ability to receive and understand information is a key to success. Being a good listener can help you learn everything from car repair to first aid for houseplants to the existence of cheap restaurants. And socially, everyone knows the benefits of being able to hear and remember information about others whom we'd like to know better.

2. Empathy. A listener who was *only* able to receive and recall large amounts of information efficiently would be hardly more likeable or valuable as a friend than a computer would be. While the ability to receive data might be admirable, personally helpful listeners are also able to empathize: to understand and "feel with" the emotions and thoughts of a speaker. An impressive body of research supports the idea that the ability to empathize is an important element in effective communication for many social roles: business supervisors, teachers, therapists and counselors, and of course friends.

It's obvious that listening empathetically can be a valuable way to help someone with a problem. But developing the ability to empathize can also have personal payoffs for you as a listener. The most

obvious one is the reward of having helped solve another person's problems. But in addition, as an empathetic listener, you can broaden your own understanding, and in doing so often learn how to deal with issues in your own life. Just as it's helpful to hear the pleasures and problems of traveling to a new place before going there yourself, listening to another person's experiences in personal issues can teach you what to think and do when you encounter similar circumstances.

3. Criticism and discrimination. In their interesting book *Teaching as a Subversive Activity,* Neil Postman and Charles Weingartner discuss this function of listening in their chapter on "Crap Detecting." They define a crap detector as someone who not only functions in a society, but *observes* it, noting its obsessions, fears, strengths, and weaknesses. Critical listeners are able to hear a speaker's words and understand the ideas without necessarily accepting them totally. The ability to listen analytically and critically differs radically from the kind of empathetic reception just discussed, but it is equally as important. Critical listeners can help individuals and societies understand themselves and recognize the accuracy of their ideas.

4. Other-affirmation. As Chapter 1 notes, a basic human need is to be recognized and acknowledged by others. Listening is one of the most fundamental means of

giving this kind of acknowledgement. The act of listening, of *choosing* to listen, is itself an affirmation of the speaker. Whenever you listen to another person you are sending a nonverbal message suggesting that he or she is important. Of course, there are varying degrees of importance, and there are also various degrees of listening intensity reflecting this range of valuing. A brief affirmation can come from pausing to exchange a few minutes of chit-chat with an acquaintance, while a much stronger message of acknowledgment is reflected in your willingness to spend hours hearing a friend talk over a personal problem.

Why We Don't Listen

Given the importance of receiving information, building empathy, critically discriminating, and affirming others, it's obvious that listening well can be valuable for both the receiver and the speaker. Yet in spite of this fact, we often do not listen with much energy or concern. Why? Sad as it may be, it's impossible to listen *all* the time, for several reasons.

Hearing Problems   If a person suffers from a physical impairment that prevents either the hearing of sounds at an adequate volume or the receiving of certain auditory frequencies, then listening will obviously suffer. Once a hearing problem has been diagnosed it's often possible to treat it. The real tragedy occurs when a hearing loss goes undiagnosed. In such cases both the person with the defect and those surrounding can become frustrated and annoyed at the ineffective communication that takes place. If you suspect that you or someone you know might have a hearing loss, it's wise to have a physician or audiologist perform an examination.

Amount of Input   The sheer amount of speech most of us encounter every day makes it impossible to carefully listen to everything we hear. According to the study cited earlier, many of us spend almost half the time we're awake listening to verbal messages—from teachers, coworkers, friends, family, salespeople, and total strangers. This means we often spend five or more hours a day listening to people talk. If you add these hours to those where we listen to radio and TV, you can see that it's virtually impossible for us to keep our attention totally focused for this length of time. Therefore, we periodically let our attention wander.

Personal Concerns   A third reason we don't always listen carefully is that we're often wrapped up in personal concerns of more immediate importance to us than the messages others are sending. It's hard to pay attention to someone else when you're anticipating an upcoming test or thinking about the wonderful time you had last night with good friends. Yet we still feel we have to "listen" politely to others, and so we continue with our charade.

Rapid Thought   Listening carefully is also difficult for a physiological reason. Although we're capable of understanding speech at rates up to 600 words per

> **To be able to really listen, one should abandon or put aside all prejudices, pre-formulations and daily activities. When you are in a receptive state of mind, things can be easily understood; you are listening when your real attention is given to something. But unfortunately most of us listen through a screen of resistance. We are screened with prejudices, whether religious or spiritual, psychological or scientific; or with our daily worries, desires and fears. And with these for a screen, we listen. Therefore, we listen really to our own noise, to our own sound, not to what is being said.**
>
> J. Krishnamuriti
> *The First and Last Personal Freedom*

minute, the average person speaks between 100 and 140 words per minute. Thus, we have a lot of "spare time" to spend with our minds while someone is talking. And the temptation is to use this time in ways that don't relate to the speaker's ideas, such as thinking about personal interests, daydreaming, planning a rebuttal, and so on. The trick is to use this spare time to understand the speaker's ideas better, rather than letting your attention wander.

"Noise" Finally, the physical and mental worlds in which we live often present distractions that make it hard to pay attention to others. The sound of traffic, music and the speech of others, as well as the kind of psychological noise discussed in Chapter 7 all interfere with our ability to hear well. Also, fatigue or other forms of discomfort can distract us from paying attention to a speaker's remarks. Consider, for example, how the efficiency of your listening decreases when you are seated in a crowded, hot, stuffy room full of moving people and other noises. In such circumstances even the best intentions aren't enough to ensure cogent understanding.

Before going any further we want to make it clear that we aren't suggesting that it's always desirable to listen intently, even when the circumstances permit. Given the number of messages to which we're exposed, it's impractical to expect yourself to listen well 100 percent of the time. This fact becomes even more true when you consider how many of the messages sent at us aren't especially worthwhile: boring stories, deceitful commercials, and remarks we've heard many times before. Given this deluge of relatively worthless information, it's important to realize that nonlistening behaviors are often reasonable. Our only concern is that you have the ability to be an accurate receiver when it really does matter.

Poor Listening Habits

Although it may not be necessary or desirable to listen effectively all the time, it's sad to realize that most people possess one or more bad habits that keep them from understanding truly important messages. As you read the following list of these poor listening behaviors, see which ones describe you.

Pseudolistening Pseudolistening is an imitation of the real thing. "Good" pseudolisteners give the appearance of being attentive: They look you in the eye, nod and smile at the right times, and even may answer you occasionally. Behind that appearance of interest, however, something entirely different is going on, for pseudolisteners use a polite facade to mask thoughts that have nothing to do with what the speaker is saying. Often pseudolisteners ignore you because of something on their mind that's more important to them than your remarks. Other times they may simply be bored, or think that they've heard what you have to say before, and so tune out your remarks. Whatever the reasons, the significant fact is that pseudolistening is really counterfeit communication.

Stage Hogging   Stage hogs are only interested in expressing their ideas and don't care about what anyone else has to say. These people will allow you to speak from time to time, but only so they can catch their breath, use your remarks as a basis for their own babbling, or to keep you from running away. Stage hogs really aren't conversing when they dominate others with their talk—they're making a speech and at the same time probably making an enemy.

Selective Listening   Selective listeners respond only to the parts of a speaker's remarks that interest them, rejecting everything else. All of us are selective listeners from time to time, as for instance when we screen out media commercials and music as we keep an ear cocked for a weather report or an announcement of time. In other cases selective listening occurs in conversations with people who expect a thorough hearing, but only get

their partner's attention when the subject turns to their favorite topic—perhaps money, sex, a hobby, or some particular person. Unless and until you bring up one of these pet subjects, you might as well talk to a tree.

A professor is one who talks in someone else's sleep.

W. H. Auden

Filling in Gaps   People who fill in the gaps like to think that what they remember makes a whole story. Since we remember half or less of what we hear, these people manufacture information so that when they retell what they listened to, they can give the impression they "got it all." Of course, filling in the gaps is as dangerous as selective listening: The message that's left is only a disorted (not merely incomplete) version of the message that could have been received.

Assimilation to Prior Messages   We all have a tendency to interpret current messages in terms of similar messages remembered from the past. This phenomenon is called *assimilation to prior input.* A problem arises for those who go overboard with this and push, pull, chop, squeeze, and in other ways mutilate messages they receive to *make sure* they are consistent with what they heard in the past. This unfortunate situation occurs when the current message is in some way uniquely different from past messages.

Insulated Listening   Insulated listeners are almost the opposite of their selective listening cousins. Instead of looking for something, these people avoid it. Whenever a topic arises they'd rather not deal with, insulated listeners simply fail to hear, or rather acknowledge it. You remind them about a problem—perhaps an unfinished job, poor grades, or the like—and they'll nod or answer you and then promptly forget what you've just said.

When we speak we do not listen, my son
  and I.
I complain of slights, hurts inflicted on
  me.
He sings a counterpoint, but not in
  harmony.
Asking a question, he doesn't wait to hear.
Trying to answer, I interrupt his refrain.
This comic opera excels in disharmony
  only.

Lenni Shender Goldstein

Defensive Listening   Defensive listeners take innocent comments as personal attacks. Teenagers who perceive parental questions about friends and activities as distrustful snooping are defensive listeners, as are insecure breadwinners who explode anytime their mates mention money, or touchy parents who view any questioning by their children as a threat to their

authority and parental wisdom. It's fair to assume that many defensive listeners are suffering from shaky public images, and avoid admitting this by projecting their own insecurities onto others.

Ambushing   Ambushers listen carefully to you, but only because they're collecting information that they'll use to attack what you have to say. The cross-examining prosecution attorney is a good example of an ambusher. Needless to say, using this kind of strategy will justifiably initiate defensiveness on the other's behalf.

Insensitive Listening   Insensitive listeners offer the final example of people who don't receive another person's messages clearly. As we've said before, people often don't express their thoughts or feelings openly but instead communicate them through subtle and unconscious choice of words and/or nonverbal clues. Insensitive listeners aren't able to look beyond the words and behavior to understand their hidden meanings. Instead, they take a speaker's remarks at face value.

It's important not to go overboard in labeling listeners as insensitive. Often a seemingly mechanical comment is perfectly appropriate. This most often occurs in situations involving *phatic* communication, in which a remark derives its meaning totally from context. For instance, the question, "How are you?" doesn't call for an answer when you pass an acquaintance on the street. In this context the statement means no more than, "I acknowledge your existence and I want to let you know that I feel friendly toward you." It is not an inquiry about the state of your health.

While insensitive listening is depressing, you would be equally discouraged to hear a litany of aches and pains every time you asked, "How's it going?"

Listening More Effectively

After reading this far you probably recognize the need for better listening in many contexts. What steps can you yourself take to become a better receiver?

Stop Talking   Zeno of Citium put it most succinctly: "We have been given two ears and but a single mouth, in order that we may hear more and talk less." It is difficult to listen and talk at the same time. This includes the silent debating, rehearsing, and retorting that often goes on in our minds. The first step to better listening, then, is to keep quiet when another person speaks.

React Appropriately   In order to help the speaker realize that you might be having problems understanding, offer positive and negative feedback. These behaviors can

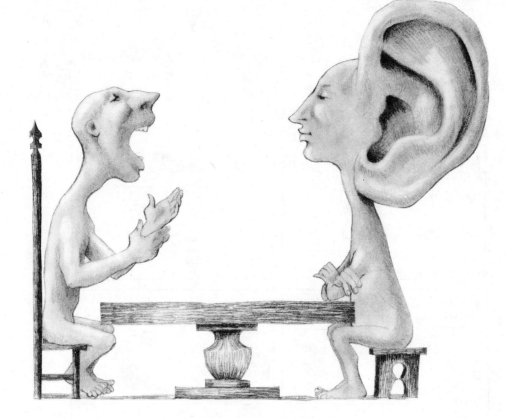

include nonverbal facial expressions: nodding, shaking your head, and so on, as well as verbal statements.

Concentrate on What Is Being Said   Focus your attention on the words, ideas, and the feelings of the speaker. Use the "extra" time you have listening to put the speaker's ideas into your own words, relate them to your experience, and think about any questions you might have.

Get Rid of Distractions   Avoid fidgeting with your pen, playing with a paperclip you've found, doodling, or writing the letter home that's been on your mind. Whenever possible, pick a listening environment that minimizes distractions such as passersby, telephone calls, loud noises, and so on. When you are stuck in a distracting setting, do your best to tune it out.

Don't Give Up Too Soon   Avoid interrupting until the other person expresses a complete thought: Clarity may be on the way! Statements that first seem obscure often make sense if you let the speaker talk for a while.

Avoid Making Assumptions If you disagree with what you hear, don't assume that the speaker is "uninformed," "lying," or otherwise behaving dishonorably.

Don't Argue Mentally Give the speaker a fair hearing; control your anger. If you argue mentally, you lose the opportunity to concentrate on what the speaker is saying. Also, it is often the case that when we mentally argue, we tend to place the other person in a fixed category, and thus cease responding to a unique person, albeit a unique person with whom we disagree.

Listen for Main Points and Supporting Evidence Critical listening will show that a speaker almost always advances one or more main points and backs them up with examples, stories, analogies, and other types of supporting material. One key to successful listening is to search for these main points, and then see if the speaker's support bears them out. A far less productive method is to dwell on an interesting story or comment while forgetting the speaker's main idea.

Share Responsibility for the Communication Remember that communication is a transaction, that we are simultaneously senders and receivers. Just as a good marriage requires both partners to give 100 percent of their effort, so a successful conversation demands the energy and skill of both parties.

Ask Questions Thus far we have been discussing listening methods basically passive in nature; that is, those that can be carried out silently. It's also possible to verify or increase your understanding in a more active way by asking questions to be sure you are receiving the speaker's thoughts and feelings accurately.

Although the suggestion to ask questions may seem so obvious as to be trivial, honestly ask yourself whether you take full advantage of this simple but effective method. It's often tempting to remain silent instead of being a questioner for two reasons. Sometimes you may be reluctant to show your ignorance by asking for further explanation of what seems as if it should be an obvious point. This reluctance is especially strong when the speaker's respect or liking is important to you. At such times it's a good idea to remember a quote attributed to Confucius: "He who asks a question is a fool for five minutes. He who does not ask is a fool for life."

A second reason people are often disinclined to ask questions is that they think they already understand a speaker. But do we in fact understand others as often or as well as we think? You can best answer by thinking about how often people misunderstand *you* while feeling certain that they know what you've meant. If you are aware that others should ask questions of you more often, then it's logical to assume that the same principle holds true in reverse.

Use Active Listening Questioning is often a valuable tool for increasing understanding. Sometimes, however, it

And, contrary to popular belief, it is usually the good talker who makes the best listener. A good talker (by which I do not mean the egomaniacal bore who always talks about himself) is sensitive to expression, to tone and color and inflection in human speech. Because he himself is articulate, he can help others to articulate their half-formulated feelings. His mind fills in the gaps, and he becomes, in Socrates' words, a kind of midwife for ideas that are struggling to be born.

This is why a competent psychiatrist is worth his weight in gold—and generally gets it. His listening is keyed for the half-tones and the dissonances that escape the untrained ear. For it is the mark of the truly good listener that he knows what you are saying often better than you do; and his playback is a revelation, not a recording.

Sydney J. Harris

won't help you receive a speaker's ideas any more clearly, and it can even lead to further communication breakdown. To see how this can be so, consider again the example of asking directions to a friend's home. Suppose the instructions you've received are to, "Drive about a mile and then turn left at the traffic signal." Now imagine that a few common problems exist in this simple message. First, suppose that your friend's idea of a mile differs from yours: Your mental picture of the distance is actually closer to two miles, where your friend's is closer to 300 yards. Next,

consider the likely occurrence that "traffic signal," really meant "stop sign;" after all, it's common for us to think one thing and say another. Keeping these problems in mind, suppose you tried to verify your understanding of the directions by asking, "After I turn at the light, how far should I go?" to which your friend replied that the house is the third from the corner. Clearly, if you parted after this exchange, you would encounter a lot of frustration before finding the elusive residence.

What was the problem here? It's easy to see that questioning might not have helped you, for your original idea of how far to drive and where to turn were mistaken. And contained in such mistakes is the biggest problem with questioning, for such inquiries don't tell you whether you have accurately received the information that has *already* been sent.

Now consider another kind of feedback—one that would tell you whether you understand what had already been said before you asked additional questions. This sort of feedback involves restating in your own words the message you thought the speaker has just sent, without adding anything new. In the example of seeking directions we've been using, such rephrasing might sound like, "So you're telling me to drive down to the traffic light by the high school and turn toward the mountains, is that it?" Immediately sensing the problem your friend could then reply, "Oh no, that's way too far. I meant that you should drive to the four-way stop by the park and turn there. Did I say stop light? I always do that when I mean stop sign!"

This simple step of restating what you thought the speaker said before going on is commonly termed *active listening,* and it is an important tool for effective listening. Remember that what is significant in active listening is to *paraphrase* the sender's words, not to parrot them. In other words, restate what you think the speaker has said in your own terms as a way of cross-checking the information. If you simply repeat the speaker's comments *verbatim,* you'll sound as if you're foolish or hard of hearing, and just as importantly, you still might be misunderstanding what's been said.

Because it's an unfamiliar way of responding, active listening may feel awkward when you first begin to use it. But by paraphrasing occasionally at first and then gradually increasing the frequency of such responses, you can begin to learn the benefits of this method without feeling foolish or sounding odd to others.

Listening to Help

So far we've talked about how becoming a better listener can help you to understand other people more often and more clearly. If you use the skills presented so far, you should be rewarded by communicating far more accurately with others every day. But there's another way in which listening can improve your relationships. Strange as it may sound, you can often help other people solve their own problems simply by learning to listen—actively and with concern.

Before we introduce various methods of listening as a method of helping, read the following situations and think about how you would respond in each of them.

1. You're speaking with a friend who has just been rejected from getting a badly wanted job. "I don't know what to do," your friend tells you. "I studied and worked two years to get that job, and it's all been for nothing."
2. Another friend confesses, "My marriage seems to be on the rocks. We hardly talk anymore. And everything triggers off a fight. we're in a rut, and it seems to be getting worse."
3. While at work or school, an acquaintance approaches you and says, "I can't decide whether to stay here or move up north. I have plenty of friends here and things are pretty good. On the other hand, I'd hate to give up a good job opportunity and find out it was a mistake. What do you think I should do?"

There are several ways in which you could have responded to these problems, none inherently good or bad. It often happens, however, that we use these ways in situations when they aren't best suited to helping others solve their problems. There's a proper time and place for each kind of response. The problem, though, usually occurs when we use these ways in the wrong situations or else depend upon one or two styles of responses for all situations.

As you read the following descriptions of ways of responding, see which ones you most frequently used in the previous exercise, and notice the results that probably would have occurred from your response.

Advising   When approached with another's problem, the most common tendency is to try to help by offering a solution. While such a response is sometimes valuable, it often isn't as helpful as people generally think.

It is always a silly thing to give advice, but to give good advice is absolutely fatal.

Oscar Wilde

Your suggestion may not offer the best course to follow, in which case it can even be harmful. There's a temptation to tell others how *we* would behave in their place, but it's important to realize that what's right for one person may not be right for another. A related consequence of advising is that it often allows others to avoid responsibility for their decisions. If, for example, a partner follows your suggestion and things don't work out, the blame can always be pinned on you. Finally, people simply may not want advice—they may not be ready to accept it, wanting instead simply to talk out their thoughts and feelings.

Judging   A judging response evaluates the sender's thoughts or behaviors in some way. The judgment may be favorable ("That's a good idea"; "You're on the right track now"), or unfavorable ("An attitude like that won't get you anywhere"). In either case this response implies that the person doing the judging is in some way

qualified to pass judgment on the speaker's thoughts or actions.

Judgmental or evaluative language is likely to make someone defensive. Thus, responding in this way might tend to put the speaker on guard and in so doing end the conversation and the possibility of helping.

Analyzing   The analyzer's response suggests that the receiver understands the sender better than the sender understands his or her own message. ("What's bothering you is. . . ."; "What you really think is. . . ."). In a sense, the analyzer tries to read the speaker's mind or provide a lesson in psychology.

There are two problems with analyzing. First, your interpretation may not be correct, in which case the sender may become even more confused by accepting it. Second, even if your analysis is accurate, sharing it with the sender might not be useful. There's a chance that it will create defensiveness (since analyzing implies superiority and the authority to evaluate).

There are times when analyzing can be a way of helping a people to see their "blind spots," but this style of responding is one many of us use too often.

Questioning   Although questioning is often a helpful way for you to understand the unclear parts of a person's statements, it can also be used as a tool to direct the other's thoughts. We've all been questioned by a parent, teacher, or other authority figure who seemed to be trying to trap us. In this way questioning is a strategy, and often implies that the person doing the asking already has some idea of what direction the discussion should take.

Supporting   Sometimes a person needs encouragement, and in these cases a supporting response might be best. But in many cases this kind of help isn't helpful at all. Telling a person who's obviously upset that "everything's all right" or joking about a problem can communicate a message that you don't accept the other's feelings as valid or that there isn't justification in the problem for feeling that way.

All these responses may be helpful at times, but they often confuse people asking for help, making them feel worse than before they shared a problem or making them defensive. Good intentions aren't always helpful.

Active Listening   Active listening involves giving feedback concerned with both the *feelings* and *thoughts* of the other person. This sort of two-barreled response is important in helping people sort out their problems. The emotional responses we have to problems are often more important than the problems themselves. For example, is the friend who was turned down for a job angry, depressed, frustrated, or confused? By reflecting back your perception of your friend's feelings, you'll help identify them. And if you guess wrong, don't worry: Your friend will correct you, and in doing so clarify the situation.

Actively listening tells the speaker that you're interested in understanding what the message is, that you care. Amazingly enough, simply feeding back people's ideas to them often helps them sort out and solve the problems for themselves. If you're lucky you probably know people who can help

you understand things better simply by sitting and listening. These people are probably active listeners, even though they don't know it.

There are several reasons why active listening works so well. First, it takes the burden off you as a friend. Simply being there to understand what's on someone's mind often makes it possible for him or her to clarify the problems. This means you don't have to know all the answers to help. Also, helping by active listening means you don't need to guess at reasons or solutions that might not be correct. Thus, both you and your friend are saved from going on a wild goose chase after incorrect solutions.

A second advantage of active listening is that it's an efficient way to get through layers of hidden meanings. Often people express their ideas, problems, or feelings in strangely coded ways. Active listening can sometimes help cut through to the real meaning. Not too long ago a student came to an instructor and asked, "How many people get Ds and Fs in this class?" The instructor could have taken the question at face value and answered it, but instead he tried active listening. He replied by saying, "Sounds like you've got some fears of doing poorly in here." After a few minutes of listening the instructor learned that the student was afraid that getting a low grade in a communication class would be equal to failing as a person.

The third advantage of active listening is that it's usually the best way to encourage people to share more of themselves with you. Knowing that you're interested will encourage less feeling of threat, and many will be willing to let down some of their defenses. In this sense active listening is simply a good way to learn more about someone, and a good foundation on which to build a relationship.

Regardless of the advantages, active listening isn't appropriate in all situations when someone wants help. Sometimes people are simply looking for information and not trying to work out their feelings. At times like this active listening would be out of place. If someone asks you for the time of day, you'd do better to simply give the information than to respond by saying, "You want to know what time it is." If you're fixing dinner and someone wants to know when it will be ready, it would be exasperating to reply, "You're interested in knowing when we'll be eating."

However, people do often hide an important feeling behind an innocent sounding statement or question, and in such cases active listening on your part can usually bring their real concern into the open. But don't go overboard with the technique. Usually, if there's a feeling hidden behind a question you'll recognize some accompanying nonverbal clue—a change in your friend's facial expression, tone of voice, posture, and so on. But it takes attention, concentration, and caring on your part.

You should realize that success in using active listening will depend on the attitude you bring to a situation. Too often people will think of active listening as a kind of gimmick they can use when some unpleasant situation arises. If you think about the technique this way it is almost sure to fail. In fact, unless you truly mean what you say, you'll come across as being manipulative, phony, and uncaring. So as you practice this listening skill try to keep these points in mind:

1. **Don't actively listen unless you truly want to help the person.** There's nothing wrong with being too preoccupied to help. But you'll be doing both yourself and the other person a disservice if you pretend to care when you really don't.

2. **Don't try to listen actively if you're not willing to take the necessary time.** Listening with feedback isn't easy. If you're willing to make the effort, you'll probably be rewarded, but you'll only lose the speaker's trust if you commit yourself and then don't follow through.

3. **Don't try to impose your ideas on the other person.** Active listening means accepting other people's feelings and trusting that they can find their own solutions. If you try to moralize, to suggest, or to change the speaker, you won't really be actively listening, and it's less likely that you'll be of much help.

4. **Keep your attention focused on the sender.** Sometimes, as you listen to others share feelings, it's easy to become defensive, to relate their thoughts to your own life, or to busy yourself thinking of an answer. Remember that active listening is a form of helping someone else. Keep your energy focused on this goal.

Readings

Anderson, Rob. *Students as Real People: Interpersonal Communication and Education.* Rochelle Park, New Jersey: Hayden, 1979.

Axline, Virginia M. *Dibs: In Search of Self.* New York: Ballantine Books, 1967.

Baddeley, Alan D. *The Psychology of Memory.* New York: Basic Books, 1976.

Barker, Larry L. *Listening Behavior.* Englewood Cliffs, New Jersey: Prentice-Hall, 1971.

Beier, Ernst G. and Evans G. Valens. *People-Reading: How We Control Others, How They Control Us.* New York: Stein and Day, 1975.

Dittmann, Allen T. "Developmental Factors in Conversational Behavior." *Journal of Communication,* 22, (1972):404–423.

Foulke, Emerson and Thomas Stricht. "Review of Research in Time-Compressed Speech." In *Time-Compressed Speech,* Sam Duker, ed. Metuchen: Scarecrow Press, 1974.

Goldhaber, Gerald M. "Listener Comprehension of Compressed Speech as a Function of the Academic Grade Level of Subjects." *Journal of Communication,* 20, (1970):167–173.

Katz, Jerrold J. and Jerry A. Foder. "The Structure of a Semantic Theory." In *Readings in the Philosophy of Language,* Jay F. Rosenberg and Charles Travis, eds. Englewood Cliffs, New Jersey: Prentice-Hall, 1971.

Kelley, Charles M. "Empathic Listening." In *Small Group Communication: A Reader,* 2nd Ed., Robert Cathcart and Larry Samovar, eds. Dubuque, Iowa: Wm. C. Brown, 1974.

Nichols, Ralph G. "Factors in Listening Comprehension." *Speech Monographs,* 15, (1948):154–163.

Nichols, Ralph G. and L. A. Stevens. *Are You Listening?* New York: McGraw-Hill, 1957.

Palamatier, Robert A. and George McNinch. "Source of Gains in Listening Skill: Experimental or Pre-Test Experience?" *Journal of Communication,* 22, (1972):70–76.

Plax, Timothy G. and Lawrence B. Rosenfeld. "Receiver Differences and the Comprehension of Spoken Messages." *Journal of Experimental Education,* 48 Fall (1979).

Postman, Neil and Charles Weingartner. *Teaching as a Subversive Activity.* New York: Delacorte Press, 1969.

Rogers, Carl R. *On Becoming a Person.* Boston: Houghton-Mifflin, 1961.

Rossiter, Charles M. "Sex of the Speaker, Sex of the Listener, and Listening Comprehension." *Journal of Communication,* 22, (1972):64–69.

Verderber, Rudolph, Ann Elder and Ernest Weiler. *A Study of Communication Time Usage by College Students.* Unpublished study, University of Cincinnati, 1976.

Weaver, Carl. *Human Listening: Processes and Behavior.* Indianapolis: Bobbs-Merrill, 1972.

Nonverbal Communication 9

9 "People don't always say what they mean . . . but their body gestures and movements tell the truth!"

"Will he ask you out? Is she encouraging you? *Know* what is really happening by understanding the secret language of body signals. You can:
Improve your sex life . . .
Pick up your social life . . .
Better your business life . . ."

"Read *Body Language* so that you can penetrate the personal secrets, both of intimates and total strangers . . .
Does her body say that she's a loose woman?
Does her body say that she's a phony?
Does her body say that she's a manipulator?
Does her body say that she's lonely?"

Unless you've been trapped in a lead mine or doing fieldwork in the Amazon Basin for the last several years, claims like these are probably familiar to you. Almost every drugstore, supermarket, and airport bookrack has its share of "body language" paperbacks. According to their claims, for only a few dollars and a fifth grade reading ability, you can learn secrets that will change you from a fumbling social failure into a self-assured mindreader who can uncover a person's deepest secrets at a glance.

While promises like these do sell lots of books (much more than texts!), they are almost always exaggerations. Don't misunderstand: There *is* a scientific body of knowledge about nonverbal communication, and it *has* answered many fascinating and valuable clues about human behavior. That's what this chapter is about. But it's unlikely the next few pages will instantly turn you into a rich, sexy, charming communication superstar.

But don't go away. Even without glamorous promises, a quick look at some facts about nonverbal communication shows that it's an important field to study. The biggest reason for its importance is that what we do often conveys more meaning than what we say. Albert Mehrabian, a psychologist working in the area of nonverbal behavior, claims that 93 percent of the emotional impact of a message comes from a nonverbal source, whereas only a paltry 7 percent is verbal. Anthropologist Ray Birdwhistell describes a 65-35 percent split between words and actions, again in favor of nonverbal messages. Even if we chose to argue with these precise figures, the point still remains: Nonverbal communication contributes a great deal to sharing meanings.

You might ask how this can be. At first glance it seems as if meanings come from words. To answer this question, imagine that you've just arrived in a foreign country in which the inhabitants speak a language you don't understand. Visualize yourself on a crowded street, filled with many types of people, from the very rich to the quite poor. In spite of these differences in wealth, there seems to be little social friction, with one exception. On one corner two people seem close to a fight. One man—he seems to be a shopkeeper—is furious at a customer, who seems to be complaining about an item he has just bought. Two police officers stroll by and obviously notice the commotion, but walk on unconcerned. Most of the pedestrians are in a great hurry, rushing off to who-knows where . . . all except for one couple. They are oblivious to everything but themselves, obviously in love.

In spite of the fact that you've never been here before, you feel comfortable because everyone seems friendly and polite. Shoppers murmur apologetically when they bump into you on the crowded sidewalks, and many people smile when your eyes meet theirs. In fact, you notice that one attractive stranger seems *very* friendly, and quite interested in you. In spite of the fact that you've been warned to watch out for shady characters, you know there's no danger here. "Why not?" you think. "It's a vacation." You smile back and both of you walk toward each other . . .

Aside from being a pleasant daydream, this little experiment should have proved that it's possible to communicate without using words. With no knowledge of the language, you were able to make a number of assumptions about what was going on in that foreign country. You obtained a picture of the economic status of some of its inhabitants, observed some conflicts and speculated about their nature, noticed something about the law enforcement policy, formed impressions about the pace of life, and became acquainted with courtship practices. How did you do all this? By tuning into the many nonverbal channels available: facial expressions, clothing, postures, gestures, vocal tones, and more. Of course, you don't have to travel abroad to recognize nonverbal messages, for they're present all the time. Because we're such a vocal society, we often ignore the other channels through which we all communicate. But they're always there.

Fie, fie upon her!
There's language in her eyes,
 her cheek, her lip.
Nay, her foot speaks; her wanton
 spirits look out at every
joint and motive in her body.

William Shakespeare
Troilus and Cressida

Before we take a closer look at each of these channels, let's examine some characteritics that all nonverbal communications share.

Characteristics of Nonverbal Communication

Nonverbal Communication Exists   Our fantasy trip to the foreign country demonstrated this fact. Even without talking it's possible to get an idea about how others are feeling. In fact, you can often learn more about others by noticing what they do than what they say. Sometimes you might suspect people seem friendly, sometimes distant, sometimes tense, excited, bored, amused, or depressed. The point is that without any formal experience you can recognize and to some degree interpret messages that other people send nonverbally. In this chapter we want to sharpen the skills you already have, to give you a better grasp of the vocabulary of nonverbal language, and to show you how this understanding can help you know yourself and others better.

Talking is talking
Dancing is dancing

Talking is talking and not talking
Dancing is dancing and not dancing

Not talking is not talking and not not talking
Not dancing is not dancing and not not dancing

Talking is not dancing
Dancing is not talking

Not talking is not not dancing
Not dancing is not not talking

Not talking is not dancing
Not dancing is not talking

Talking is dancing
Dancing is talking

Dancing is talking
Talking is dancing

Dancing is talking and not talking
Talking is dancing and not dancing

Not dancing is not talking and not not talking
Not talking is not dancing and not not dancing

Dancing is not dancing
Talking is not talking

Not dancing is not not dancing
Not talking is not not talking

Not dancing is not dancing
Not talking is not talking

Dancing is dancing
Talking is talking

Douglas Dunn

First of all, he had to make it clear to those potential companions of his holiday that they were of no concern to him whatsoever. He stared through them, round them, over them—eyes lost in space. The beach might have been empty. If by chance a ball was thrown his way, he looked surprised; then let a smile of amusement lighten his face (Kindly Preedy), looked round dazed to see that there *were* people on the beach, tossed it back with a smile to himself and not a smile *at* the people, and then resumed carelessly his nonchalant survey of space.

But it was time to institute a little parade, the parade of the Ideal Preedy. By devious handlings he gave any who wanted to look a chance to see the title of his book—a Spanish translation of Homer, classic thus, but not daring, cosmopolitan too—and then gathered together his beach-wrap and bag into a neat sand-resistant pile (Methodical and Sensible Preedy), rose slowly to stretch at ease his big frame (Big-Cat Preedy), and tossed aside his sandals (Carefree Preedy, after all).

William Sansom
A Contest of Ladies

You Can't Not Communicate   The fact that communication without words does take place brings us to the second important feature of nonverbal communication. To understand what we mean here, think back to a recent time you spent with another person. Suppose we asked you not to communicate any messages at all while with your partner. What would you have done? Closed your eyes? Withdrawn into a ball? Left the room? You can probably see that even these behaviors communicate messages that mean you're avoiding contact.

Take a minute and try *not* communicating. Find a partner and spend some time trying not to disclose any messages to each other. What happened?

The impossibility of not communicating is extremely significant because it means that each of us is a kind of transmitter that cannot be shut off. No matter what we do, we send out messages that say something about ourselves. If, for instance, someone were observing you now, what nonverbal clues would they get about how you're feeling? Are you sitting forward or reclining back? Is your posture tense or relaxed? Are your eyes wide open or do they keep closing? What does your facial expression communicate now? Can you make your face expressionless? Don't people with expressionless faces communicate something to you?

The fact that we are all constantly sending nonverbal clues is important because it means that we have a constant source of information available about ourselves and others. If you can tune into these signals, you'll be more aware of how others feel and think, and you'll be better able to respond to their behavior.

Nonverbal Communication Transmits Feelings Whereas feelings are communicated quite well nonverbally, thoughts don't particularly lend themselves to nonverbal channels. Think back to the fantasy you just completed. Do you recall the different messages that you sent and received? Most people find that nonverbal communication expresses how they *feel,* unlike verbal messages, which usually relate what they *think.*

You can test this another way. Here's a list that contains both thoughts and feelings. Try to express each item nonverbally, and see which ones come most easily:

1. You're tired
2. You're in favor of capital punishment
3. You're attracted to another person in the group
4. You think marijuana should be legalized
5. You're angry at someone in the group

This experience shows that, short of charades, thoughts don't lend themselves to nonverbal expression, but feelings obviously do.

Nonverbal Communication Is Ambiguous
Some words of caution before introducing you to a fourth feature of nonverbal communication: A great deal of ambiguity surrounds nonverbal behavior. To understand what we mean, consider this: How would you interpret silence from your spouse, date, or companion after an evening in which you both laughed and joked a lot? Can you think of at least two possible meanings for this nonverbal behavior? Or suppose that a much-admired person with whom you've worked suddenly begins paying more attention to you than ever before. What could the possible meanings of this be?

The point is that although nonverbal behavior can be extremely revealing, it can have so many possible meanings that it's foolish to think that your interpretations will always be correct. It's important to recognize nonverbal messages as *clues* that need to be checked out for accuracy, and not facts. Popular advice on this subject notwithstanding, it's *not* usually possible to read a person like a book.

Writer (to movie producer Sam Goldwyn): Mr. Goldwyn, I'm telling you a sensational story. I'm only asking for your opinion, and you fall asleep.

Goldwyn: Isn't sleeping an opinion?

Much Nonverbal Communication Is Culture-Bound Besides nonverbal communication being ambiguous, it also varies from one culture to another. Depending on your background, you may interpret a particular nonverbal behavior differently than someone raised in different circumstances. Also, the meaning you attribute to a particular nonverbal behavior may be the same meaning attributed to some *other* nonverbal behavior by a member of a culture different from yours. Finally, although a particular nonverbal behavior may have meaning for you, in another culture it may be perceived as little more than idiosyncratic or random behavior.

Consider the following three nonverbal behaviors:

1. The little finger pointed straight up.
2. A rapid crossing of the index fingers.
3. The drawing of the index finger over an eyebrow after the finger has been licked briefly.

If you are a member of the predominant American culture, these three behaviors would probably appear meaningless. However, as Morsbach tells us, in Japan each is meaning-laden. The first gesture refers to a girlfriend, wife, or mistress; the second alludes to a fight; and the third is an indirect way to indicate to someone that he or she is a liar. Three examples of nonverbal behaviors that appear random and meaningless in one culture are recognized as patterned and meaningful in another.

Now, consider the following situation: A teacher is standing in front of her class and talking. Some students maintain eye contact with her while others do not. Which children are conveying respect for the teacher, the ones who maintain eye contact, or the ones who don't? Depending upon your own cultural background, the answer may be the former or the latter. For example, for Anglo children, maintaining eye contact is a sign of respect: Anglo children are taught to keep eye contact when their teacher speaks. Black children, on the other hand, are taught that looking is a sign of *dis*-respect.

Finally, consider the following example: A Japanese businessman sits across from an American businessman as they begin to discuss a trade agreement. The Japanese gentleman sits with his feet flat on the floor, his hands in his lap, and his torso erect. The American perceives that the Japanese is uncomfortable, tense, and likely to disagree with whatever he proposes. The Japanese businessman, on the other hand, recognizes that he has adopted a position identified as relaxed in his culture. The meanings attributed to the same behavior differ according to the cultural backgrounds of the participants.

Verbal and Nonverbal Communication

Although this chapter deals with nonverbal communication, don't get the idea that our words and actions are unrelated. Quite the opposite is true: Verbal and nonverbal communication are interconnected in every communication act, though not always in the same way. Let's take a look at the various relationships between our words and other types of expression.

Repeating   First, nonverbal behaviors can *repeat* what is said verbally. If someone asked you for directions to the nearest drugstore, you could say, "North of here about two blocks," and then repeat your instructions nonverbally by pointing north. This kind of repetition is especially useful when we're describing an idea that can also be viewed visually, such as size, shape, direction, and other such physically demonstrable concepts.

Substituting   Nonverbal messages may also *substitute* for verbal ones. For example, instead of saying, "North of here about two blocks," you could point north and add, "about two blocks." The usefulness of substitution goes far beyond simply describing physical ideas. For instance, the more you know someone, the easier it is to use nonverbal expressions as a kind of shorthand to substitute for words. When you see a familiar friend wearing a certain facial expression, it isn't necessary to ask, "What kind of day did you have?" In the same way, experience has probably shown you that certain kinds of looks, gestures, and other clues say far better than words, "I'm angry at you," or, "I feel great."

In spite of the usefulness of nonverbal communication as a substitute for words, it's often dangerous to trust your interpretations and unspoken messages entirely. Even with the people you know best there's room for misunderstanding, and the potential for jumping to wrong conclusions increases the less you know the other person. Remember our warning: nonverbal communication is ambiguous.

Complementing   Another way in which verbal and nonverbal messages can relate is called *complementing*. If you saw a student talking to a teacher, and her head was slightly bowed, her voice low and hesitating, and she shuffled slowly from foot to foot, you might conclude that she felt inferior to the teacher, possibly em-

I suppose it was something you said
That caused me to tighten
And pull away.
And when you asked,
"What is it?"
I, of course, said,
"Nothing."

Whenever I say, "Nothing,"
You may be very certain there is something.
The something is a cold, hard lump of
Nothing.

Lois Wyse

barrassed about something she did. The nonverbal behaviors you observed provided the context for the verbal behaviors—they conveyed the relationship between the teacher and student. Complementing nonverbal behaviors signal the attitudes that the interactants hold toward one another.

Accenting   Nonverbal behaviors can also *accent* verbal messages. Just as we use italics in print to underline a word or idea, we can emphasize some part of a face-to-face message in various ways: Pointing an accusing finger adds emphasis to criticism (as well as probably creating defensiveness in the receiver); shrugging one's shoulders accents confusion; and hugging can highlight excitement or affection. As you'll see later in this chapter, the voice plays a big role in accenting verbal messages.

Regulating Nonverbal behavior also serves to *regulate* verbal behavior. By lowering the voice at the end of a sentence ("trailing off"), we indicate that the other person may speak. We also convey this information through the use of eye contact and by the way we position our bodies. Young children are often yelled at for interrupting adults. What adults fail to understand is that children have not as yet learned all the subtle cues indicating when the other person may speak. Through a rough series of trials and errors (*very* rough in some homes), children finally learn how to "read" other people well enough to avoid interrupting behaviors.

Contradicting Finally—and often most significantly—nonverbal behavior can often *contradict* the spoken word. If you said, "North of here about two blocks" and pointed south, your nonverbal message would contradict what you said. While sending such incompatible messages might sound foolish at first, there are times when we deliberately do just that. One big use of double messages (as they're often called) is to politely but clearly send a message that might be difficult to handle if it were expressed in words. For instance, think of a time when you became bored with a conversation while your companion kept rambling on. At such a time the most straightforward statement would be, "I'm tired of talking to you and want to go meet someone else." Although it might feel good to be so direct, this kind of honesty is often considered impolite for anyone over five years of age.

Instead of being blunt, people frequently rely on nonverbal methods of sending the same message. While nodding politely and murmuring "huh-huh" and "no kidding?" at the appropriate times, a communicator can signal a desire to leave by looking around the room, turning slightly away from the speaker, or even making a point of yawning. In most cases clues such as this are enough to end the conversation without the awkwardness of expressing outright what's going on. Courtship is one area in which double messages abound. Even in these liberated times the answer "no" to a romantic proposition may mean "yes." Of course, it may also really mean an emphatic "no." The success of many relationships has depended on the ability of one partner to figure out—mostly using nonverbal messages—when a double message is being sent, and when to take the words at face value.

So far we've been talking about cases where a communicator deliberately contradicts a verbal message with nonverbal signals. There are other times when we unintentionally say one thing with our words and another with our actions. Have you ever tried to look confident when you were really afraid? Often the facade is almost perfect; then, just when you're convinced that you're looking like a calm, cool character, you notice some behavior that is an obvious signal of your nervousness: shaky knees, sweaty palms, quivering voice. This kind of double message is the downfall of many of us at one time or another: students in beginning public speaking classes, or nervous applicants in job interviews, for example.

As we discuss the different kinds of nonverbal communication, we'll point out a number of ways in which people contradict themselves by either conscious or unconscious behaviors. Thus, by the end of this chapter you should have a better idea of how others feel, even when they can't or won't tell you with their words.

Types of Nonverbal Communication

So far we've talked about the characteristics of nonverbal communication and how our unspoken messages relate to our use of words. Now it's time to look at the many types of nonverbal communication.

Clothing The way we dress tells others something about us. The armed forces, for instance, have developed uniforms partly as a way of showing who has what particular job and who's in charge. Thus, uniforms are a sort of nonverbal badge that describes the wearer's place in the military social system. Although many have a tendency to criticize the military as a rigid system that puts people into strictly defined classes, in many ways we also use clothing to categorize people.

Think about the people you know. Can you tell anything about their political or social philosophies by the way they dress? A good place to begin your survey is with the faculty at your school. Is there any relationship between the way instructors dress and their teaching style? Take a look at your friends. Do you find that the people who spend time together share the same ideas about clothing? Is there a "uniform" for political radicals and one for conservatives? Is there a high fashion "uniform" that tells the public who's in style and who's out of it?

A student proved to himself how clothing labels a person's social position by trying an experiment. He spent a week hitchhiking back and forth from Santa Barbara to Los Angeles, a distance of about 100 miles. Every other day he would alternate his clothing style. On Monday, Wednesday, and Friday he wore old Levi's, sandals, and a tie-dyed sweatshirt. On Tuesday, Thursday, and Saturday he put on stay-pressed bell-bottomed pants, well-shined leather shoes, and a freshly ironed shirt. Other than his clothing, he kept all factors constant: He began at the same time each day; stood in the same spot; and signaled with his thumb in exactly the same way. The results seemed to prove how much clothes can say to others. As he described:

It was incredible! On my three grubby days I got rides from people who looked just like I did. Two of them drove old V.W. buses, and the third had a '55 Ford pickup truck. They all wore Levi's, boots, and all had pretty much the same lifestyle. On the days when I dressed up, I got rides in shiny new Oldsmobiles and Cadillacs from people who were completely opposite from the ones I'd driven with the day before. The very first thing one guy said after picking me up was how nice it was to see a young person who wasn't one of those "hippie types!"

As well as illustrating the influence clothing has in our culture, this experiment points out a real danger inherent in reading many nonverbal messages: We find ourselves stereotyping others on skimpy evidence, and often our interpretations are

If one wears a shoe known to be a runner's shoe, those knowledgeable in these matters can recognize another of their kind. Shoes are ranked in terms of status in the runner's culture, but for the purposes of achieving recognition as a member, it is sufficient merely to be sporting a running shoe; an Interval 305 New Balance or Brooks 270 will do the job.

Although any running shoe suffices to communicate "I am a runner," the kind of shoe worn does articulate the message further. For example, a person sporting a pair of Eugen Brutting Marathons, a shoe with a distinctive diamond embossed with the letters EB, communicates that his or her commitment to running is serious. These shoes cost approximately $12 more than other popular running shoes. They are known for their ultralight yet substantive construction. A person wearing them communicates that he or she knows a great deal about shoes, that he or she trains long and hard and for fast times.

Jeffrey E. Nash
Decoding the Runner's Wardrobe

mistaken. By jumping to conclusions about another human from these surface appearances, we may very well be stereotyping ourselves out of some important relationships.

At this point you might be thinking of the old saying, "You can't judge a book by its cover." How valid is such a statement? In an attempt to answer this, psychologist Lewis Aiken conducted a study focusing on "wearer characteristics." His goal was to see if there were any relationship between the type of clothing a person chooses to wear and personality. Aiken focused his study on female subjects and found that clothes do offer some clues about the characteristics of the wearer. For instance, Aiken found that women who had a high concern for decoration and style in dress

also scored above average on traits such as conformity, sociability, and nonintroversion. Women who dressed for comfort also scored high in the areas of self-control and extroversion. A great interest in dress correlated positively with compliance, stereotypic thinking, social conscientiousness, and insecurity. Those who dressed in high conformity to style also rated above average on social conformity, restraint, and submissiveness. And finally, women who stressed economy in their dress rated high on responsibility, alertness, efficiency, and precision.

To see if Aiken's results held for men as well as women and to bring his research up to date, Lawrence Rosenfeld and Tim Plax conducted a follow-up investigation. They gave a battery of psychological examinations to a large number of male and female college students, and also administered a test that measured the

"A general! Goodness gracious, you don't <u>look</u> like a general!"

subjects' attitudes toward clothes on four dimensions: clothing consciousness, exhibitionism, practicality, and the desire to design clothes.

Upon analyzing the results, some definite relationships between personality type and approach to clothing did emerge. For instance, both men and women who were not especially conscious of clothing style proved to be more independent than their more stylish counterparts. Highly exhibitionistic males were less sympathetic than other groups, and exhibitionistic women were more detached in their relationships. Men who dressed in a highly practical manner rated low on leadership orientation and were less motivated toward friendship relationships, whereas those less concerned with practicality were more success oriented and forceful.

Results such as these are fascinating, for they show that to some degree we *can* get an idea about human "books" by their covers. At the same time it's important to remember that research results are generalizations, and that not every clothes-conscious or exhibitionistic dresser fits into the pattern just described. Again, the best course is to treat your nonverbal interpretations as hunches which need to be checked out and not as absolute facts.

The Face and Eyes   Clothes might be the first place we look for clues to a person's character, but once the impact of clothing has passed, the face and eyes are probably the most noticed parts of the body. This doesn't mean, however, that the nonverbal messages from the face and eyes are the easiest to read. The face is a tremendously complicated channel of expression to interpret for the following reasons:

1.   It's hard to describe the number and kind of expressions we commonly produce with our face and eyes. For example, researchers have found that there are at least eight distinguishable positions of the eyebrows and forehead, eight more of the eyes and lids, and ten for the lower face. When you multiply this complexity by the number of emotions we experience, you can see why it would be almost impossible to compile a dictionary of facial expressions and their corresponding emotions.

2.   Facial expressions change with incredible speed. For example, slow-motion films have been taken that show expressions fleeting across a subject's face in as short a time as a fifth of a second.

Also, it seems that different emotions show most clearly in different parts of the face: happiness and surprise in the eyes and lower face; anger in the lower face, brows, and forehead; fear and sadness in the eyes; and disgust in the lower face.

3.   We learn to control facial expressions early in life. Thus, most of us are fairly successful at disguising or censoring undesired messages. In spite of this censoring, the rapid speed at which expressions can change, and the inability of senders to see their own faces and make sure they send the desired messages, means that each of us does convey a great deal of "true" information, whether we want to or not.

Two prominent researchers in this area, Paul Ekman and Wallace Friesen, talk about three ways in which we falsify messages by controlling our facial expression.

Simulating   Sometimes we hide a lack of any feelings at all by *simulating* an expression we don't really feel. For example, suppose someone you know only casually tells you that a friend was in an auto accident. You may not be particularly upset by this news, but you feign an expression of upset because you feel the situation calls for it. The real feeling you had was close to neutral, and you created the upset expression to meet the demands of the social situation.

Neutralizing   At other times we avoid expressing an undesired emotion by *neutralizing* our expression. For example, suppose just as you get into the shower the doorbell chimes. You have to shut off the water, dry yourself, jump into a robe or some clothing, and rush to the door before the person who rang walks off—all in about twenty seconds. Your expression as you race to the door is probably one of anger, or at least irritation. But just as you open the door you neutralize the expression, tone it down. The neutral mask covers the expression of the real feeling.

Masking A third technique of falsifying involves *masking* a true emotion with one seemingly more appropriate. Boring classes may result in half-closed eyes, frequent yawns, and a dull, glazed-over expression, but they also give rise to a common mask for boredom: an "interested" face, one with wide-open eyes, a brow wrinkled to convey thought, and the expression of other more situation-appropriate responses.

In spite of the complex ways in which we strive to control our facial expressions, you can still pick up messages by watching a person's face. One of the easiest ways is to look for expressions that seem to be overdone. Often when people try to fool themselves or others they'll emphasize their masks to a point where their expressions seem too exaggerated to be true. Another way to detect feelings is by watching for expressions at moments when those displaying them aren't thinking about what their faces are showing. We've all had the experience of glancing into another car while stopped in a traffic jam or looking around at a sporting event and seeing expressions that the wearer would probably never show in more guarded moments. At other times it's possible to watch a micro-expression as it flashes across someone's face. For just a moment we see

> The face is the mirror of the mind, and eyes without speaking confess the secrets of the heart.
>
> St. Jerome

a flash of emotion quite different from the one a speaker is trying to convey. Finally, you may be able to spot contradictory expressions on different parts of someone's face: Eyes say one thing, but the expression of mouth or eyebrows might be sending quite a different message.

The eyes themselves can send several kinds of messages. Meeting another's glance with your eyes is usually a sign of involvement, whereas looking away signals a desire to avoid contact. (As we mentioned earlier, this is why solicitors on the street—panhandlers, salespeople, petitioners—try to catch your eye.) Once they've managed to establish contact with a glance it becomes harder for the approached person to draw away. A friend explained how to apply this principle to hitchhiking: "When I'm hitching a ride, I'm always careful to look the drivers in the eye as they come toward me. Most of them will try to look somewhere else as they pass, but if I can catch a driver's eye, the car will almost always stop." Most of us remember trying to avoid a question we didn't understand by glancing away from the teacher. At times like these we usually became very interested in our textbooks, fingernails, the clock—anything but the teacher's stare. Of course, the teacher always seemed to know the meaning of this nonverbal behavior and ended up picking on those of us who signaled our uncertainty.

Eyes also can communicate positive or negative attitudes. When someone glances toward us with the proper facial expression, we get a clear message that the looker is interested in us, thus the expression "making eyes." At the same time, when our long glances toward others are avoided, we can be pretty sure that the others aren't as interested in us as we are in them. (Of course, there are all sorts of courtship games in which the receiver of a glance pretends not to notice any message by glancing away, yet signals interest with some other part of the body.)

The eyes communicate both dominance and submission. We've all played the game of trying to stare down somebody, and in real life there are also times when downcast eyes are a sign of giving in. In some religious orders, for example, subordinate members are expected to keep their eyes downcast when addressing a superior.

Even the pupils of our eyes communicate. E. H. Hess and J. M. Polt of the University of Chicago measured the amount of pupil dilation while showing men and women various pictures. The results of the experiment were interesting: A person's eyes grow larger in proportion to the degree of interest he or she has in an object. For example, men's pupils grew about 18 percent larger when looking at

pictures of a naked woman, and the rate of dilation for women looking at a naked man's picture was 20 percent. Interestingly enough, the greatest increase in pupil size occurred when women looked at a picture of a mother and infant. A good salesperson can increase profits by being aware of pupil dilation. As Edward Hall describes, he was once in a Middle East bazaar, where an Arab merchant insisted that a customer looking at his jewelry buy a certain piece to which the shopper hadn't been paying much attention. But the vendor had been watching the pupils of the buyer's eyes and had known what the buyer really wanted.

Posture   Another way we communicate nonverbally is through our posture. To see if this is true, stop reading for a moment and notice how you're sitting. What does your position say nonverbally about how you feel? Are there any other people near you now? What messages do you get from their present posture? By paying attention to the postures of those around you, as well as to your own, you'll find another channel of nonverbal communication that can furnish information concerning how people feel about themselves and others.

The English language indicates the deep links between posture and communication. English is full of expressions that tie emotional states with body postures:

1. "I won't take this lying down!"
2. "He can't stand on his own two feet."
3. "She has to carry a heavy burden."
4. "Take a load off your back."
5. "You're all wrapped up in yourself."
6. "Don't be so uptight!"

Such phrases show that an awareness of posture exists for us, even if it's often unconscious. The main reason we miss most posture messages is that they aren't too obvious. It's seldom that people who feel weighed down by a problem hunch over so much that they stand out in a crowd. And when we're bored we usually don't lean back and slump enough to embarrass the person with whom we're bored. In interpreting posture, then, the key is to look for small changes that might be shadows of the way people feel inside.

For example, a teacher who has a reputation for interesting classes told us how he uses his understanding of micropostures to do a better job:

Because of my large classes I have to lecture a lot, and that's an easy way to turn students off. I work hard to make my talks entertaining, but you know that nobody's perfect, and I do have my off days. I can tell when I'm not doing a good job of communicating by picking out three or four students before I start my talk and watching how they sit throughout the class

period. As long as they're leaning forward in their seats, I know I'm doing okay, but if I look up and see them starting to slump back, I know I'd better change my approach.

Psychologist Albert Mehrabian has found that other postural keys to feelings are tension and relaxation. He says that we take relaxed postures in nonthreatening situations and tighten up when threatened. Based on this observation he says we can tell a good deal about how others feel simply by watching how tense or loose they seem to be. For example, he suggests that watching tenseness is a way of detecting status differences: the lower-status person is generally the more rigid and tense-appearing, whereas the one with higher status is more relaxed. This situation is the kind that often happens when we picture a "chat" with the boss (or professor or judge) where we sit ramrod straight while our "superior" leans back in a chair.

The same principle applies to social situations where it's often possible to tell who's uncomfortable by looking at pictures. Often you'll see someone laughing and talking as if perfectly at home, with posture shouting nervousness. Some people never relax, and their posture shows it.

Why have hands? They are, from time to time, useful. This has been, in many cases, established. They are mankind's only really trustworthy vocabulary, the nerves and muscles of the spirit made manifest.

Kenneth Patchen

Gestures   While we can use our entire body to communicate through postures, we also express feelings with just one body part through gesturing. Like other forms of nonverbal communication, gestures can either reinforce or contradict a speaker's words. We've all seen the reinforcing power that comes from certain body movements. For instance, imagine the gestures that would accompany the following statements:

1. "What can I do about it?"
2. "I can't stand it anymore!"
3. "Now let me tell you something!"
4. "Easy now. It'll be all right."

It was easy to envision what gestures should accompany each message, wasn't it? You can see what an important role these movements play by imagining a speaker expressing the same words without

gesturing. Somehow the speaker would seem less involved or sincere. In fact, an absence of gestures is usually a good indication that the speaker may be feeling unenthusiastic about the subject being discussed.

Sometimes gestures provide a clue to unspoken feelings—ones that even the sender may be unaware of. Sigmund Freud, pioneer explorer of the subconscious, recognized this in 1905 when he wrote, "He that has eyes to see and ears to hear may convince himself that no mortal can keep a secret. If his lips are silent, he chatters with his fingertips; betrayal oozes out of him at every pore." The report of one psychotherapist, P. Wachtel, gives a dramatic example of how gestures can provide clues to inner feelings:

Mrs. L sat leaning back, with one hand holding the other. Her hands seemed to be acting out a struggle to prevent expression through gesturing, mildly reminiscent of the efforts of Dr. Strangelove to prevent his arm from making a Hitler salute. The hand being held continued to begin movements which were prevented by the holding hand.

Of course, such telltale gesturing isn't restricted to the psychiatrist's office. One clear example of someone whose feelings show up through gestures is the fidgeter, who assures us that "everything is fine" while almost ceaselessly biting a fingernail, flicking a cigarette, or bending a paperclip. Even when the fidgeter is aware of these gestures and tries to control them, the nervousness usually finds another way of leaking out, such as toe tapping, leg crossing and uncrossing, or other restless movements.

Besides nervousness, you can often detect other emotions from a person's gestures. It's possible to observe anger by looking beyond a smile and noticing whitened knuckles and clenched fists. When a person would like to express friendship or attraction, but for some reason feels inhibited, you can sometimes notice a slight reaching out or maybe even an opening of hands. We've even seen those who proclaim to all how open and honest they want to be while their gestures suggest something different: talking from behind a hand, folding their arms across their chests, or turning away from us. In one article, Paul Scheflen, a psychiatrist, tells how a person's sexual feelings can be signaled through gestures. He describes "preening behaviors" that draw attention to the sender's body and advertise a "come-on" message. Movements such as stroking or combing the hair, glancing in a mirror, and rearranging the clothing are often signals of sexual interest in another person.

Ekman and Friesen describe another kind of double message—the "lie of omission." Deceivers nonverbally show true feelings by failing to accompany words with appropriate gestures. This is the kind of behavior we see from people who say they are excited or happy while sitting almost motionless with hands, arms, legs, and posture signaling boredom, discomfort, or fatigue.

Touch Besides being the earliest means we have of making contact with others, touching is essential to our healthy development. During the nineteenth and early twentieth centuries a large percentage of children born every year died from a disease then called *marasmus*, which translated from Greek means "wasting away." In some orphanages the mortality rate was nearly 100 percent, but even children in the most "progressive" homes, hospitals, and other institutions died regularly from the ailment. When researchers finally tracked down the causes of this disease, they found that the infants suffered from lack of physical contact with parents or nurses, rather than from lack of nutrition, medical care, or other factors. The infants hadn't been touched enough, and died as a result. From this knowledge came the practice of "mothering" children in institutions—picking the baby up, carrying it around, and handling it several times each day. At one hospital that began this practice, the death rate of infants fell from between 30 and 35 percent to below 10 percent.

As children develop, their need for being touched continues. In his excellent book *Touching: The Human Significance of the Skin,* Ashley Montagu describes research suggesting that allergies, eczema, and other health problems are in part caused by a person's lack of mother-contact while an infant. Although Montagu says that these problems develop early in life, he also cites cases where adults suffering from conditions as diverse as asthma and schizophrenia have been successfully treated by psychiatric therapy that uses extensive physical contact.

Touch seems to increase a child's mental functioning as well as physical health. L. J. Yarrow conducted surveys showing that babies who have been given plenty of physical stimulation by their mothers have significantly higher IQs than those receiving less contact.

The society we live in places less importance on touch than on other, less immediate senses, such as sight or hearing. Our language is full of visual and aural figures of speech, such as: "Seeing is believing"; "I'll be hearing from you"; "Here's looking at you"; and "Sounding something out." As Bernard Gunther points out, when leaving someone we say, "See you later," never "touch," "smell," or "taste" you later.

In spite of the need for making physical contact with others, North American society discourages much touching. Anyone who has traveled to other countries, particularly in Latin America, southern Europe, and parts of Africa, has noticed the differences in the amount of contact between citizens there and in the United States, Canada, and northern Europe.

For most Americans, the amount of touching decreases with age. Sixth-graders touch each other less than first-graders. Parents touch their older children less often than their younger ones. Within our culture there are differences between the touching behavior of various groups. For instance, men touch each other much less than they touch women. While this might seem perfectly natural to someone brought up in a culture holding that touch between members of the same sex suggests homo-sexuality, a look at other cultures shows that prolonged hand contact, embracing, and even types of kissing goes on be-

tween the most masculine of men and the most feminine of women.

What touching does go on between adults in North American culture is highly prescribed by unwritten social rules. In the 1960s Sidney Jourard conducted a survey exploring touching behavior. He first divided the body into fourteen areas (such as top of head, face, hands, thighs, etc.), and asked 300 students in which areas they gave and received touches most often when interacting with parents, same-sex friends and opposite-sex friends.

Jourard found that body contact occurs most frequently between friends of the opposite sex, and is usually confined to upper portions of the body. The data for Jourard's report was collected during 1963 and 1964. During the intervening years there has been much talk about the need for more touch. But has the actual amount of contact changed? Is one group more accessible to touch now than in 1964? Are different body parts more accessible? Do certain people have greater access to others? To answer these questions, Lawrence Rosenfeld and two of his students, Sallie Kartus and Chett Ray, repeated Jourard's study in 1976.

A large number of unmarried male and female undergraduate students between eighteen and twenty-two years old completed a questionnaire asking how often and where on their bodies during the previous twelve months they were touched by their mother, father, closest same-sex friend, and closest opposite-sex friend. The body diagram presented to the subjects was divided into fourteen areas, starting with 1 at the top of the head, and ending with 14 at the toes (see Fig. 9–1).

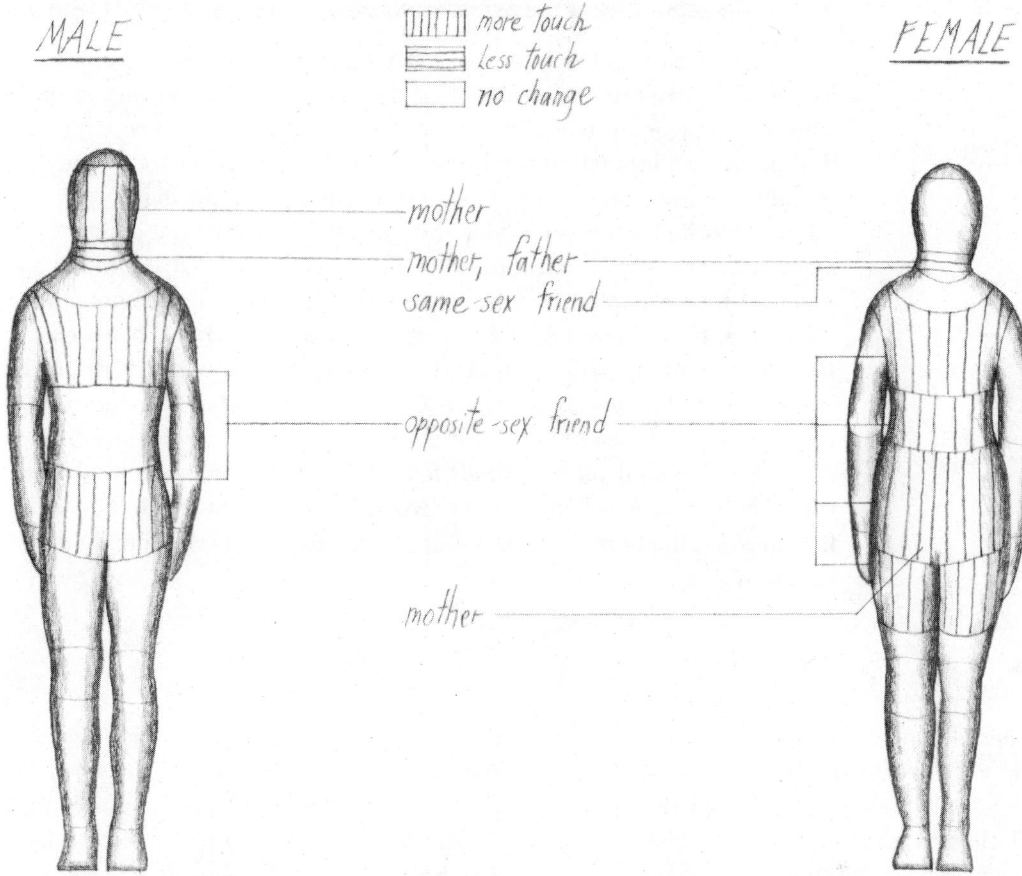

MALE

⊞⊞	more touch
☰	less touch
☐	no change

FEMALE

mother
mother, father
same-sex friend

opposite-sex friend

mother

Figure 9-1

Regardless of the increase in talk about touch in our society, there was very little change in body accessibility. Touching remained about the same between parents and their children and also between same-sex friends. However, touch between opposite-sex friends increased.

Data such as this paints a clear, if depressing, view of touching in our society. As young children, most Americans receive at least a modest amount of physical love and intimacy from their parents. The next time most can expect to receive this level of physical caring won't come until they have chosen a partner, sometime in late adolescence. Even then, the nurturing seemingly brought by physical contact will most often come only from one's partner—a heavy demand for one person to carry.

Associated with (but not always the same as) the kind of love and intimacy we've been discussing is the sexual side of touching. It's obvious that sex can be one way of expressing care for a partner. But

We can turn now to the safer and more tender intimacies of the dance-floor. At parties, discotheques, dance-halls and ballrooms, adults who are strangers to one another can come together and move around the room in an intimate frontal embrace. Individuals who are already friendly can also use the situation to escalate a non-touching relationship into a touching one. The special role that social dancing plays in our society is that it permits, in its special context, a sudden and dramatic increase in body intimacy in a way that would be impossible elsewhere. If the same full frontal embrace were performed between strangers, or partial strangers, outside the context of the dance-floor, the impact would be entirely different. Dancing, so to speak, devalues the significance of the embrace, lowering its threshold to a point where it can lightly be indulged in without fear of rebuff. Having permitted it to occur, it then gives a chance for it to work its powerful magic. If the magic fails to work, the formalities of the situation also permit retreat without ignominy.

Desmond Morris
Intimate Behavior

especially in a touch-starved culture, sex can also serve another purpose not necessarily connected with intimate love or affection: It may simply be a socially acceptable way of touching and being touched by another human being. While it's possible to argue that there's nothing wrong with making this kind of contact, it's sad to think that a sexual act is one of the very few ways to touch another person acceptably in a manner more personal than a handshake. While we're only speculating, see if this idea makes sense to you: If we lived in a culture where physical contact was more acceptable, perhaps many people could achieve the touching they seem to need without resorting to sex out of desperation. Then sex would be able to

exist in its proper role, as one form of contact, to be valued and enjoyed when the time is right instead of being sometimes overused by people who see it as the only way to bridge the gap between themselves and others.

Voice   The voice itself is another channel of nonverbal communication. If you think about it for a moment, you'll realize that a certain way of speaking can give the same word or words many meanings. For example, look at the possible meanings from a single sentence just by changing the word emphasis:

This is a fantastic communication book. (Not just any book, but *this* one in particular.)

This is a *fantastic* communication book. (This book is superior, exciting.)

This is a fantastic *communication* book. (The book is good as far as communication goes; it may not be so great as literature or drama.)

This is a fantastic communication *book.* (It's not a play or record, it's a book.)

It's possible to get an idea across without ever expressing it outright by accenting a certain word in a sentence. In *Nonverbal Communication in Human Interaction,* Mark Knapp quotes an example from *Newsweek* on how this is done. It describes how Robert J. McCloskey, a State Department official in the Nixon Administration, was able to express the government's position in an off-the-record way:

McCloskey has three distinct ways of saying, "I would not speculate:" spoken without accent, it means the department doesn't know for sure; emphasis on the "I" means "I wouldn't, but you may—and with some assurance;" accent on "speculate" indicates that the questioner's premise is probably wrong.

Our voice communicates in many other ways—through its tone, speed, pitch, number, and lengths of pauses, volume, and nonfluencies (such as stammering, use of "uh," "um," and "er"). All these factors together can be called *paralanguage,* and they can do a great deal to reinforce or contradict the message our words convey.

Sarcasm is one instance in which we use both emphasis and tone of voice to change a statement's meaning to the opposite of its verbal message. Experience this yourself with the following three statements (first time through say them literally, and then say them sarcastically):

1. "Darling, what a beautiful little gown!"
2. "I really had a wonderful time on my blind date."
3. "There's nothing I like better than calves' brains on toast."

Albert Mehrabian and others have conducted experiments indicating that when the vocal factors (tone of voice, nonfluencies, emphasis, and so forth) contradict the verbal message (words), the vocal factors carry more meaning. They had subjects evaluate the degree of liking communicated by a message in which vocal clues conflicted with the words and found that the words had little effect on the interpretation of the message.

Communication through paralanguage isn't always intentional. Often our voices give us away when we're trying to create an impression different than our actual feelings. For example, you've probably had experiences of trying to sound calm and serene when you were really exploding with inner nervousness. Maybe your deception went along perfectly for a while—just the right smile, no telltale fidgeting of the hands, posture appearing relaxed—and then, without being able to do a thing about it, right in the middle of your relaxed comments your voice squeaked! The charade was over.

In addition to reinforcing or contradicting messages, some vocal factors influence the way a speaker will be perceived by others. For example, breathiness in a man causes him to be perceived as artistic, and in a woman causes her to be perceived as petite, pretty, yet shallow. Both men and women suffer being viewed as the same stereotypes when they speak with a flat voice: They are perceived as sluggish, cold, and withdrawn. And both men and women suffer stereotyping associated with an increase in speaking rate: They are perceived as more animated and extroverted. Nasality is probably the most socially offensive vocal cue, giving rise to a host of perceived undesirable characteristics.

The degree to which vocal factors communicate is extensive, as Lawrence Rosenfeld and Jean Civikly have pointed out in *With Words Unspoken: The Nonverbal Experience*. From vocal cues *alone* (people in these studies could not see the person speaking), we can determine age, differentiate "big" from "small" people, and judge personality characteristics, such as dominance, introversion, sociability, and certain emotions (although fear and nervousness, love and sadness, and pride and satisfaction are often confused). Interestingly, from vocal cues alone we can determine a person's status—and we can do this on the basis of *single word cues* (we don't need more than a few seconds worth of a speech sample).

Vocal cues are being used for more than just social purposes. There are now a number of available devices that can analyze the characteristics of a speaker's voice to determine whether the words being uttered are the truth or lies. One such device is called the *Psychological Stress Evaluator* (P.S.E.). This machine measures those muscular tremors in the voice that cause extremely small variations in pitch. While these changes are inaudible to the human ear, the P.S.E. can give clues as to whether the speaker is under tension, possibly due to lying.

Although machines such as the P.S.E. are relatively new and still being tested for reliability, they have already been put to interesting uses. Several court cases have been dropped because the defendants' voices indicated innocence. In one of the century's major crimes, George O'Toole, a former C.I.A. employee, examined the recorded voice of Lee Harvey Oswald, the presumed assassin of President John F. Kennedy. According to O'Toole's analysis, Oswald was telling the truth when he stated that he did not shoot Kennedy. As the technology to evaluate vocal clues becomes more precise, perhaps mysteries such as the Kennedy assassination will be more quickly and accurately resolved.

Proxemics and Territoriality   Proxemics is the study of how people and animals use the space around them. Before we discuss this fascinating area of research, try the following experiment.

Choose a partner, go to opposite sides of the room, and face each other. Very slowly begin walking toward each other while carrying on a conversation. You might simply talk about how you feel as you experience the activity. As you move closer, try to be aware of any change in your feelings. Continue moving slowly toward each other until you are only an inch or so apart. Remember how you feel at this point. Now, while still facing each other, back up until you're at a comfortable distance for carrying on your conversation.

During this experiment your feelings will most likely change at least three times. During the first phase, when you were across the room from your partner, you probably felt unnaturally far away. Then, as you neared a point about three feet distant, you probably felt like stopping; this is the distance at which two people in our culture normally stand while conversing socially. If your partner wasn't someone you're emotionally close to, you probably began to feel quite uncomfortable as you moved through this normal range and came closer; it's possible that you had to force yourself not to move back. Some people find this phase so uncomfortable that they can't get closer than twenty inches or so to their partner.

The reason for your discomfort has to do with your spatial needs. Each of us carries around a sort of invisible bubble of *personal space* wherever we go. We think of the area inside this bubble as our own—almost as much a part of us as our own bodies. As you moved closer to your partner, the distance between your bubbles narrowed and at a certain point disappeared altogether: Your space had been invaded, and this is the point at which you probably felt uncomfortable. As you moved away again, your partner retreated out of your bubble, and you felt more relaxed.

Of course, if you were to try this experiment with someone close to you—your husband, wife, girlfriend or boyfriend—you might not have felt any discomfort at all, even while touching. On the other hand, if you'd been approaching someone who made you uncomfortable—a total stranger or someone you disliked— you probably would have stopped farther away from them. The reason for this is that our personal bubbles vary in size according to the person we're with and the situation we're in. And it's precisely the varying size of our personal space—the distance that we put between ourselves and others—which gives a nonverbal clue about our feelings.

Anthropologist Edward T. Hall has defined four distances we use in our everyday lives. He says that we choose a particular one depending upon how we feel toward others at a given time, and that by "reading" which distance people take, we can get some insight into their feelings.

Intimate distance   The first of Hall's zones begins with skin contact and ranges out to about eighteen inches. We usually use intimate distance with people who are emotionally very close to us, and then mostly in private situations—making love, caressing, comforting, protecting. By allowing someone to move into our intimate distance we let them enter our personal space. When we do this voluntarily, it's usually a sign of trust: We've willingly lowered our defenses. On the other hand, when someone invades this most personal area without our consent, we usually feel threatened. This explains the feeling you may have had during the last exercise when your partner intruded into your space without any real invitation from you. It also explains the discomfort we sometimes feel when forced into crowded places such as buses or elevators with

> Once I heard a hospital nurse describing doctors. She said there were beside-the-bed doctors, who were interested in the patient, and foot-of-the-bed doctors, who were interested in the patient's condition. They unconsciously expressed their emotional involvement—or lack of it—by where they stood.
>
> Edward Hall

strangers. At times like these the standard behavior in our society is to draw away or tense our muscles and avoid eye contact. This is a nonverbal way of signaling, "I'm sorry for invading your territory, but the situation forced it."

In courtship situations a critical moment usually occurs when one member of a couple first moves into the other's intimate zone. If the partner being approached does not retreat, this usually signals that the relationship is moving into a new stage. On the other hand, if the reaction to the advance is withdrawal to a greater distance, the initiator should get the message that it isn't yet time to get more intimate. We remember from our dating experiences the significance of where on the car seat our companions chose to sit. If they moved close to us, it meant one thing; if they stayed jammed against the passenger's door, we got quite a different message.

Personal distance   This second spatial zone ranges from eighteen inches at its closest point to four feet at its farthest. Its

closer phase is the distance at which most couples stand in public. But if someone of the opposite sex stands this near one partner at a party, the other partner is likely to feel uncomfortable. This "moving in" often is taken to mean that something more than casual conversation is taking place. The far range of personal distance runs from about two-and-a-half to four feet. It's the zone just beyond the other person's reach. As Hall puts it, at this distance we can keep someone "at arm's length." This choice of words suggests the type of communication that goes on at this range: The contacts are still reasonably close, but they're much less personal than the ones that occur a foot or so closer.

Test this for yourself. Start a conversation with someone at a distance of about three feet, and slowly move a foot or so closer. Do you notice a difference? Does this distance affect your conversation?

Social distance   This third zone ranges from four to about twelve feet out. Within it are the kinds of communication that usually occur in business situations. Its closer phase, from four to seven feet, is the distance at which conversations usually occur between salespeople and customers and between people who work together. Most people feel uncomfortable when a salesclerk comes as close as three feet, whereas four or five feet nonverbally signals, "I'm here to help you, but I don't mean to be too personal or pushy."

We use the far range of social distance— seven to twelve feet—for more formal and impersonal situations. This is the range at which we sit from our boss (or other authority figure) as he or she stares across the desk at us. Sitting at this distance signals a far different and less relaxed type of conversation than if we were to pull a chair around to the boss's side of the desk and sit only three or so feet away.

Public distance   This is Hall's term for the furthest zone, running outward from twelve feet. The closer range of public distance is the one that most teachers use in the classroom. In the further reaches of public space—twenty-five feet and beyond—two-way communication is almost impossible. In some cases it's necessary for speakers to use public distance due to the size of their audience, but we can assume that anyone who voluntarily chooses to use it when he or she could be closer is not interested in having a dialogue.

When our spatial bubble is invaded, we respond with what are called *barrier behaviors,* behaviors designed to create a barrier (or fix a broken one) between ourselves and other people. You may wish to invade someone's personal space and note the reaction. At first the person is most likely to simply back away, probably without realizing what is happening. Next, your partner might attempt to put an object between you, such as a desk, a chair, or some books clutched to the chest, all in an effort to get some separation. Then, the other person will probably decrease eye contact (the "elevator syndrome," in which we can crowd in and even touch one another so long as we avoid eye contact). Furthermore, your reluctant partner might sneeze, cough, scratch, and exhibit any variety of behaviors to discourage your antisocial behavior. Finally, in the end, if none of these behaviors achieve the desired goal of getting some space between the

two of you the other person might "counterattack," gently at first ("Move back, will you?"), but then more forcefully (probably with a shove).

Writers sometimes confuse personal space with a related concept: *territoriality.* Whereas personal space is the invisible bubble we carry around, the bubble that serves as an extension of our physical being, territory remains stationary. Any geographical area, such as a room, house, neighborhood, or country to which we assume some kind of "rights" is our territory. What's interesting about territoriality is that there is no real basis for the assumption of proprietary rights of "owning" some area, but the feeling of "owning" exists nonetheless. My room in my house is *my room* whether I'm there or not (unlike my personal space which is carried around with me) and it's my room because I say it's my room. Although I could probably make a case for my room *really being* my room (as opposed to belonging to another family member or to the mortgage holder on the house), what about the desk I sit at in each class? I feel the same way about the desk. It's *my desk,* even though it's certain that the desk is owned by the school and is in no way really mine.

How can you tell if you are territorial? Ask yourself: Is there some piece of land, some area, which you would defend against others? Are you uncomfortable when someone comes into your room uninvited, or when you're not there? Does the thought of your neighborhood showing

an increase in crime make you want to fight back? Does the thought of defending your country sound like a good idea? Ethographers (people who study animal behavior and attempt to make parallels with human behavior) argue that we are, indeed, territorial *in nature;* that is, like other animals, we human beings are biologically programmed to defend our territory.

Territoriality in animals serves a number of functions, such as providing a defended area for food and mating, and a place to hide from enemies. A territory also aids in the regulation of population density since only those controlling certain parts of the territory (usually the best pieces of land) tend to mate, thereby keeping the population in balance.

It is difficult to determine the advantages territoriality has for humans as a species. However, certain advantages do exist for individuals, especially for those with high status. Generally we grant people with higher status more personal territory and greater privacy. We knock before entering our supervisor's office, whereas he or she can usually walk into our work area without hesitating. In traditional schools professors have offices, dining rooms, and even toilets that are private, whereas the students, who are presumably less important, have no such sanctuaries. In the military greater space and privacy usually come with rank: Privates sleep forty to a barracks, sergeants have their own private rooms, and generals have government-provided houses.

Environment To conclude our look at nonverbal communication we want to emphasize the ways in which physical settings, architecture, and interior design affect our communication. Begin your thinking by recalling for a moment the different homes you've visited lately. Were some of these homes more comfortable to be in than others? Certainly a lot of these kinds of feelings are shaped by the people you were with, but there are some houses where it seems impossible to relax, no matter how friendly the hosts. We've spent what seemed like endless evenings in what Mark Knapp calls "unliving rooms," where the spotless ashtrays, furniture coverings, and plastic lamp covers seemed to send nonverbal messages telling us not to touch anything, not to put our feet up, and not to be comfortable. People who live in houses like this probably wonder why nobody ever seems to relax and enjoy themselves at their parties. One thing is quite certain: They don't understand that the environment they have created can communicate discomfort to their guests.

There's a large amount of research that shows how the design of an environment can shape the kind of communication that takes place in it. In one experiment at Brandeis University Maslow and Mintz found that the attractiveness of a room influenced the happiness and energy of people working in it. The experimenters set up three rooms: an "ugly" one, which resembled a janitor's closet in the basement of a campus building; an "average" room, which was a professor's office; and a "beautiful" room, which was furnished with carpeting, drapes, and comfortable furniture. The subjects in the experiment were asked to rate a series of pictures as a way of measuring their energy and feelings of well-being while at work. Results of the experiment showed that while in the ugly room, the subjects became tired and bored more quickly and took longer to complete their task. When they moved to the beautiful room, however, they rated the faces they were judging higher, showed a greater desire to work, and expressed feelings of importance, comfort, and enjoyment. The results teach a lesson that isn't surprising: Workers generally feel better and do a better job when they're in an attractive environment.

Many business people show an understanding of how environment can influence communication. Robert Sommer, a leading environmental psychologist, described several such cases. In *Personal Space: The Behavioral Basis for Design,* he points out that dim lighting, subdued noise levels, and comfortable seats encourage people to spend more time in a restaurant or bar. Knowing this, the management can control the amount of customer turnover. If the goal is to run a high-volume business that tries to move people in and out quickly, it's necessary to keep the lights shining brightly and not worry too much about soundproofing. On the other hand, if the goal is to keep customers in a bar or restaurant for a long time, the proper technique is to lower the lighting and use absorbent building materials that will keep down the noise level.

Furniture design can control the amount of time a person spends in an environment too. From this knowledge came the Larsen chair, which was designed for Copenhagen restaurant owners who felt their customers were occupying their seats too long without spending enough money. The chair is constructed to put an uncomfortable pressure on the sitter's back if occupied for more than a few minutes. (We suspect that many people who are careless in buying furniture for their homes get much the same result without trying. One environmental psychologist we know refuses to buy a chair or couch without sitting in it for at least half an hour to test its comfort.)

Sommer also describes how airports are designed to discourage people from spending too much time in waiting areas. The uncomfortable chairs, bolted shoulder to shoulder in rows facing outward, make conversation and relaxation next to impossible. Faced with this situation, travelers are forced to move to restaurants and bars in the terminal, where they're not only more comfortable but where they're likely to spend money.

Casino owners in places such as Las Vegas also know how to use the environment to control behavior. To keep gamblers from noticing how long they've been shooting craps, playing roulette and blackjack, and feeding slot machines, they build their casinos without windows or clocks. Unless wearing a wristwatch, the customer has no way of knowing how long he or she has been gambling, or, for that matter, whether it's day or night.

In a more therapeutic and less commercial way physicians have also shaped environments to improve communications. One study showed that simply removing a doctor's desk made patients feel almost five times more at ease during office visits. Sommer found that redesigning a convalescent ward of a hospital greatly increased the interaction between patients. In the old design seats were placed shoulder to shoulder around the edges of the ward. By grouping the chairs around small tables so that patients faced each other at a comfortable distance, the amount of conversations doubled.

Even the design of an entire building can shape communication among its users. Architects have learned that the way housing projects are designed will control to a great extent the contact neighbors will have with each other. People who live in apartments near stairways and mailboxes have many more neighbor contacts than do those living in less heavily traveled parts of the building, and tenants generally have more contacts with immediate neighbors than with people even a few doors away. Architects now use this information to design buildings that either encourage communication or increase privacy, and house hunters can use the same knowledge to choose a home that gives them the neighborhood relationships they want.

Sometimes the matter of designing an environment can become absurd. During 1968 the United States, South Vietnam, and North Vietnam spent eight months arguing over the shape of a table at which they would hold their peace talks. The argument centered on the nonverbal statement that the design of the conference room would make. The North Vietnamese wanted a square table, which would have given the National Liberation Front (NLF) guerillas a separate side all to themselves. As the Communists saw it, this arrangement would have given the guerillas equal status as an independent government. The United States and South Vietnamese were not about to give in to the demand. They wanted two rectangular tables, one seating themselves and the other for the North Vietnamese and NLF. This design would have kept the guerillas from having a whole table side to themselves, and symbolically denied them clear-cut status as an equal power. Several thousand lives later both sides finally compromised on a round table, which having no sides at all, allowed each side to claim victory.

So far we've talked about how designing an environment can shape communication, but there's another side to consider. Watching how people use an already existing environment can be a way of telling what kind of relationships they want. For example, Sommer watched students in a college library and found that there's a definite pattern for people who want to study alone. While the library was uncrowded, students almost always chose corner seats at one of the empty rectangular tables. Finally each table was occupied by one reader. New readers would then choose a seat on the opposite side and far end of an occupied table, thus keeping the maximum distance between themselves and the other readers. One of Sommer's associates tried violating these "rules" by sitting next to and across from other female readers when more distant seats were available. She found that the approached women reacted defensively, either by signaling their discomfort through shifts in posture, gesturing, or by eventually moving away.

Campuses are full of conscious and unconscious architectural symbolism. While the colleges at Santa Cruz evoke images of Italian hill towns as they might have been if the peasants had concrete, the administration building is another story. It appears to anticipate the confrontations between students and administration that marked the sixties. At Santa Cruz, administrative offices are located in a two-story building whose rough sloped concrete base with narrow slit windows gives it the look of a feudal shogun's palace. The effect is heightened by the bridge and landscaped moat that one crosses to enter the building. "Four administrators in there could hold off the entire campus," joked one student.

Sym Van Der Ryn *Chief Architect, State of California*

Research on classroom environments is rather extensive. Probably the most detailed study was conducted by Raymond Adams and Bruce Biddle. Observing a variety of classes from grades one, six, and eleven, the principal finding was that the main determinant of whether a student was actively and directly engaged in the process of classroom communication was that student's seating position. This finding held even when students were assigned seats, indicating that location, and not personal preferences, determined interaction.

Other studies by Robert Sommer and his colleagues found that students who sit opposite the teacher talk more, and those next to the teacher avoid talking at all. Also, the middle of the first row contains the students who interact most, and as we move back and to the sides of the classroom, interaction decreases markedly.

With an overwhelming lack of imagination we perpetuate a seating arrangement reminiscent of a military cemetery.

This type of environment communicates to students that the teacher, who can move about freely while they can't, is the one who is important in the room, is the only one to whom anyone should speak, and is the person who has all the information. The most advanced curriculum has little chance of surviving without a physical environment that supports it.

As we draw this discussion of nonverbal communication to a close, there are some points we'd like to reemphasize.

1. In a normal two-person conversation the words or verbal components of the message carry far less of the social meaning of the situation than do the nonverbal components. This statistic may have been difficult for you to believe when we cited it at the beginning of the chapter, but by this time you know how many channels nonverbal communication includes. Our hope is that the information and experiences of the chapter have placed some importance on nonverbal communication in your life.

2. When compared with verbal language, nonverbal behavior is very limited. Our nonverbal communication is concerned mostly with the expression of feelings, likings, or preferences, and these usually *reinforce, contradict,* or *accent* the message we're expressing verbally.

3. Although nonverbal behaviors are more powerful in expressing feelings than are words, they're ambiguous and difficult to "read" accurately. Nonverbal behaviors always bear checking out.

4. Many gestures, glances, postures, and other behaviors are culturally learned. They do not necessarily apply to other cultures or even to subcultures within our society. At this point most research on nonverbal behaviors has been done on middle- and upper-middle-class college students and shouldn't be automatically generalized to other groups.

5. Remember the importance of congruency—the matching of your verbal and nonverbal expressions. Contradicting messages from two channels are a pretty good indication of deliberate or unconscious deception, and matching signals reinforce a message.

We haven't tried to teach you *how* to communicate nonverbally in this chapter—you've always known this. What we do hope you've gained here is a greater *awareness* of the messages you and others send, and we further hope that you can use this new awareness to understand your relationships, improve them, and make them more interpersonal.

Readings

Adams, Raymond and Bruce Biddle. *Realities of Teaching: Explorations with Video Tape.* New York: Rinehart and Winston, 1970.

Aiken, Lewis R. "The Relationship of Dress to Selected Measures of Personality in Undergraduate Women." *Journal of Social Psychology,* (1963):119–128.

Ardrey, Robert. *The Territorial Imperative.* New York: Dell, 1966.

Bakker, Cornelius B. and Marianne Bakker-Rabadau. *No Trespassing! Explorations in Human Territoriality.* San Francisco: Chandler and Sharp, 1973.

Birdwhistell, Ray L. *Kinesics and Context.* Philadelphia: University of Pennsylvania Press, 1970.

Burgoon, Judee and Thomas Saine. *The Unspoken Dialogue.* Boston: Houghton Mifflin, 1978.

Byers, P. and H. Byers. "Nonverbal Communication and the Education of Children." In *Functions of Language in the Classroom,* C. B. Cazden, V. P. John and D. Hymes, eds. New York: Teachers College Press, 1972.

Deasy, C. M. "When Architects Consult People." *Psychology Today,* 3, (March 1970):10.

Ekman, Paul and Wallace V. Friesen. *Unmasking the Face: A Guide to Recognizing Emotions from Facial Expressions.* Englewood Cliffs, N.J.: Prentice-Hall, 1975.

Feldman, Saul D. "The Presentation of Shortness in Everyday Life. Height and Heightism in American Society: Toward a Sociology of Stature." In *Lifestyles: Diversity in American Society,* 2nd Ed., S. D. Feldman and G. W. Thielbar, eds. Boston: Little, Brown and Company, 1975.

Gunther, Bernard. *Sense Relaxation Below Your Mind.* New York: Macmillan, 1968.

Hall, Edward T. *The Hidden Dimension*. Garden City, N.Y.: Anchor Books, 1969.

Hess, E. H. and J. M. Polt, "Pupil Size as Related to Interest Value of Visual Stimuli." *Science,* 132, (1960):349–350.

Jourard, Sidney M. "An Exploratory Study of Body Accessibility." *British Journal of Social and Clinical Psychology,* 5, (1966):221–231.

Keyes, Ralph. "The Height Report." *Esquire* (November, 1979):31–43.

Knapp, Mark L. *Nonverbal Communication in Human Interaction,* 2nd Ed. New York: Holt, Rinehart and Winston, 1978.

Leathers, Dale G. *Nonverbal Communication Systems*. Boston: Allyn and Bacon, 1978.

Maslow, A. and N. Mintz. "Effects of Aesthetic Surroundings: Initial Effects of Those Aesthetic Surroundings upon Perceiving 'Energy' and 'Well-Being' in Faces." *Journal of Psychology,* 41, (1956):247–254.

Mehrabian, Albert. *Nonverbal Communication*. Chicago: Aldine-Atherton, 1972.

Molloy, John T. *Dress for Success*. New York: Wyden, 1975.

Montagu, Ashley. *Touching: The Human Significance of the Skin*. New York: Harper and Row, 1971.

Morsbach, H. "Aspects of Nonverbal Communication in Japan." *Journal of Nervous and Mental Disease,* 157, (1973):262–277.

Rosenfeld, Lawrence B. and Jean M. Civikly. *With Words Unspoken: The Nonverbal Experience*. New York: Holt, Rinehart and Winston, 1976.

Rosenfeld, Lawrence B., Sallie Kartus and Chett Ray. "Body Accessibilty Revisited." *Journal of Communication,* 26, (1976):27–30.

Rosenfeld, Lawrence B. and Timothy G. Plax. "Clothing as Communication." *Journal of Communication,* 27, (1977):24–31.

Scheflen, Albert E. *How Behavior Means*. Garden City, N.Y.: Anchor Books, 1974.

Sommer, Robert. *Personal Space: The Behavioral Basis of Design*. Englewood Cliffs, N.J.: Prentice-Hall, 1969.

Sommer, Robert. *Tight Spaces*. Englewood Cliffs, N.J.: Prentice-Hall, 1978.

Taylor, Anne P. and George Vlastos. *School Zone: Learning Environments for Children*. New York: Van Nostrand Reinhold, 1975.

Taylor, H. M. "American and Japanese Nonverbal Behavior." In *Papers in Japanese Linguistics* 3, J. V. Neustupny, ed. Melbourne: Monash University, 1974.

Thompson, James J. *Beyond Words: Nonverbal Communication in the Classroom*. New York: Citation Press, 1973.

Wachtel, P. "An Approach to the Study of Body Language in Psychotherapy." *Psychotherapy,* 4, (1967):97–100.

Wilson, Glenn and David Nias. "Beauty Can't Be Beat." *Psychology Today,* 10, (September 1976):96–98, 103.

10 And the whole earth was of one language and one speech. And it came to pass, as they journeyed from the east, that they found a plain in the land of Shinar; and they dwelt there.

And they said to one another, go to, let us make brick, and burn them thoroughly. And they had brick for stone, and slime had they for mortar.

And they said, go to, let us build us a city and a tower, whose top may reach into heaven; and let us make us a name, lest we be scattered abroad upon the face of the whole earth.

And the Lord came down to see the city and the tower, which the children of men builded.

And the Lord said, behold, the people is one, and they have all one language; and this they begin to do: and now nothing will be restrained from them, which they have imagined to do.

Go to, let us go down, and there confound their language, that they may not understand one another's speech.

So the Lord scattered them abroad from thence upon the face of all the earth; and they left off to build the city.

Therefore is the name of it called Babel; because the Lord did there confound the language of all the earth; and from thence did the Lord scatter them abroad upon the face of all the earth.

Genesis 11:1–9

Sometimes it seems as if *none* of us speaks the same language. How often have you felt that nobody understood what you were saying? *You* knew what you meant, but people just didn't seem to understand you. How often have the tables been turned— you couldn't understand somebody else's

ideas? And how many times have you had the feeling that people were deliberately playing tricks with words, using language to fool you or to hide what was on their minds?

In this chapter we'll examine these problems by taking a quick look at the relationship between words and what they represent. We'll show you ways language trips people up and techniques you can use to make language work better. We'll also discuss how language describes how we see the world and shapes our view of it. Finally, we'll look at ways in which the type of language that communicators use reflects their attitudes, both toward themselves and each other.

The Nature of Language

Let's begin by examining some characteristics of language. Because we use words almost constantly, we often assume words are ideally suited to convey meaning. Actually, several points should be considered for our verbal messages to be accurate and successful.

Language Is Symbolic Probably the most important characteristic of language is its symbolic nature. Words represent "things"—objects, processes, ideas—but words are not the things they represent. For instance, the word "coat" is not the same as the piece of clothing it describes. Only fools would expect the letters c-o-a-t to keep them warm in a snowstorm. Yet people often forget the symbolic nature of language and confuse words with their referents. For example, students who want to receive high grades may cram facts into their heads just long enough to regurgitate

them into a bluebook. They forget that the letters such as "A" or "B" are only symbols, and that a few lines of ink on paper don't necessarily represent true learning. In the same way, simply saying the words, "I care about you" doesn't necessarily reflect the truth, although for many disappointed lovers this lesson is a painful one.

Meanings Are in People, Not in Words
Showing a dozen people the same symbol and asking them what it means is likely to get twelve different answers. Does an American flag summon up associations of soldiers giving their lives for their country? Fourth of July parades? Institutionalized bigotry? Mom's apple pie? What does a cross represent? The gentleness and wisdom of Jesus Christ? Fire-lit rallies of Ku Klux Klansmen? A childhood Sunday school? The necklace one's sister always wears?

Like these symbols, words can be interpreted in many different ways. And this interpretation is the basis for many misunderstandings. Two people may have an argument about "feminism" without either ever realizing that they are using the word to represent entirely different things. The same goes for "communism," "Republicans," "health food," and thousands upon thousands of other symbols. Words don't mean, people do—and often in widely different ways.

The symbolic nature of language is, thus, the source of many communication

> "I don't know what you mean by 'glory,'" Alice said.
>
> Humpty Dumpty smiled contemptuously. "Of course you don't—till I tell you. I meant 'there's a nice knock-down argument for you!'"
>
> "But 'glory' doesn't mean 'a nice knock-down argument,'" Alice objected.
>
> "When I use a word," Humpty Dumpty said, in a rather scornful tone, "it means just what I choose it to mean—neither more nor less."
>
> "The question is," said Alice, "whether you can make words mean so many different things."
>
> "The question is," said Humpty Dumpty, "which is to be master—that's all."
>
> Lewis Carroll
> *Through the Looking Glass*

problems. But the difficulties don't end with an understanding of symbolism. The terms and the structures used to assemble language contain many other problems that complicate the transmission of messages. Let's look at a number of these linguistic dangers, and at how to cope with them in making communication more effective.

Problems Inherent in Language

Intentional Orientation   Although a word is a symbol and not the thing it represents, people often respond to a word *as if* it were the thing. This tendency is referred to as an *intentional orientation,* as opposed to an *extensional orientation* (seeing people, objects, and events as they are, not as they are labeled).

In a recent letter to Ann Landers, a woman complained that her parents opposed her impending marriage. Why? Because the man she was marrying was a *nurse.* The parents could not separate the label "nurse" from the actual person, and attributed to him all the beliefs they attached to the label, such as femininity.

How do people respond to the word "snake"? If they break out in a cold sweat, cringe a little, or have an otherwise aversive response, they're exhibiting an intentional orientation. Finally, there is the classic story of the psychology professor who placed a cookie on the desk of each one of his students in a certain class. The students came in, thought the gift was an excellent idea, and ate the cookies. Remarks ranged from "very good" to "excellent." The professor then announced that the cookies were made from dog biscuits. Some smiled, but more felt nauseous. These students responded to the *word,* and not the *thing,* the tasty cookie.

Polarization   Our language fosters a strong tendency to polarize objects, to see matters as "black" or "white," as either one thing or the other. Most objects, however, can only be categorized between the two

Each one of us is alone in the world. He is shut in a tower of brass and can communicate with his fellows only by signs, and the signs have no common value, so that their sense is vague and uncertain. We seek pitifully to convey to others the treasures of our heart, but they have not the power to accept them, and so we go lonely, side by side but not together, unable to know our fellows and unknown by them. We are like people living in a country whose language they know so little that with all manner of beautiful and profound things to say, they are condemned to the banalities of the conversation manual. Their brain is seething with ideas and they can only tell you that the umbrella of the gardener's aunt is in the house.

W. Somerset Maugham
The Moon and Sixpence

extremes. How does language polarize the world? It provides a vocabulary with few midpoints and a great many opposites.

Try the following short exercise. First, write down the opposite of each of the following words:

tall _____

heavy _____

happy _____

strong _____

legal _____

This exercise probably took you no more than a few seconds. Now, write down the word that represents the *midpoint* between the two opposites. Did you find the second task easy? Probably not. In fact, you might have been unable to provide meaningful midpoints at all.

What's the midpoint between "tall" and "short"? *Average?* That's not very descriptive. In fact, most of the midpoint adjectives that could be used in this exercise are nonspecific and vague.

Consider the final word: "legal." If legal and illegal could be clearly distinguished, we would have little need for lawyers. One student suggested that the midpoint between legal and illegal was "doing it and not getting caught."

Fact-Inference Confusion We can make statements about things we observe as well as about things we do not observe. The problem is that the grammar of our language does not distinguish between the two. "She is driving an MG sports-car" is *grammatically* equivalent to "She is seething with rage," yet the first statement is a matter of fact while the second is inferential. While we can directly observe the car and her driving it, we cannot directly observe her seething rage. Any statement we make about rage is based on a few observations and conclusions drawn from those observations.

The problems crop up when we start talking about other types of deviant behavior. We say of a person who drinks too much that he "is" an alcoholic, and we say of people who think bizarre thoughts that they "are" schizophrenic. This person is a drug addict and that person is a homosexual. Others are sadomasochists, pedophiliacs, juvenile delinquents. The English language is constructed in such a way that we speak of people *being* (certain things) when all we know is that they do certain things . . .

That kind of identity is a myth. Admittedly, if a person believes the myth, the chances rise that he will assume the appropriate, narrowly defined role. Believing that one is an addict, an alcoholic, a schizophrenic, or a homosexual can result in relinquishing the search for change and becoming imprisoned in the role.

Edward Sagarian

There's nothing wrong with making inferences as long as we identify them as such. The danger comes when we confuse them with facts, which are (in fact) quite different. Facts are based on observations, whereas inferential statements may not be; factual statements can only be made by the observer, whereas anyone can make an inferential statement; facts are certain, whereas inferences are only probable; and facts are directly verifiable, whereas inferences are not.

Allness   No one can say everything about anything; yet our language, especially the word "is," makes this statement seem true. "John is a poor student." Is that all John is? Could John also be a father, a son, a mechanic, a taxpayer, a movie-goer, or a friend? The statement that John is a poor student implies two erroneous ideas: (1) a poor student is *all* John is, and (2) this information is all people need to know about John to understand him *completely*.

Static Evaluation   When people form a statement about a person, event, or thing, they tend to hold the opinion for a long period of time, and to avoid changing it, even though what it refers to may change a great deal. "John is a poor student" may suggest that John was, and will always be a poor student. One may reasonably ask *when* was John a poor student, and in *what* classes?

By not keeping pace with changing times, people may find themselves holding attitudes and beliefs that do not correspond with the actual world. Alfred Korzybski provides us with a good illustration of this discrepancy. A large fish in the same tank with a small fish may endanger the life of the small fish (that could serve as food). So, to prevent the small fish from being eaten, a glass partition is placed in the tank which separates the two. The large fish slams into the partition several times and eventually comes to realize that the glass cannot be penetrated. Once the large fish makes this evaluation, the partition may be removed. Even though the situation has changed, the large fish continues to believe that it cannot eat the small fish.

The confusing nature of language often leads people to behave like the "dumb" fish. Having once labeled a person or thing, they cling to that label even after the label is no longer accurate. Saying that "John is handsome, boring, or immature," isn't as correct as saying, "The John I encountered yesterday seemed to be. . ." There's a big difference between saying, "Beth is a phony" and, "Beth seemed phony the other night." The second statement describes the way someone behaved at one point in time, and the first categorizes Beth as if she had always been a phony. This kind of verbal generalizing may cause teachers to think of students as "slow learners" or "troublemakers" because of past test scores or reports.

Troublesome Words

So far, this discussion has covered the problems inherent in the nature of language. Now we'll examine some particularly tricky classes of words.

Equivocal Words   One kind of semantic misunderstanding is caused by equivocal words; that is, words that can be interpreted in more than one way. Misunderstandings from equivocal words happen almost every day, usually when we least expect them. Not long ago we ordered dinner in a Mexican restaurant and noticed that the menu described each item as coming with rice or beans. We asked the waitress for a "tostada with beans." But when the order arrived, we were surprised to find that instead of a beef tostada with beans on the side, the waitress had brought a tostada *filled* with beans. At first we were angry at her for botching a simple order, but then we realized that it was as much

our fault for not making the order clear as it was hers for not checking.

Often equivocal word problems are more serious. A nurse gave one of his patients a real scare when he told him that he "wouldn't be needing" his robe, books, and shaving materials any more. After that statement, the patient became quiet and moody for no apparent reason. When the nurse finally asked the patient why, he discovered that his statement led the poor man to think he was going to die soon although he had really meant that he'd be going home soon.

Most of the words people use can be interpreted in a number of ways. A good rule to remember for avoiding such misunderstandings is: If a word can be interpreted in more than one way, it probably will be.

Relative Words   Relative words gain their meaning by comparison. For example, do you attend a large or small school? This depends on what you compare it to. Alongside a campus such as the University of Michigan, with over 30,000 students, your school may look small; but compared with a smaller institution, it might seem quite large. Relative words such as "fast" and "slow," "smart" and "stupid," "short" and "long" are clearly defined only through comparison.

Using relative terms without explaining them can lead to communication problems. Have you ever responded to someone's question about the weather by saying it was warm, only to find out the person thought it was cold? Have you followed a friend's advice and gone to a "cheap" restaurant only to find that it was twice as expensive as you expected? Or have you at one time learned that classes you heard were "easy" turned out to be hard? The problem in each case resulted from failing to link the relative word to a more measurable term.

Emotive Words   Emotive words seem to describe something but really announce the speaker's attitude toward it. Do you like that old picture frame? If you do, you'd probably call it an "antique," but if you think it's ugly, you'd likely describe it as "a piece of junk." Whether the picture frame belongs on the mantle or in the garbage can is not a matter of fact but of opinion, although it's easy to forget this when you use emotive words.

Here's a list of emotive words:

If you approve, say	If you disapprove, say
thrifty	cheap
traditional	old-fashioned
extrovert	loudmouth
cautious	coward
progressive	radical
information	propaganda
strategic withdrawal	retreat
military victory	massacre
eccentric	crazy

Bertrand Russell, the philosopher, provided a good method for seeing how emotive words work: "conjugating irregular verbs." First, examine an action or personality trait, and then show how it can be viewed either favorably or unfavorably, according to the label people give it. For example:

I'm casual.

You're a little careless.

He's a slob.

Or try this one:

I read love stories.

You read erotic literature.

She reads pornography.

Or:

I'm thrifty.

You're money conscious.

He's a tightwad.

Now perform a few conjugations with the following statements:

I'm tactful.

I'm conservative.

I'm quiet.

I'm relaxed.

My child is high spirited.

I have a lot of self-pride.

Indiscriminate Terms   Although the world is filled with diversity, language denies this variety by providing us with single words that refer to many similar items. Most nouns are indiscriminate terms. For instance, how many varieties are there for "teacher," "student," or "book"? Each of these nouns serves as a category into which we dump many diverse ideas and deny the uniqueness of the original referents.

Sometimes a word says more than we intend it to. In such cases the chosen word can unintentionally describe a whole class of objects, though it was only intended to describe specific members of that class. For example, an instructor may tell students to study "everything we've covered so far" for an exam, causing them to lose sleep, and neglect other work. When the day of the test comes however, the students discover that the instructor really meant for them to study everything since the last-midterm. Evidently, the words "everything we've covered so far" were too broad.

Classifying is not inherently wrong or bad. It would be impossible to deal with things in the world without some classifying and categorizing. Consider the problems inherent in seeing everything as unique. For example, how much food would go uneaten and spoil if people couldn't decide what it was? It's usually efficient and necessary to observe only a few key properties of an object before a person classifies and deals with the item. Nevertheless, while generalizing is necessary, this process shifts our focus from the unique to the common properties. Such habitual generalization can easily gloss over the differences which make people, places, and things exciting.

Fiction Words   Semanticists use the label "fiction word" to describe terms such as freedom, truth, democracy, and justice. Fiction words make communication difficult because for many people the terms elicit strong emotional reactions that have little to do with dictionary meanings. The danger of such words comes from assuming their meaning is clear. For example, candidates for office declare that they favor "peace," and many people automatically vote for them, assuming these candidates' election will initiate a new era of international friendship. Later, voters learn that their candidates' ideas of peace involved bombing into submission any country with different governmental policies.

Consider the following statement: "In many cases revolutions are justifiable ways of getting rid of repressive governments." How would people respond to such a statement? Statements such as these are vague—they mean different things to different people. Is this referring to a violent or nonviolent revolution? Or are all revolutions alike? If people defend one revolution, will they necessarily defend them all? And what about "repressive governments"? Does everybody share the same idea about this term? Probably not, yet few take much time trying to find a common definition. In discussions with statements such as the one above, people speak languages that only seem to be alike.

Abstract Words   Much of language is too abstract. Often people use words that cover more territory than is necessary, and in so doing not only make themselves harder to understand but also start us thinking in differing ways. Any idea can be described on a number of levels, some more abstractly than others. Consider the printed material you're reading now. Most people would call it a book. But narrowing the description, one could label it a "communication book," or more specifically, *Interplay*. The description can become more and more precise: Chapter 10 of

Interplay, or even page 261 of Chapter 10 of *Interplay.* In each case the description focuses more specifically on the object, excluding other items that were members of the same categories.

Instead of going down the abstraction ladder to more concrete terms, language can become more abstract. Rather than labeling *Interplay* as a book, it could be described as educational literature, nonfiction writing, or printed material, each description growing less specific. In essence, the more precise the description, the less likely the chance of being mis-understood.

Abstract language frequently damages communication. For instance, imagine someone who has had a bad experience traveling abroad, and so blames an entire country. ("Yeah, those damn Hottentots are a bunch of thieves. If you're not careful they'll steal you blind. I know, because one of 'em stole my camera last year.") You can see here how lumping people into abstract categories ignores the fact that for every thieving Hottentot there are probably 100 honest ones. This kind of thinking leads to mistaken assumptions that keep people apart: "None of those kids are any damn good!"; "You can't trust anybody in business"; "Those cops are all a bunch of goons." Each of these statements is too general, and says more than people really intend.

Examples like these show how thinking in abstract terms can lead to ignoring important individual differences. In this sense semantics isn't "just" a matter of words. People who use highly abstract language begin to *think* in generalities, ignoring uniqueness. And expecting people to act a certain way can become a self-fulfilling prophecy. If people think all police officers are brutal, they're more likely to react in a defensive, hostile way toward them, which increases the chance that police officers will react to these people as a threat. If people think teachers don't care about classes, then students' defensive indifference is likely to change a potentially helpful instructor into someone who literally doesn't care.

Failing to recognize abstractions can lead to a great deal of unnecessary grief. One couple was convinced that their child was abnormal because she hadn't learned to talk by the age of two. The parents wouldn't listen when someone tried to explain that some kids begin talking later than others and that there was nothing to worry about. "But something must be wrong with Billy," the parents said, pointing to a book on child development. "It says right here that children should be talking by one year, and Billy only makes noises." The parents, however, had failed to read the first chapters of the book, which stressed that the term "child" is an abstraction—that there's no such thing as the "typical" child.

What can people do to reduce excessive use of abstract language? Probably the best thing is to pay attention to everyday conversation. Every so often (especially during an emotional argument) people should ask themselves if they can translate abstract language into less vague terms.

People often discover they've been using words that are difficult to explain.

Another way to reduce the use of unnecessary abstractions is through the use of *operational definitions*. Instead of defining a word with more words, an operational definition *points,* as it were, to the behaviors, actions, or properties that a word signifies.

We use operational definitions all the time: "The student union is that building with all the bikes in front"; "What I'd like more than anything is thirty acres of land on the Columbia River"; "My idea of a good time is eating a triple-decker, three-flavor, chocolate-dipped ice cream cone." Each of these statements is relatively clear. Rather than using vague, more abstract language, they show in observable terms what the speaker is talking about. S. I. Hayakawa points out that the best examples of operational definitions in our everyday lives are found in cookbooks. Cookbooks describe a dish by telling what ingredients are combined in what amounts by what operations. ("To make a pizza, begin with the crust. Mix one-fourth cup water with two cups flour . . .")

Many definitions aren't operational. These definitions never point to more clearly understandable operations; instead, they explain words with more words. A nonoperational, highly abstract cookbook might define a pizza as "a delectable, flavorful treat that is both hearty and subtle." Obviously, it would be extremely difficult to learn very much about a pizza from such a description. In the same way it's far clearer to define words such as "freedom" and "democracy" operationally rather than abstractly.

The Language of Deception

So far we've discussed cases where people use overly vague abstractions unintentionally. But other instances occur when people use abstractions to deliberately obscure others' intentions. Euphemisms (from the Greek word meaning "to use words of good omen") are pleasant terms substituted for blunt ones. Euphemisms soften the impact of information that might be unpleasant. Unfortunately, this pulling of linguistic punches often obscures the accuracy of a message.

He can compress the most words into the smallest ideas of any man I ever met.

Abraham Lincoln

Advertisers provide numerous examples of euphemisms. "Rinsing" and "tinting" hair creates a better impression than dyeing, and "dentures" seem less unattractive than false teeth! "Preowned" cars sound in better condition than second-hand ones, just as "credibility gap" skirts the issue of calling a politician a liar.

The war in Vietnam produced a great many euphemisms, perhaps more than any other event in current history. For instance, "pacification of the enemy infrastructure" meant blasting the Viet Cong out of a village, and "redeployment of troops" and "Vietnamization" both referred to American withdrawal of fighting personnel.

Although more people are developing a healthy skepticism toward euphemisms, there's still the danger that a few high-level abstractions will slip through. Therefore, it's necessary to keep on guard—to ask what those fine-sounding words refer to, and what they mean in specific, operational terms to the person who spoke them.

Language Shapes Our world

In addition to clarifying and obscuring meaning, language, specifically vocabulary and grammar, actually structures our perceptions.

The Sapir-Whorf Hypothesis   Anthropologists have long known that the culture people live in shapes their perceptions of reality. Some social scientists believe that one's cultural perspective is at least partially shaped by the language the members of that culture speak. Benjamin Lee Whorf and Edward Sapir asserted this idea in their writings.

After spending several years with various North American Indian cultures, Whorf

found that their patterns of thinking were shaped by the language they spoke. For example, Nootka, a language spoken on Vancouver Island, contains no distinction between nouns and verbs. The Indians who speak Nootka view the entire world as being constantly in process. While English speakers see something as fixed or constant (noun), Nootka speakers view it as constantly changing. Thus, the Nootka speaker might label a "fire" as a "burning," or a house as a "house-ing." In this sense our language operates much like a snapshot camera, whereas Nootka works more like a moving-picture camera.

What does this have to do with communication? Because of the static, unchanging nature of our grammar, we often regard people and things as never changing. Someone who spoke a more process-oriented language would view people quite differently, perhaps recognizing their changeable nature.

The Sapir-Whorf hypothesis has never been conclusively proved or disproved. In spite of its intellectual appeal, some critics point out that it is possible to conceive of flux even in static languages like English. Supporters of the hypothesis respond that while it is *possible* to conceptualize an

STRAIGHT, *strāt, adj.* direct, unbent, even; adjusted; honest, candid, forthright, true, reliable, veracious; clear, accurate, trustworthy; heterosexual. (From the *Thesaurus of Synonyms and Antonyms,* and *Webster's New Collegiate Dictionary.*)

We are constantly being compared and contrasted; gay sensibilities versus straight sensibilities; gay lifestyles versus straight lifestyles; gay audiences versus straight audiences; gay press versus straight press; and here at the Greater Gotham Business Council, gay businesses versus straight businesses.

If *they* are *straight,* then what, really, are *we?*

The *Thesaurus of Synonyms and Antonyms* lists the following as antonyms for the word *straight:* crooked, curved, unreliable, confused, false, ambitious, evasive. It lists the following as synonyms for the words *crooked:* twisted, dishonest, distorted, deformed, warped, corrupt.

If *they* are *straight,* are *we,* therefore, all of the above?

I've considered using the word *heterosexuals* when referring to *them,* but I find it too long and too clinical. *Heteros* or *hets* is short and easy to say, but opens us up to being called *homos.*

The ad for the Oscar Wilde Memorial Bookstore in New York City says, "Think Straight, Be Gay," a sentiment with which I am in full agreement. But if we *think,* and therefore we *are,* what does that make them? Queers?

Breeders gets right to the point, and of course we can always use the Yiddish word my grandfather used when he referred to non-Jews: *yenim,* "the others." This, however, can get confusing: sexual preferences and religious beliefs get mixed.

May I suggest, then, when the subject comes up that we refer to those with different sexual preferences in a term that *does not* reflect negatively on *us.* Instead of calling them *straights,* I propose that we call them *non-gays.*

Edward Sherman

idea in different languages, some languages make it easier to recognize a term than others.

Suppose that an English speaker just returned from a visit to New York and someone asks this traveler what kind of place it is. "Oh, it's a terrible place," the traveler says. Now examine this response.

Saying that New York *is* terrible (or great) implies two things: (1) that the judgment is a total one covering everything about the city; and (2) that New York is an unchanging place. The word *is* implies eternal sameness, when in fact the "things" named are changing, dynamic processes. New York today isn't the same place it was last year or will be tomorrow, and the traveler's experiences there aren't necessarily the same as others have had. The traveler would have been more correct answering, "My impressions while visiting New York in January 1980 were that the streets were crowded, the people I encountered behaved rudely, and the prices for food, lodging, and entertainment were too high." This way of talking isn't always practical, but it's certainly more accurate than judging New York in absolute terms.

Alfred Korzybski, who originated the discipline of General Semantics, operated in a way consistent with Whorf and Sapir's hypothesis. He suggested changing English by adding a device to remind us of the way things change. He proposed that we qualify important words by attaching subscripts to them. For example, instead of saying, "I didn't like Joe," one might say, "I didn't like Joe last Tuesday." This device would make it harder to think in abstract, general terms.

Some cultures allow their members to change names whenever they wish. Perhaps this practice would make it easier to see how none of us are the same person and how we all change.

Labels: Products and Ideas Within our own culture advertisements are probably the best example of how attitudes can be created through the use of words. Semanticists like to tell a story that illustrates this point. In a department store experimenters set up two stacks of handkerchiefs side by side on a table. The merchandise in each was identical; the only difference being the signs above each pile. One read "Fine Linen Handkerchiefs—$1.50 each," while the other said "Nose Rags—35¢." As expected, the "handkerchiefs" sold out quickly, and the "nose rags" were hardly touched. In this case names didn't reflect reality as much as create it.

Advertising isn't the only field in which words shape attitudes. Not too long ago a new course was introduced into high schools and junior highs across the country. In the course students learned such things as the biology of human reproduction, the causes and dangers of venereal disease, and in some instances methods of preventing unwanted pregnancies. School administrators usually called the course "Sex Education." But almost everywhere it was taught, a large number of parents and other community members raised protests. Their arguments usually centered around this theme: "School is no place to teach kids about sex." Often these protests developed into mass meetings, newspaper editorials, and letter-writing campaigns that opposed the teaching of such a "delicate" and "personal" subject.

The protests threatened what educators considered an important program, one that would ensure the future health and happiness of many students. Being well acquainted with the course, educators

believed that nothing in the class material would threaten the moral values that the protesters felt were under attack. But somehow the public had to be shown the true aims of the program. As time passed, many teachers and administrators began to realize that much of their problem was caused by the name of the course. Once schools recognized that the word "sex" threatened so many people, the solution was simple. Rather than teach "Sex Education," the schools announced they would offer classes in "Social Hygiene" or "Family Health." There was no basic change in the subjects taught, just the name of the course. And amazingly, most of the protests died away. The public was satisfied once they were sure that the schools were no longer dabbling in sex.

The words we use to describe people's roles or functions in society can also shape the way they feel about themselves. Much of people's self-esteem is derived from the importance they feel their work has, a perception which often comes from the titles for their roles. For example, a theater owner had trouble keeping ushers working for more than a week or two. The ushers tired quickly of their work, which consisted mostly of taking tickets, selling popcorn, and showing people to their seats. Then, with only one change, the manager ended the personnel problems. The manager simply "promoted" all the ushers to the "new" position of "assistant manager." And believe it or not, the new title was sufficient to make the employees happy. The new name encouraged them to think more highly of themselves and to take new pride in their work.

Self-Concept The significance of words in shaping our self-concept goes beyond job titles. Racist and sexist language greatly affect the self-concepts of the people discriminated against. An article in the *New York Times Magazine* by Casey Miller and Kate Swift points out some of the aspects of our language that discriminate against women, suggesting women are of lower status than men. Miller and Swift write that, except for words referring to females by definition, such as "mother" and "actress," English defines many nonsexual concepts as male. The underlying assumption is that people in general are men. Also, words associated with males have positive connotations, such as "manly," "virile," "courageous," "direct," "strong," and "independent," whereas words related to females are fewer and have less positive connotations, such as "feminine wiles" and "womanish tears."

Most dictionaries, in fact, define "effeminate" as the opposite of masculine, although the opposite of "feminine" is closer to "unfeminine." Any language expressing stereotyped sexual attitudes or assuming the superiority of one sex over another is sexist, so adding feminine endings to nonsexual words, such as "poetess" for female poet, is as sexist as "separate but equal" is racist.

Whereas sexist language usually defines the world as made up of superior men and inferior women, racist language usually defines it as composed of superior whites and other inferior racial groups. Words and images associated with "white" are usually positive, whether it's the hero-cowboy in white or connotations of white as "pure," "clean," "honorable," "innocent," "bright," and "shiny." The words and images associated with black are often negative, a concept that reaches from the clothes of the villain-cowboy to

connotations such as "decay," "dirt," "smudge," "dismal," "wicked," "unwashed," and "sinister."

To the extent that our language is both sexist and racist, our view of the world is affected. For example, men are given more opportunity than women to see themselves as "good," and in the same way whites are given more opportunity than blacks. Language shapes the self-concepts of those it labels in such a way that members of the linguistically slighted group see themselves as inferior.

Many linguistic changes beginning in the late 1960s were aimed primarily at teaching speakers and writers a new vocabulary in order to change the destructive connotations that accompany many of our words. For example, "black is beautiful" is an effort to reduce perceived status differences among blacks and whites.

Changes in writing style were also designed to counter the sexual prejudices inherent in language, particularly eliminating the constant use of "he" and introducing various methods either to eliminate reference to a particular sex, or to make reference to both sexes. Throughout this book we have used a number of techniques for avoiding sexist language: switching to the sexually neutral plural (they); using the passive voice to eliminate sexed pronouns; employing the "he or she" structure; carefully balancing individual masculine and feminine pronouns in illustrative material; and even doing total rewrites to delete conceptual sexual bias. Another solution, proposed by Casey Miller and Kate Swift, could be to use *tey* for "he" and "she," *ter(s)* for "his" and "her(s)," and *tem* for "him" and "her."

The plural forms remain intact, with the use of "they," "their(s)," and "them." What would have happened if we had chosen to implement this solution to the problem?

Language Reflects Our Attitudes

Besides shaping perceptions, language often reflects the speaker's attitudes. In their fascinating book *Language Within Language,* Morton Wiener and Albert Mehrabian describe several ways in which the forms and structures of verbal expressions offer clues about our feelings and beliefs.

Liking   One needn't be a communication scholar to realize that people often express liking or disliking indirectly. We've all sensed another's disapproval or approval without knowing exactly how it was communicated. Wiener and Mehrabian suggest several indirect verbal methods for signifying liking or disliking. The fact that most of them are not chosen consciously doesn't diminish their impact.

Demonstrative pronoun choice   While several pronouns can correctly refer to a person, some are more positive than others. Consider the difference between saying, "These people want our help" and the equally accurate, "Those people want our help." Most people would probably conclude that the first speaker is more sympathetic than the second. In the same way, speakers sound more positive when they say "Here's Tom" than if they say, "There's Tom." The difference in such cases is one of grammatical *distance.*

People generally suggest attraction by indicating closeness and dislike by linguistically removing themselves from the object of their conversation.

Sequential placement   Another way to signify attitude is to place positive items earlier in a sequence. For example, notice the difference between discussing "Jack and Jill" and referring to "Jill and Jack." Or consider how people respond to questions about courses they are taking or friends they intend to invite to an upcoming party. In many cases the first person or subject mentioned is more important or better liked than subsequent ones. (Of course, sequential placement isn't always significant. You may put "toilet bowl cleaner" at the top of your shopping list simply because it's closer to the market door than champagne.) Wiener and Mehrabian point out an interesting example of the sequencing principle that often occurs in psychotherapy, where the patient mentions a certain subject first, not because it it is more likeable, but because it's the easiest one to discuss. Even here the same principle applies: Positive subjects often precede negative ones.

Negation   People usually express liking in a direct, positive manner while they use more negative language with less favorable subjects. Imagine, for instance, that a person asks a friend's opinion about a book, movie, or restaurant. Consider the difference between the response, "It was good'' and, "It wasn't bad." In the same way, the positive, "I'd like to get together with you" is a stronger indication of liking than the more negative, "Why don't we get together?"

Duration   The length of time people spend discussing a person or subject can also be a strong indicator of attraction to either the subject or to the person with whom they're talking. If a person asks a new acquaintance about work and receives the brief response, "I'm a brain surgeon" with nothing more, the questioner would probably suspect that either the subject was a sensitive one or that this person wasn't interested in the questioner. Of course, there may be other reasons for short answers, such as preoccupation of the speaker, but one good yardstick for measuring liking is the time others spend communicating with us.

Only presidents, editors, and people with tapeworms have the right to use the editorial "we."

Mark Twain

Responsibility   Besides indicating liking or interest, language can also reflect a speaker's unconscious willingness to take responsibility for his or her statements, as the following categories show.

The "it" statement   Notice the difference between the sentences of each set:

"It bothers me when you're late."

"I'm worried when you're late."

"It's nice to see you."

"I'm glad to see you."

"It's a boring class."

"I'm bored in the class."

"It" statements externalize the subject of the conversation. The subject is neither the person talking nor the one listening, but some "it" that is never really identified. Whenever people hear the word "it" used this way, they should ask themselves what "it" refers to. They inevitably find that the speaker uses "it" to avoid clearly identifying to whom the thought or feeling belongs.

The "you" statement   The word "you" also allows the speaker to disown comments that might be difficult to express:

"You get frightened" instead of

"I get frightened . . ."

"You wonder . . ." instead of

"I wonder . . ."

"You start to think . . ." instead of

"I'm starting to think . . ."

The "we" statement   The word "we" can sometimes bring people together by pointing out their common beliefs. But in other cases the word becomes a device for diffusing the speaker's responsibility, a device that refers to a nebulous collection of people that doesn't really exist. Just as "you" and "we" often really means "I." "We all believe . . ." means "I believe . . ." and "We ought to . . ." means "I

"My hand is doing this movement . . ."

"Is *it* doing the movement?"

"I am moving my hand like this . . . and now the thought comes to me that . . ."

"The thought 'comes' to you?"

"I have the thought."

"You *have it?*"

"*I think.* Yes. I think that I use 'it' very much, and I am glad that by noticing it I can bring it all back to me."

"Bring it back?"

"*Bring myself back.* I feel thankful for this."

"*This?*"

"Your idea about the 'it'."

"*My idea?*"

"I feel thankful towards you."

Claudio Naranjo

want to . . ." (You might notice that this text uses a lot of "we's." Do you find your beliefs included enough to think the word is justified?)

Questions   In the manner of "you" statements, questions often make the other person defensive. They can also be used as a form of flattery ("Where did you get that lovely tie?"), or as a replacement for "I" statements (the most common). Some therapists argue that there are very few *real* questions, that most questions hide some statement that the person does not want to make, possibly out of fear.

"What are we having for dinner?" may hide the statement, "I want to eat out," or "I want to get a pizza."

"How many textbooks are assigned in that class?" may hide the statement, "I'm afraid to get into a class with too much reading."

"Are you doing anything tonight?" can be a less risky way of saying, "I want to go out with you tonight."

"Do you love me?" safely replaces the statement, "I love you," which may be too embarrassing, too intimate, or too threatening for the person to state directly.

In all these cases the questioners avoid the risk of expressing themselves first. Of course, you never use questions this way, do you?

The "but" statement   Statements that take the form X-but-Y can be quite confusing. A closer look at this construction explains why. "But" has the effect of cancelling the thought that proceeds it:

"You're a really swell person, but I think we ought to stop seeing each other."

"You've done good work for us, but we're going to have to let you go."

"This paper had some good ideas, but I'm giving it a grade of D because it's late."

These "buts" often mask the speaker's real meaning behind more pleasant-sounding ideas. A more accurate and less confusing way of expressing complex ideas is to replace "but" with "and." In this way you can express a mixture of attitudes without eliminating any of them.

Language reflects attitudes. Language shapes attitudes. Language can clarify or obscure. Symbols stand for ideas, but not always the same ones. Our brief look at language shows that words and things aren't related in the straightforward way that we might assume. Because it's so difficult to understand each other's ideas through words, it's tempting to look for better alternatives. As you'll see in the next chapter, other ways of communicating do exist. But often we're faced with no other choice but to do the best we can with our often inadequate means of verbal expression. Perhaps the most we can do is to proceed with caution, trying our best to understand each other and always realizing that the task is a difficult one.

Readings

Alexander, Hubert G. *Meaning in Language.* Glenview, Ill.: Scott, Foresman and Co., 1969.

Berryman, Cynthia L. and James R. Wilcox. "Attitudes Toward Male and Female Speech: Experiments on the Effects of Sex-Typical Language." *Western Journal of Speech Communication,* 44, (1980):50–59.

Bois, J. Samuel. *The Art of Awareness.* Dubuque, Iowa: Wm. C. Brown, 1973.

Chase, Stuart. *The Tyranny of Words.* New York: Harvest Books, 1938.

Clark, Virginia P., Paul A. Eschholz and Alfred F. Rosa, eds. *Language: Introductory Readings,* 2nd Ed. New York: St. Martin's Press, 1977.

Condon, John C. *Semantics and Communication,* 2nd Ed. New York: Macmillan, 1975.

Davis, Ossie. "The English Language Is My Enemy." In *Language: Concepts and Processes,* Joseph A. De Vito, ed. Englewood Cliffs, N.J.: Prentice-Hall, 1973.

DeVito, Joseph A., ed. *Language: Concepts and Processes.* Englewood Cliffs, N.J.: Prentice-Hall, 1973.

Fabun, Don. *Communications: The Transfer of Meaning.* Beverly Hills, Calif.: Glencoe Press, 1968.

Francis, W. Nelson. "Word-Making: Some Sources of New Words." In *Language: Introductory Readings,* 2nd Ed., Virginia P. Clark, Paul A. Eschholz and Alfred F. Rosa, eds. New York: St. Martin's Press, 1977.

Hayakawa, S. I. *Language in Thought and Action.* New York: Harcourt, Brace and Jovanovich, 1964.

Hayakawa, S. I. *The Use and Misuse of Language.* Greenwich, Conn.: Fawcett Books, 1962.

Korzybski, Alfred. *Science and Sanity.* Lancaster, Penn.: Science Press Printing Co., 1933.

Lakoff, Robin. *Language and Woman's Place.* New York: Harper Colophon Books, 1975.

Miller, Casey and Kate Swift. "One Small Step for Genkind." *New York Times Magazine* (April 16, 1972). Reprinted in *Language: Concepts and Processes,* Joseph A. DeVito, ed. Englewood Cliffs, N.J.: Prentice-Hall, 1973.

Miller, Casey and Kate Swift. *Words and Women.* Garden City, N.Y.: Anchor Press, 1976.

Newman, Edwin. *A Civil Tongue.* Indianapolis: Bobbs-Merrill, 1976.

Rich, Andrea L. *Interracial Communication.* New York: Harper and Row, 1974.

Ritchie-Key, Mary. *Male/Female Language.* Metuchen, N.J.: Scarecrow Press, 1975.

Rosenfeld, Lawrence B. "The Confrontation Policies of S. I. Hayakawa: A Case Study in Coercive Semantics." *Today's Speech,* 18, (1970):18–22.

Sagarian, Edward. "The High Cost of Wearing a Label." *Psychology Today* (March 1976): 25–27.

"The Euphemism: Telling It Like It Isn't," *Time* (September 19, 1969):26–27.

Whorf, Benjamin Lee. *Language, Thought and Reality,* John B. Carroll, ed. Cambridge, Mass.: M.I.T. Press, 1956.

Wiener, Morton and Albert Mehrabian. *A Language Within Language: Immediacy, a Channel in Verbal Communication.* New York: Appleton-Century-Crofts, 1968.

11 Once upon a time there was a world with no conflicts.

The leaders of each nation recognized the need for cooperation and met regularly to solve any potential problems before they could grow. They never disagreed on areas needing attention or on ways to handle these areas, and so there were never any international tensions, and of course there was no war.

Within each nation things ran just as smoothly. The citizens always agreed on who their leaders should be, so elections were always unanimous. There was no social friction between various groups. Age, race, and educational differences did exist, but each group respected the others and all got along harmoniously.

Personal relationships were always perfect. Strangers were always kind and friendly to each other. Neighbors were considerate of each other's needs. Friendships were always mutual, and no disagreements ever spoiled people's enjoyment of one other. Once people fell in love—and everyone did—they stayed happy. Partners liked everything about each other and were able to satisfy each others' needs fully. Children and parents agreed on every aspect of family life, and never were critical or hostile toward each other. Each day was better than the one before.

Of course, everybody lived happily ever after.

This story is obviously a fairy tale. Regardless of what we may wish for or dream about, a conflict-free world just doesn't exist. Even the best communicators, the luckiest people, are bound to wind up in situations when their needs don't match the needs of others. Money, time, power, sex, humor, asthetic taste, as well as a thousand other issues arise, and keep us from living in a state of perpetual agreement.

For many people the inevitability of conflict is a depressing fact. They think that the existence of ongoing conflict means that there's little chance for happy relationships with others. Effective communicators know differently. They realize that while it's impossible to *eliminate* conflict, there are ways to *manage* it effectively. And those effective communicators know the subject of this chapter—that managing conflict skillfully can open the door to healthier, stronger, and more satisfying relationships.

What Is Conflict?

Stop reading and make a list of as many different conflicts as you can recall. Include both conflicts you've experienced personally and ones which only involve others.

This list will probably show you that conflict takes many forms. Sometimes there's angry shouting, as when parents yell at their children. In other cases, conflicts involve polite discussion, as in labor-management negotiations or legal trials. Sometimes conflicts are carried on through hostile silence, as angry couples act when conducting an unspoken feud. And finally, conflicts may wind up in physical fighting between friends, enemies, or even total strangers.

Whatever forms they may take, all interpersonal conflicts share certain similarities. Joyce Frost and William Wilmot provide a thorough definition of conflict. They state that conflict is *an expressed struggle between at least two inter-dependent parties who perceive incompatible goals, scarce rewards, and interference from the other parties in achieving their goals.* Let's look at the various parts of this definition so as to develop a clearer idea of conflicts in people's lives.

Expressed Struggle   Another way to describe this idea is to say that both parties in a conflict know that some disagreement exists. For instance, you may be upset for months because a neighbor's loud stereo keeps you from getting to sleep at night, but no conflict exists between the two of you until the neighbor learns about your problem. Of course, the expressed struggle doesn't have to be verbal. You can show your displeasure with somebody without saying a word. A dirty look, the silent treatment, or avoiding the other person are all ways of expressing yourself. But one way or another, both parties must know that a problem exists before they're in conflict.

Perceived Incompatible Goals   All conflicts look as if one party's gain will be another's loss. For instance, consider the neighbor whose stereo keeps you awake at night. Does somebody have to lose? If the neighbor turns down the noise, then he loses the enjoyment of hearing the music at full volume; but if the neighbor keeps the volume up, they you're still awake and unhappy.

But the goals in this situation really aren't completely incompatible—solutions do exist that allow both parties to get what they want. For instance, you could achieve peace and quiet by closing your windows or getting the neighbor to close his. You might use a pair of earplugs. Or perhaps the neighbor could get a set of earphones, allowing the music to play at full volume without bothering anyone. If any of these solutions prove workable, then the conflict disappears.

Unfortunately, people often fail to see mutually satisfying answers to their problems. And as long as they *perceive* their goals to be mutually exclusive, then, although the conflict is unnecessary, it is still very real.

Perceived Scarce Rewards   Conflicts also exist when people believe there isn't enough of something to go around. The most obvious example of a scarce resource is money—a cause of many conflicts. If a person asks for a raise in pay and the boss would rather keep the money or use it to expand the business, then the two parties are in conflict.

Time is another scarce commodity. As authors and family men, all three of us are constantly in the middle of struggles about how to use the limited time we have to spend. Should we work on this book? Visit with our wives? Play with our children? Enjoy the luxury of being alone? With only twenty-four hours in a day, we're bound to wind up in conflicts with our families, editors, students, and friends—all of whom want more of our time than we have available to give.

> **I'm lonesome; they are all dying; I have hardly a warm personal enemy left.**
>
> James McNeill Whistler

Interdependence   However antagonistic they might feel toward each other, the parties in a conflict are usually dependent upon each other. The welfare and satisfaction of one depends on the actions of another. If this weren't true, then even in the face of scarce resources and incompatible goals there would be no need for conflict. Interdependence exists between conflicting nations, social groups, organizations, friends, and lovers. In each case, if the two parties didn't need each other to solve the problem, they would go separate ways. In fact, many conflicts go unresolved because the parties fail to understand their interdependence. One of the first steps towards resolving a conflict is to take the attitude that "we're all in this together."

Conflict Is Natural and Inevitable

Frost and Wilmot's definition asserts that conflicts are bound to occur, even to the most happy, successful, lucky people. It's vitally important to recognize the inevitability of conflict, for failing to do so can lead to a lot of unnecessary grief. Expecting life to be free of conflict is like expecting the weather to be perfect every day. If you maintain this kind of hope, you're bound to be disappointed. On the other hand, having a more realistic attitude about the weather can help you get through (and even take advantage of) stormy days.

Even after we recognize the inevitability of conflict, most people tend to view it as an unpleasant though necessary activity (similar to figuring out income taxes or visiting the dentist). A quick look at our culture reveals several reasons for this bad image. The first relates to unrealistic teaching. From the time children can understand speech, most of them are raised on a diet of fairy tales that paint the ideal world as free of conflicts. The storybook ending of living "happily ever after" implies that if people are truly good they live harmonious lives that are free of any friction. Many TV shows perpetuate this image. While TV characters do have problems, they're inevitably simple enough to be cleared up before the final commercial, hardly a reflection of real life.

While TV and newspapers show that conflicts exist in the real world, most of the struggles these media describe cannot be called constructive. Soldiers and innocent civilians die in wars, angry demonstrators riot, and social groups shout angrily at each other. This sort of hostility and violence is hardly a testimonial to the benefits of conflict.

In addition, many families present conflict as dangerous and undesirable. Some parents are verbally or physically abusive to each other and their children. Because people learn from models, their children may grow up to be the same kind of fighters as were their parents. This is why so many adults who are child-beaters were, as children, victims of abuse themselves. In other cases, the horror of viewing destructive aggression may lead children to avoid conflicts when they grow up.

At the other end of the spectrum, families in which conflicts are not acknowledged create the idea that confrontations are to be avoided. Many parents never acknowledge the conflicts that they feel with each other, even to themselves. When disagreements do come up, they're handled privately—"Not in front of the children." Many parents feel compelled to keep up a "couple front," making it look to the children as if adults agree on everything. Parental advice and commands repeatedly suggest that conflict is bad:

"Now don't get angry. . . ."

"Don't talk back."

"There's nothing to fight about."

"If you can't say something nice, don't say anything."

Moreover, adults without noticeable conflicts are presented as models:

"She doesn't have an angry bone in her body."

"He's such a nice person."

"They're always so friendly."

Teachings such as these are confusing to children, who *know* that they experience conflict. What's a youngster to do when a brother or sister won't share, when parents are critical, when friends are uncooperative or cruel? Surely turning the other cheek isn't *always* the answer.

While children hear so much preaching about being nice, they're also being presented with messages that praise aggressiveness. Sports heroes frequently

---

Well-washed and well-combed domestic pets grow dull; they miss the stimulus of fleas.

Francis Galton

---

wind up in fights, often to the noisy approval of fans. Sarcasm and humor are often used as effective putdowns by the same adults who talk so much about kindness. Grownups who preach about pleasantness threaten ominously, "If you don't stop fighting you'll be sorry!"

Why is it that overt disagreement seems to be such a taboo in our society? What forces so many people to express their conflicts indirectly in such destructive, crazy ways? The answer lies in what Herbert Simons has termed a "system view" of conflict. Communicators that hold this view believe (usually not consciously) that maintaining the status quo is an extremely important goal, and that people should avoid rocking the boat in any way—even when the present system is clearly unsatisfactory.

The tendency to keep an unsatisfying system running smoothly occurs in many settings. Both managers and employees continue plugging away at old ways of doing business rather than face the challenge of developing better methods. Teachers and students often look with hostility at each other across a gap of mutual mistrust and fear. Many families suffer through what Thoreau called lives of "quiet desperation," rather than speaking up and trying to change their lives.

Yet many people support the status quo only because they don't acknowledge that conflicts can be positive, and because they don't possess the skills to manage their disagreements constructively. This chapter should help people develop a more powerful awareness of the skills involved in managing conflicts.

So far, we've discussed beliefs about conflict that apply equally to both sexes. In addition, most of us have been exposed to the idea that men and women "ought" to deal with disagreements in different ways. Probably the biggest difference has to do with emotions. The cultural stereotype of female behavior holds that women have a great capacity for expressing emotions, while men are generally expected to be more "logical" and issue-oriented. Thus, for many people of both sexes, it's more appropriate to hear a woman say she's disappointed or confused than it does to hear a man send the same messages. The same holds true for nonverbal expressions. While most people wouldn't be surprised to see a woman cry, the same behavior coming from a man is usually more of a shock.

Just as many people are used to perceiving women as extremely emotional, so they also find it easier to accept assertiveness when it comes from a man. Even in these relatively more liberated times, many people find the widely circulated guide "How To Tell a "Businessman from A Businesswoman" amusing:

A businessman is aggressive; a businesswoman is pushy.

He loses his temper because he's so involved in his job; she's bitchy.

He follows through; she doesn't know when to quit.

He's firm; she's stubborn.

He isn't afraid to say what he thinks; she's opinionated.

In the last decade, there has been increasing recognition that such stereotypes have more to do with cultural conditioning than with biology. Yet even the most ardent liberationists will admit that many people—both men and women—still accept and live by these attitudes.

Styles of Conflict

People have their individual styles of handling conflict—characteristic approaches they take when their needs appear incompatible with what others want. Sometimes a style is helpful and sometimes not. In either case people should recognize their own styles so they can make the styles work for them.

Individual Styles   What's your style of handling conflict? Let's find out by inventing two hypothetical characters— Sally and Ralph—and see how they manage a problem that you might find familiar.

Sally and Ralph have been friends for several years, ever since they moved into the same apartment building. While they had always exchanged favors in a neighborly way, lately Ralph has been

depending more and more on Sally. He asks her to care for his cat and houseplants almost every other weekend while he travels, borrows food and cash without returning it, and drops in to talk about his unhappy love life at least once a week. Until lately, Sally hasn't minded much, but now she's getting tired of Ralph's behavior.

Take a look at the six alternatives below and rank them in the order you'd choose. Mark your most likely response as number 1, your next most likely as number 2, and so on.

1. Steer clear of Ralph as much as possible. Pretend not to be home when he drops by. Make excuses for why you can't help him with his problems.

2. Do the favors for Ralph, hoping that he'll stop imposing soon. After all, nobody's perfect and it isn't worth making an issue over this.

3. Do the favors for Ralph, but casually hint about the inconvenience involved.

4. Tell Ralph about the inconveniences that resulted from helping him, but state that you're willing to do a few favors for him as a friend, even though they're something of a nuisance. After all, friends ought to help each other out, even if it causes some trouble. You just want him to meet you halfway.

5. Tell Ralph that you're fed up with his demands, that you don't mind helping once in awhile, but that his continued imposition will jeopardize your friendship.

6. Tell Ralph how his requests make you feel and ask him to work with you to find a way to solve his problems that's less of a strain for you.

Make sure you've ranked your responses before going on. Each one of the choices above represents a different orientation to the conflict between Sally and Ralph. A close examination will show the different ways that people handle their own conflicts, and give you an idea of the styles which you use most often.

1. Avoidance/withdrawal. People who avoid conflicts usually believe that it's easier to put up with the status quo than to face the problem head on and try to solve it. This attitude usually doesn't make sense, for the costs of avoiding an issue are high. Avoiding the issue uses up a great deal of energy without resolving the aggravating situation. In addition, avoiders usually lose a chunk of their self-respect since they so clearly downplay their own concerns in favor of the other person's. Finally, failing to deal with a problem can often result in spoiling an entire relationship.

Every time Sally hides from Ralph or changes the subject so he won't ask her for a favor, she becomes uncomfortable and probably leaves Ralph feeling the same way. After this goes on for awhile, it's likely that whatever enjoyment Sally and Ralph had found together will be eclipsed by their new way of relating and the friendship will degenerate into an awkward, polite shell.

This kind of avoidance is particularly sad since the immediate fears of dealing with an issue are usually way out of proportion to what is likely to happen. This isn't to blame avoiders, who may not know any better way to act. We simply want to point out the typically unsatisfactory results of such a conflict style.

In a few cases, however, avoidance may be the best course. If a conflict is short-lived, it might not be worth resolving. For example, you might let a friend's annoying grumpiness pass, knowing that the friend has been sick lately but will soon feel better. If the issue is genuinely a minor one, you might decide not to confront a person with it. You may have a neighbor, for instance, whose lawn sprinklers occasionally hit your newly washed car. In your opinion, this may not even be worth mentioning. Or you might reasonably choose to keep quiet if the conflict occurs in an unimportant relationship, such as an acquaintance whose language you find offensive but don't see often enough to make an issue of.

So far we've discussed withdrawal as a means of avoiding conflict. In *The Intimate Enemy,* psychologist George Bach talks about people who back off from issues as a way of expressing aggression. Bach claims there are two types of aggression: clean fighting and dirty fighting. Either because they can't or won't express their feelings openly, dirty fighters sometimes resort to "crazymaking" techniques to vent their resentments. These behaviors are called "crazymaking" because of the effect they have on the person they're directed against.

Crazymaking avoiders refuse to face an issue in order to punish their partner. For instance, suppose Ralph had sensed some uneasiness in Sally lately and asked if anything was bothering her. "No, nothing really," Sally replies. This leaves Ralph feeling confused and gives Sally a kind of

mean satisfaction at punishing Ralph for the sins he unknowingly committed. An even more insidious kind of avoidance occurs when the crazymaker withholds common pleasantries of the relationship—without announcing what's going on. Courtesy, affection, humor, doing the dishes, these and many other gifts can become weapons of passive-aggressive communicators.

2. Accommodation. Accommodators deal with conflict by giving in, putting the other's needs ahead of their own. Certainly, accommodation is sometimes appropriate, such as when the other person's needs really are more important than yours. For

Pseudoaccommodating is another style of crazymaking. In this stratagem, the communicator disguises aggression by pretending to give in. People with this style make agreements for the sake of peace but then don't keep them. In the short run this style gets the people two results: peace and quiet, and the chance to do what they want. Of course, in the long run this behavior can damage relationships.

3. Smoothing over. In terms of assertiveness, people who smooth conflicts over are more bold than withdrawers or accommodators. They may let you know what they want, but in a way that doesn't reflect how strongly they feel. The goal here is to preserve an image that "everything is OK" above all else. Sometimes people who smooth over get what they want and sometimes they don't, but in either case they fail to communicate the full extent of their message.

Just as withdrawal and accommodation are useful orientations in certain situations, so is the smoothing over approach. If the other person is liable to react defensively to the statement about conflict and if the relationship really is more important than the concerns of either party, then smoothing the matter over may be an adequate response. The danger from such a style, however, is that it doesn't usually resolve the problem or prevent it from reoccurring.

Aggressive crazymakers use several smoothing-over strategies. Subject changing is a perfect example. Subject changers briefly mention the issue that's concerning them ("I sure wish it was a little quieter around here sometimes so I could get my work done."), and then drop the subject when the other person responds. It's easy to

instance, if a friend wants to have a serious talk and you feel playful, you'd most likely honor the friend's request, particularly if the person was facing some kind of crisis and wanted your help. In most cases, however, accommodators fail to assert themselves either because they don't value themselves sufficiently, or because they don't know how to ask for what *they* want.

There are also crazymakers who use accommodation as an aggressive tactic. Guiltmakers accommodate others but try to extract payment by punishing the other person. We've all seen guiltmakers in action. "Go on," they say, "go ahead and use the car. I didn't really need to do those errands and buy food today anyhow . . ." Or, "No really, I'll be happy to help. I'm feeling a little sick, but it will pass."

see how this style of hinting can get annoying.

Crisis ticklers, on the other hand, bring up what's bothering them without ever mentioning it explicitly. For instance, instead of expressing concern about spending too much, a crisis tickler might say, "Gee, things are sure getting expensive lately." But the crisis tickler would back off if the partner asked if anything was wrong.

Joking can be an extremely aggressive though subtle crazymaking behavior. Jokers use humor to smooth over conflicts by kidding about a subject that is actually quite serious, or by making jokes when a partner wants to deal with a conflict. The joker can handle any protests about such kidding by saying, "Gee, I was just trying to lighten things up a little." Jokers can also disguise their own aggressive feelings by joking about them. While the jokes might earn a few laughs, this kind of humor often diminishes the issue, thus keeping jokers from getting what they want.

4. Compromising. Unlike the three previous orientations, compromisers bring their concerns into the open and try to satisfy both their own needs and those of others. The only problem with compromising is that by definition nobody is totally satisfied with the outcome.

While compromising may be preferable to avoidance or power plays, it does have its problems. First, if the people involved see a compromise coming they might inflate their demands, still attempting to get everything they want. This situation occurs in labor negotiations, where both parties begin discussions with exaggerated claims. While this strategy may appeal to gameplayers, it minimizes trust. More commonly, compromises are unsatisfying because they often leave one or both parties unhappy. For example, if Sally grudgingly agrees to help Ralph occasionally, she will still resent his behavior and he won't be getting enough assistance. The best to be said for compromises is that they're more attractive than some of the previous alternatives for handling conflicts.

5. Competition. We're so familiar with competition as a style of conflict that it doesn't need much explanation. The main element in competition is power: whoever has the most clout wins. The kindest thing to be said about this orientation is that it's honest. It may also be a satisfactory style in those rare cases when there clearly are "good guys" and "bad guys," but such instances are not common.

The biggest problem with power is that in a competitive situation both parties often lose. International politics offers an obvious example: If World War III ever starts, who will win? The same kind of total loss all too often occurs in interpersonal conflicts. For example, in many contested divorces who

People always say they are not themselves when tempted by anger into betraying what they really are.

Edgar Watson Howe

---

besides the lawyers really win when the contesting couple spend thousands of dollars, experience intense pain and bitterness, and in many cases confuse and sadden the lives of their children?

6. Integration. Communicators who handle their conflicts in an integrated way are concerned about their own needs as well as those of the other person. But unlike compromisers, they won't settle for only a partially satisfying solution. Let's imagine that Sally cares about herself and also about Ralph, and that the relationship is also important to Ralph who isn't just interested in exploiting Sally. They may be able to talk matters out and find a way of being friends, which gives both of them the things they want.

While integration sounds as if it is the perfect way of handling all conflicts, it does have drawbacks: It takes time and effort to find integrative solutions, and the process can be both frustrating and tiring. The relationship has to be extremely important to both partners for this method to work. And there are times when there simply isn't a totally satisfying solution to a problem, despite the best efforts of everyone. Even though the attempt to work matters through can affirm the goodwill of everyone, it's disappointing to try so hard and come up short.

We'll have more to say about integrative styles of handling conflicts later in this chapter.

Which Style to Use?   A look at your own behavior and that of others will show you that very few people use the same conflict style all the time. For instance, take someone whose coworkers may describe as a power-oriented competitor. This person uses his position and knowledge as weapons to get what he wants from others with whom he works. But while he is a fighter on the job, his behavior is completely different with his friends away from work. With them he's a collaborator, interested in discovering their needs and working to solve them as well as his own.

His style fits still another pattern with his children. Rather than deal with problems involving them he'll avoid the issue in any way possible: making jokes, pretending to "forget" about his promises to discuss a problem, or retreating into his work. Many of us are like this man, changing our behaviors to suit various circumstances.

The person in this example changes conflict styles depending on whom he's dealing with; but this isn't the only determinant of which style to use. Sometimes people switch styles depending on the issue involved. For instance, you might be inclined to compromise on an issue that isn't vitally important to you, while you'd be more likely to confront others when the problem is a critical one.

Another factor governing our choice of conflict style is the mood we happen to be in. On some days you're probably most inclined to be an accommodator, giving in to the demands or desires of others. But at other times you might be feeling more angry or grouchy, and be inclined to compete, even on unimportant issues.

Many communicators use one or two styles exclusively because these ways of relating are the only ones they know. We've already seen that patterns of thinking and acting are formed early in life, and during these first critical years (and often beyond) many people see only avoiding, smoothing over, and competition. Not knowing that there are other alternatives which might be more effective, they use these styles throughout their lives to handle their own conflicts. This lack of awareness about effective communication styles explains why so many educators see a need for training parents in communication skills, so that children will grow from the start learning ways of relating that will help them throughout adulthood.

Even when aware of different conflict styles, some communicators rely heavily on only one or two. These behaviors are usually ones that worked well in the past, and so the tendency is to continue relying on them, even though their usefulness may be gone. Frost and Wilmot cite the example of the man who is "stuck" in the style of a 1960s protestor, seeing every issue as a fight against the establishment. This man identifies reflexively with the underdog, without considering whether the underdog is correct. He sees those in power as always evil and wrong, and tries to use any power at his disposal to defeat those "enemies." This man finds enemies where none exist, and creates problems unnecessarily.

Another common example of relying on longstanding but obsolete behavior is the student who accommodates and withdraws from those in authority because standing up to such people in the past met with punishment. It may make sense to give in to a harsh parent or authoritarian teacher when you're small and powerless, but such behavior isn't necessary as an adult, especially when others are willing and interested in dealing constructively with problems.

It should now be clear that there's no single "best" style of dealing with conflict. What's appropriate behavior for communicating with a police officer you believe has unfairly given you a speeding ticket might not be the best way to act with a neighbor whose dog is digging up your garden. And the right way to talk to your neighbor might not work at all when discussing the way you've drifted apart with an old friend. The key to success, then, is to develop a *repertoire* of conflict styles so that when issues come up you'll be able to choose the way of communicating that works best for the given situation. Before introducing a new style of communicating to add to that repertoire, we next want to offer some guidelines to tell whether the styles of communication you're presently using are helping or hindering your present conflicts.

Functional and Dysfunctional Conflict

Some bacteria are "good," aiding digestion and cleaning up waste, while others are "bad," causing infection. There are helpful forest fires which clean out dangerous accumulations of underbrush and harmful ones which threaten lives and property. In the same way, some conflicts can be beneficial. They provide a way for relationships to grow by solving the problem at hand and often improving other areas of interaction as well. Other conflicts can be harmful, causing pain and leaving a relationship weaker. Communication scholars usually describe harmful conflicts as *dysfunctional* and beneficial ones as *functional*.

What makes some conflicts functional and others dysfunctional? Usually the difference doesn't rest in the subject of the conflict, for it's possible to have good or poor results on almost any issue. Sometimes certain individual styles of communication are more productive than others, as you've just learned. In other cases the success or failure of a conflict will depend on the method of resolution the parties choose. We'll talk more about types of conflict resolution later in this chapter. We want now to describe several symptoms that distinguish functional and dysfunctional conflicts.

Polarization   In a dysfunctional conflict biases are rampant. Participants see themselves as "good" and the other person as "bad"; their actions as "protective" and the other's as "aggressive"; their behavior as "open and trustworthy" and the other's as "sneaky and deceitful." Researchers Robert Blake and Jane Mouton found that people engaged in this kind of polarization underestimate the commonalities shared with the other person, and so miss areas of agreement and goodwill.

By contrast, participants in a functional conflict realize that the other person's needs may be legitimate too. A person who is allergic to cigarette smoke recognizes that smokers aren't necessarily evil people who delight in tormenting them, while the smoker sympathizes with the other's need for cleaner air. In issues such as this functional conflict is marked by mutual respect.

Unwillingness to Cooperate   Participants in a dysfunctional conflict see each other as opponents and view the others' gain as their loss: "If you win, I lose" is the attitude. This belief keeps partners from looking for ways to agree or find solutions that can satisfy them both. People rarely try to redefine the situation in more constructive ways, and seldom give in, even on noncritical issues.

The Chinese have a story based on three or four thousand years of civilization. Two Chinese coolies were arguing heatedly in the midst of a crowd. A stranger expressed surprise that no blows were being struck. His Chinese friend replied, "The man who strikes first admits that his ideas have given out."

Franklin Delano Roosevelt

A more functional approach recognizes that by cooperating it may be possible to find an answer that leaves everyone happy. Even nations basically hostile to each other often recognize the functional benefits of cooperating. For example, the United States and the Soviet Union have clear-cut differences in certain areas, yet work together in fields such as disease control, halting air piracy, and disarmament. This same kind of cooperation is possible in interpersonal conflicts. We will have a great deal to say about cooperative problem solving later in this chapter.

Coercion   In destructive conflicts the participants rely heavily on power to get what they want. "Do it my way, or else" is a threat commonly stated or implied in dysfunctional conflicts. Money, favors, friendliness, sex, and sometimes even physical coercion become tools for forcing the other person to give in. Needless to say, victories won with these kind of power plays don't do much for a relationship.

More enlightened communicators realize that power plays frequently are a bad idea, not only on ethical grounds but because they often have a way of backfiring. Since it's rare that a party in a relationship is totally powerless, it's possible to win a battle only to lose a war. One classic case of the dysfunctional consequences of using power to resolve conflicts occurs in families where authoritarian parents make their children's requests into "unreasonable demands." It's easy enough to send a five-year-old out of a room for some real or imagined misbehavior, but when that child grows into a teen-ager he or she has many ways of striking back.

Escalation In destructive conflicts the problems seem to grow larger instead of smaller. As you read in Chapter 7, defensiveness is reciprocal: If you attack me, the tendency is for me to strike back even harder. We've all had the experience of seeing a small incident get out of hand and cause damage out of proportion to its importance.

One clear sign of functional conflict is that in the long run the behavior of the participants solves more problems than it creates. We say "long run" because facing up to an issue instead of avoiding it frequently makes life more difficult for a while. In this respect handling conflicts functionally is rather like going to the dentist: You may find it a little (or even a lot!) painful for a while, but you're only making matters worse by not facing the problem.

Losing Sight of the Original Issue In dysfunctional conflicts the partners often bring in issues having little or nothing to do with the original problem. Take for example a couple who originally are having trouble deciding whether to spend the holidays at his or her parents' home. As they begin to grow frustrated at their inability to solve the dilemma, one of them—let's say the man—angrily remarks, "Your mother is always trying to latch onto us!," to which the woman replies, "If you want to talk about latching on, what about *your* folks? Ever since they loaned us that money they've been asking about every dime we spend." "Well," the man retorts, "if you could ever finish with school and hold down a decent job, we wouldn't have to worry about money so much. You're always talking about wanting to be an equal partner, but I'm the one paying all the bills around here."

You can imagine how the conversation would go from here. Notice how the original issue became lost as the conflict expanded. It's obvious that this kind of open-ended hostility is unlikely to solve any of the problems it brings up, not to mention the potential for creating problems not even existing before.

One characteristic of communicators who handle conflict well is their ability to keep focused on one subject at a time. Unlike those dysfunctional battlers whom Bach calls "kitchen sink fighters," skillful communicators might say, "I'm willing to talk about how my parents have been acting since they made us that loan, but first let's settle the business of where to spend the holidays." In other words, for functional problem solving, the rule is "one problem at a time."

So far we've looked at the differences between the *processes* of functional and dysfunctional conflicts. Now let's compare the *results* of these different styles.

Dysfunctional conflict typically has three consequences. First, none of the parties are likely to get what they were originally seeking. In the short run it may look as if one person might win in a dispute while the other loses, but most often both parties suffer in some way. For instance, an instructor might win by forcing his unpopular grading system on students who clearly would lose out if they received grades lower than the ones they believed they deserved. But in situations such as this, instructors also fail to get what they want, for instead of trying to truly understand and master the material, the students will most likely become preoccupied with beating the system by simply memorizing facts, trying to "psych out" the forthcoming exams, or even cheating. Obviously this behavior prevents good learning, which means that the instructor has failed just as much as the students have lost the fairness and the interesting instruction they sought. In the long run, everyone has lost.

A second consequence of dysfunctional conflicts is that they threaten the future of the relationship. Let's return to that feuding couple. It's easy to imagine how the resentments of both partners would affect their behavior. For example, it's unlikely that either would feel affectionate after such an exchange, and so we might expect their sex life to deteriorate. As their disappointment grows, they would probably be less willing to help each other in their usual ways. The wife might be less cooperative about doing her share of cooking and cleaning, while the husband wouldn't offer advice on how to complete school assignments. Thus, if this couple can't solve their original problems, it's likely that dissatisfaction with each other will grow like a cancer until it has poisoned most every part of their relationship. This effect of individual conflicts on an overall relationship explains why it's important to deal successfully with seemingly inconsequential matters such as arriving on time for appointments or who takes out the trash, for every time partners don't resolve a small conflict they weaken their entire relationship.

Failure to resolve interpersonal problems is also personally destructive to each participant. We discussed the range of emotions in Chapter 5. Take a moment now and think about the feelings you've experienced when you were a party in an unresolved conflict. It's likely that you felt (and still may feel) inadequate, foolish, unworthy, unlikeable, or unloveable. Poorly managed conflicts have a strong effect on our self-esteem and can bring about effects that can linger on for years, threatening both our peace of mind and our future relationships with others.

In contrast to these dismal outcomes, functional conflicts have positive results. One benefit to skillfully handling issues is that interpersonal involvement increases. When we engage in a conflict productively, we get excited, motivated to act. In contrast to an apathetic person, the functional communicator is determined to do something to make the relationship better.

Skillfully handled conflict also promotes growth in a relationship. Along with restoring harmony, dealing with a conflict teaches people things about each other they didn't know before. They learn more about each other's needs and how such needs can be satisfied. Feelings are clarified. Backgrounds are shared. Of course growth can occur in nonconflict situations too; the point here is that dealing with problems can be an opportunity for getting to know each other better. Moreover, conflicts provide the opportunity for new kinds of sharing. We often fail to know where another person stands on an issue until that issue is confronted.

Constructive conflict also provides a safe outlet for the feelings of frustration and aggression that are bound to occur in any relationship. When people accept the inevitable fact that they'll occasionally disagree with each other, they can be willing to let their partners express that disagreement, and in so doing defuse a great deal of it. One characteristic of good interpersonal communicators is that they allow each other to blow off steam without taking offense.

Finally, functional conflicts allow each person involved to establish his or her personal identity within the relationship. To see how important this individual identity is, think back to the early stages of your relationships. (Try to recall a wide variety:

romantic, friendship, business, academic.) In many cases the earliest stages of relationships are marked by such a desire to promote harmony that the members behave unnaturally: They're so polite, so concerned with each other's happiness that they ignore their own needs and wants. In this effort to keep everything smooth, the parties give up a bit of themselves. But when conflicts finally do surface, each gives the other a chance to show where he or she stands, to say, "I understand what you want, but let me tell you what's important to *me*." When this and later conflicts are handled skillfully, they allow the relationship to grow while at the same time letting each person remain an individual.

Resolving Interpersonal Conflicts

After reading the last section you can see that "functional" is the key word when dealing with interpersonal conflicts. You need to find effective ways of communicating *during* a conflict, and of course you want to create an *outcome* satisfying for everyone concerned. In the next few pages we'll look at three styles of resolving conflict. While each has its advantages and drawbacks, you'll see that some ways of managing disputes are more functional than others.

Win-Lose   Win-lose conflicts are ones in which one party gets what he or she wants while the other comes up short. People resort to this method of resolving disputes when they perceive a situation as being an "either-or" one: Either I get my way or you get your way. The most clear-cut examples of win-lose situations are certain games such as baseball or poker in which the rules require a winner and a loser. Some interpersonal issues seem to fit into this win-lose framework: two coworkers seeking a promotion to the same job, say, or a couple arguing over how to spend their limited money.

Power is the distinguishing characteristic in win-lose problem solving, for it's necessary to defeat an opponent to get what you want. The most obvious kind of power is physical. Some parents threaten their children with warnings such as "Stop misbehaving or I'll send you to your room." Adults who use physical power to deal with each other usually aren't so blunt, but the threat often exists nonetheless. For instance, behind the legal system is the implied threat, "Follow the rules or we'll lock you up."

Real or implied force isn't the only kind of power used in conflicts. People who rely on authority of many types engage in win-lose methods without ever threatening physical coercion. In most jobs supervisors have the potential to use authority in the assignment of working hours, job promotions, desirable or undesirable tasks, and of course in the power to fire an unsatisfactory employee. Teachers can use the power of grades to coerce students to act in desired ways.

Intellectual or mental power can also be a tool for conquering an opponent. Everyone is familiar with stories of how a seemingly weak hero defeats a stronger enemy through cleverness, showing that brains can triumph over brawn. In a less admirable way, crazymakers can defeat their partners in effective, if destructive ways: by inducing guilt, avoiding issues,

> **The test of a man or woman's breeding is how they behave in a quarrel.**
>
> George Bernard Shaw

withholding desired behaviors, pseudo-accommodating, and so on.

Even the usually admired democratic principle of majority rule is a win-lose method of resolving conflicts. However fair it may be, this system results in one group getting its way and another being unsatisfied.

There are some circumstances in which the win-lose method may be necessary, as when there are truly scarce resources, and where only one party can achieve satisfaction. For instance, if two suitors want to marry the same person, only one can succeed. And to return to an earlier example, it's often true that only one applicant can be hired for a job. But don't be too willing to assume that your conflicts are necessarily win-lose. Many situations seeming to require a loser can be resolved to everyone's satisfaction.

There is a second kind of situation wherein win-lose is the best method of conflict. Even when cooperation is possible, if the other person insists on defeating you, then the most logical response might be to defend yourself by fighting back. "It takes two to tango," the old cliché goes, and it also often takes two to cooperate.

A final and much less frequent justification for trying to defeat another person occurs when the other party is clearly behaving in a wrongful manner, and where defeating that person is the only way to stop the wrongful behavior. Few people would deny the importance of restraining a person who is deliberately harming others, even if the belligerent person's freedom is sacrificed in the process. It seems justifiable to coerce others into behaving as we think they should only in the most extreme circumstances.

Lose-Lose In lose-lose methods of problem solving neither side is satisfied with the outcome. While the name of this approach is so discouraging that it's hard to imagine how anyone could willingly use the method, in truth lose-lose is a fairly common approach to handling conflicts.

Compromise is the most respectable form of lose-lose conflict resolution. In compromising, all the parties are willing to settle for less than they want because they believe that partial satisfaction is the best result they can hope for. In *Interpersonal Conflict Resolution,* Albert Filley makes an interesting observation about our attitudes towards this method. Why is it, he asks, that if someone says, "I will compromise my values," we view the action unfavorably; yet we talk admiringly about parties in a conflict who compromise to reach a solution? While compromises may be the best obtainable result in some conflicts, it's important to realize that both people in a dispute can often work together to find much better solutions. In such cases "compromise" is often a negative concept.

Most of us are surrounded by the results of bad compromises. Consider a common example, namely the conflict between one person's desire to smoke cigarettes and another's need for clean air. The win-lose outcomes on this issue are obvious: either the smoker abstains or the nonsmoker gets polluted lungs—neither solution is very satisfying. But a compromise whereby the smoker only gets to enjoy a rare cigarette or must retreat outdoors to smoke, and the non-smoker still must inhale some fumes or feel like an ogre is hardly better. Both sides still have lost considerable comfort and goodwill.

The costs involved in still other compromises are even greater. For example, if a divorced couple compromise on childcare by haggling over custody and then finally grudgingly split the time with their youngsters, it's hard to say that anybody has won.

Compromises aren't the only lose-lose solutions, or even the worst ones. There are many instances in which the parties both strive to be winners, but as a result of the struggle both wind up losers. On the international scene, many wars illustrate this sad point. A nation that gains military victory at the cost of thousands of lives, large amounts of resources, and a damaged national consciousness hasn't truly won much. On the interpersonal level the same principle holds true. Most of us have seen battles of pride in which both parties strike out and both suffer. It seems as if there should be a better alternative, and fortunately there often is.

No-Lose In this type of problem solving the goal is to find a solution satisfying the needs of everyone involved. Not only do the partners avoid trying to win at each other's expense, but there's a belief that by working together it's possible to find a solution in which everybody reaches their goals without needing to compromise.

One way to understand how no-lose problem solving works is to look at a few examples.

A boss and his employees get into a conflict over scheduling. The employees often want to shift the hours they're scheduled to work in order to accommodate personal needs, while the boss needs to be sure that the operation is fully staffed at all times. After some discussion they arrive at a solution that satisfies everyone: The boss works up a monthly master schedule indicating the hours during which each employee is responsible for being on the job. Employees are free to trade hours among themselves, as long as the operation is fully staffed at all times.

A conflict about testing arises in a college class. Due to sickness or other reasons a certain number of students need to take exams on a makeup basis. The instructor doesn't want to give these students any advantage over their peers, and doesn't want to go through the task of making up a brand new test for just a few people. After working on the problem together, instructor and students arrive at a no-lose solution. The instructor will hand out a list of twenty possible exam questions in advance of the test day. At examination time five of these questions are randomly drawn for the class to answer. Students who take makeups will draw from the same pool of questions at

I will not play at tug o' war.
I'd rather play at hug o'war,
Where everyone hugs
Instead of tugs,
Where everyone giggles
And rolls on the rug,
Where everyone kisses,
And everyone grins,
And everyone cuddles,
And everyone wins.

Shel Silverstein

the time of their test. In this way, makeup students are taking a fresh test without the instructor having to create a new exam.

A newly married husband and wife found themselves arguing frequently over their budget. The wife enjoyed buying impractical but enjoyable items for herself and the house, while the husband feared that such purchases would ruin their carefully constructed budget. Their solution was to set aside a small amount of money each month for purchases. The amount was small enough to be affordable, yet gave the wife a chance to escape from their spartan lifestyle. Addtionally, the husband was satisfied with the arrangement since the luxury money was now a budget category by itself, which got rid of the "out of control" feeling that came when his wife made unexpected purchases. The plan worked so well that the couple continued to use it even after their income rose, by increasing the amount devoted to luxuries.

While solutions such as these might seem obvious when you read them here, a moment's reflection will show you that such cooperative problem solving is all too rare. People faced with such conflicts often resort to such dysfunctional styles of communicating as withdrawing, avoiding, or competing, and wind up handling the issues in a manner resulting in either a win-lose or lose-lose outcome. As we said earlier, it's a shame to see one or both parties in a conflict come away unsatisfied when they could both get what they're seeking by communicating in a no-lose manner.

In order for no-lose problem solving to work, it's essential to follow several steps.

1. Define the needs of both parties. The place to begin is by deciding what it is that you want or need. Sometimes the answer is obvious, as in our earlier example of the neighbor whose loud stereo music kept others awake. In other instances, however, an immediate problem hides the real need. For example, the parents of a three-year-old girl were aggravated by the routine that had developed around their daughter's bedtime every night. Instead of going to sleep quietly, the child spent about forty-five minutes badgering her folks. First she wanted a drink of water, then to go to the bathroom, then to be tucked in, then to be reassured there were no wolves under her bed, and on and on.

When they first thought about this problem, the parents said their need was to have the little girl go to sleep shortly after going to bed. After talking for a while, however, they realized that they didn't really care whether she stayed awake for a while, since they figured she'd go to sleep when she was tired. What they really wanted was to be left alone so they could spend a few precious hours together undisturbed before turning in themselves. While this newly defined need doesn't seem too different from their first statement, you'll soon see that the difference really is a significant one.

Because one's needs aren't always immediately clear, it's sometimes a good idea to think about a problem alone, before approaching the other person involved.

Once your own wants are clear it's time to find out what the other person needs. (This is when to use the listening skills described in Chapter 8.) When the parents began to talk about their daughter's needs with her, they learned some interesting facts. In their haste to have some time together, the parents had given the little girl the impression that they didn't care about her at night. Feeling insecure, the child used her various complaints as a way of getting her parents' attention and expressions of love.

Once the parents realized this fact, it became clear that they needed to find a solution that would leave their little girl feeling secure and at the same time allow them to have uninterrupted evenings together.

When they're really communicating effectively, partners can help each other clarify what it is that they're seeking. Truly believing that their happiness depends on the other's satisfaction, they actively try to analyze what obstacles need to be overcome.

2. Generate possible solutions. In this step the partners try to think of as many ways to satisfy both their needs as possible. They can best do so by "brainstorming" —inventing as many potential solutions as they can. The key to success in brainstorming is to seek quantity without worrying too much about quality. The rule here is to prohibit criticism of all ideas, no matter how outlandish they might sound. An idea seeming farfetched can sometimes lead to a more workable one. Another rule of brainstorming is that ideas aren't personal property. If one person makes a suggestion, the other should feel free to modify or change it without having to worry about spoiling the original thought. Once the partners get over feeling possessive about ideas, the level of defensiveness in the conversation drops and both people can work together to find the best solution without worrying about whose it is.

The parents and their daughter brainstormed a number of possible solutions to their bedtime problem. Their list consisted of starting the bedtime routine earlier, not allowing the daughter to get up once she had been tucked in, letting the daughter stay up until she feel asleep and then carrying her to bed, allowing only two or three "getups," and spending more time together before bedtime. While some of these were clearly unacceptable to the parents and others didn't suit their daughter, the family listed all the ideas they could think of at this point, preparing themselves for the next step in no-lose problem solving.

3. Evaluate the possible solutions and choose the best one. This is the place to critically evaluate the list of ideas you generated in the previous step. Again, the key point is to avoid taking sides and arguing about solutions. Instead, your goal should be to work cooperatively with your partner to decide which proposal has the best chance of satisfying both your needs. Remember that in most cases your happiness depends on the other person being satisfied as well.

The best solution to the bedtime problem seemed to be to spend more time together before lights out for the daughter. The family came up with a plan whereby the mother and father would each read a story to their little girl, and then each in turn would spend five minutes talking with her about anything she wanted, promising not to allow any interruptions at all to their time together. This was the daughter's idea, and she announced that if she could have this "special time," she would know that she was an important person to her parents and would not need to interrupt them after her bedtime.

4. Implement the solution. Now the time comes to try out the idea you just selected and to see if it does in fact satisfy everyone's needs. Your chances of success here will be increased if everyone involved understands exactly what it is you've decided to do. The key questions to answer are *who* does *what* to *whom*, and *when?*

Before the family tried out their solution, they went over the agreement to make sure it was clear. This step proved to be important, for a potential misunderstanding existed. The mother and father often received phone calls during the evening, and the daughter wanted to be sure that these calls wouldn't interrupt her talks. After thinking this over, the parents agreed that they could return the calls later. This sort of clarification is important if agreements are going to work.

5. Follow up the solution. You can't be sure a solution will work until you try it out. After you've tested it for a while, it's a good idea to plan a meeting to talk over how things are going. You may find that you need to make some changes or even rethink the whole problem.

After the parents and daughter had tried their new bedtime routine out for a few weeks, they found it was basically successful. One problem remained, however. The father's business required him to be away from home one or two evenings a week, and the daughter felt cheated when she didn't get her special times with him. When faced with this difficulty the parents returned to Step 2 and developed several possible ways to solve the new problem. They decided together that the best solution was for the father to phone his little girl sometime during the afternoons when he wouldn't be returning home and to spend five minutes talking just with her. This left the daughter feeling loved and important, the father feeling good for not neglecting his little girl, and the mother happy about not having to struggle with a complaining child at bedtime.

This no-lose method is especially attractive when you consider the alternatives we've already discussed. It's easy to see how such a system can work well for solving individual conflict; but just as significantly, communicating in this manner can improve entire relationships.

You can see for yourself how well your present styles of managing conflicts affect your relationships, and how well new styles you might try work by asking the following questions:

a. How much do we learn about each other? A conflict should help us gain new information, especially in the area of the conflict. We should be more aware of each other's likes and dislikes, needs, wants, and desires. The more we learn about each other, the more beneficial the conflict is to our relationship.

b. How effectively do we influence each other? After a conflict we should be more aware of the power each of us has to influence the other, and we should be more willing, now, to accept that influence. To the extent that we avoid coercion and the use of crazymakers, conflict is beneficial. We are more effective at influencing each other.

c. How much do we fear and trust each other? A constructive conflict should leave us fearing each other less, and trusting each other more.

d. Do we seek revenge? The extent to which we conduct a fair fight, a no-lose or win-win one, determines the extent to which either of us seeks revenge. If we understand each other, engage in conflict sincerely, and work hard to satisfy both our concerns, no one should seek revenge, and the relationship should be more stable and enduring.

e. How good do we feel about ourselves? A constructive conflict should raise our self-worth and increase how good we feel about ourselves.

f. How good do we feel about our relationship? Just as a constructive conflict increases our feelings of self-worth, it should increase the positive feelings we have for our relationship. We should feel closer to each other, and look at our relationship as more important than it was before the conflict.

Of course, some conflicts are going to be better than others in terms of the ultimate effects on our relationship. But every conflict has the potential to help our relationship grow and become more meaningful.

Readings

Bach, George R. and Peter Wyden. *The Intimate Enemy.* New York: Avon, 1968.

Bach, George R. and Ronald M. Deutsch. *Pairing.* New York: Avon, 1970.

Ellis, Donald G. and B. Aubrey Fisher. "Phases of Conflict in Small Group Development." *Human Communication Research,* 1, (1975): 195–212.

Filly, Alan C. *Interpersonal Conflict Resolution.* Glenview, Ill.: Scott, Foresman, 1975.

Frost, Joyce Hocker and William W. Wilmot. *Interpersonal Conflict.* Dubuque, Iowa: Wm. C. Brown, 1978.

Gordon, Thomas. *Parent Effectiveness Training.* New York: Peter H. Wyden, 1970.

Jandt, Fred E. *Conflict Resolution Through Communication.* New York: Harper and Row, 1973.

Rosenfeld, Lawrence B. *Now That We're All Here . . . Relations in Small Groups.* Columbus, Ohio: Charles E. Merrill, 1976.

Simons, Herbert. "Persuasion in Social Conflicts: A Critique of Prevailing Conceptions and a Framework for Future Research." *Speech Monographs,* 39, (1972):227–247.

Thomas, Kenneth. "Conflict and Conflict Management." In *Handbook of Industrial and Organizational Psychology,* Marvin D. Dunnette, ed. Chicago: Rand McNally, 1976.

Name Index

Subject Index

games 61
gestures 232-233

hearing 194, 196-197
    problems of 201
helplessness, fallacy of 123-124
honesty 178

Identity Self 36
indiscriminate terms 258, 260
intentional orientation 254
interpersonal communication,
    definition of 16-17, 19
interpretation and perception
    101-103
intimacy, depth and breadth of
    136-137
investment thesis 142-143
"it" statements 270

Johari Window 54-56
Judging Self 36-37

labels 266-267
language, characteristics of
    252-254
    self-concept and 267-268
leadership 89, 91
listening, active 212-213
    improvement of 205-209
    myths of 194-196
    obstacles to 201-205
    process of 196-198

Managerial Grid 161-162
model, communication 11-15
    self-disclosure 54-56

needs, affection 4
    control 4
    ego 4
    inclusion 4

physical 2-3
safety 3-4
self-actualization 4-5
need complementarity 141
noise, definition of 14
nonverbal communication,
    characteristics of 217-222
    verbal communication and
    222

organization 197-198
    perception and 100-101
overgeneralization, fallacy of
    122

pastimes 59-61
perception and age 87-88
    culture 96, 98
    fatigue 87
    health 87
    hearing 83-84
    height 88-89
    occupation 93-95
    sex 89-93
    sight 84-85
    smell 81
    taste 80-81
    touch 82-83
perfection, fallacy of 119-120
personal space 238-241
personality and self-acceptance
    42
    self-disclosure 68
    self-esteem 42, 44
playmates, imaginary 151-152
polarization 254, 289
posture 230-232
proxemics 238-241
proximity thesis 143
pseudolistening 202-203
pupil dilation 230

questions 271

Rational-Emotive Therapy 117-
    128

reflected appraisal 28-31
    requirements of 30
relationships and context 134-
    136
    intimacy 136-137
    time 137-138
relationships, stages of 143-149
    in children 148-149
relative words 257
rituals 59

Sapir-Whorf hypothesis 264-
    266
selective perception 99-100
self-alienation 68
self-concept, age and 34
    changing 48-50
    defensiveness and 170-172
    definition of 26-27
    development of 27-34
    dimensions of 34-37
    maintaining 37-42
    self-disclosure and 68-69
self-disclosure, avoidance of
    63-64, 66, 69-72, 113
    definition of 56-59
    in families 62-63, 66-67
    friendship and 66
    mental health and 67-68
    model of 54-56
    sex differences and 61-64, 66
self-fulfilling prophecy 44-48,
    261
sex differences and emotions
    112
    friendship 155-156
    perception 81-82, 84, 85, 87
    roles 89-93, 112
    self-disclosure 61-64, 66
shoulds, fallacy of 120-122
shyness 109, 153

significant others 28, 30-31, 46
similarity thesis 138, 140
social comparison 28, 32-34
social exchange theory 141-142
social penetration 137
static evaluation 256-257
suicide 5-6

supportive behaviors 165-166, 168-170

Tennessee Self-Concept Scale 34
territoriality 238, 241, 243
touch 233-236
trust 66, 71, 178-179

vocal cues 236-238
voice 236-238
vultures 38-39

"we" statements 270-271

"you" statements 270